American Labor in the Southwest

Contributing Authors

Rodney Anderson

Edward D. Beechert

James Byrkit

Arthur Carstens

David H. Dinwoodie

James C. Foster

George N. Green

John M. Hart

David Maciel

Paul Mandel

H. L. Mitchell

Monsignor Charles O. Rice

Earl Bruce White

AMERICAN LABOR IN THE SOUTHWEST

The First One Hundred Years

James C. Foster, *editor*

The University of Arizona Press
Tucson, Arizona

About the Editor

James C. Foster, author of numerous books and articles on labor relations, worked as a machinist in a union shop and became a member of the United Steel Workers. In 1974, he joined the faculty of Arizona State University at Tempe, to teach history and coordinate the Labor Studies Program. He also organized the Arizona Labor History Council, made up of college instructors, high school teachers, and members of organized labor. In 1981, he accepted a position at the University of Wisconsin at Parkside, to set up a college credit program for union members, in the Industrial Relations Department. Dr. Foster holds a Ph.D. degree from Cornell Univesity in history and labor relations.

THE UNIVERSITY OF ARIZONA PRESS

Copyright © 1982
The Arizona Board of Regents
All Rights Reserved

This book was set in 10/12 V-I-P Baskerville
Manufactured in the U.S.A.

Library of Congress Cataloging in Publication Data

American labor in the Southwest.

Includes bibliographical references and index.
1. Trade-unions—The West—History—Addresses, essays, lectures.   2. Alien labor, Mexican—The West—History—Addresses, essays, lectures.
2. Alien labor, Mexican—The West—History—Addresses, essays, lectures.   I. Foster, James C. (James Carl)
HD6508.A447   331.88'0979   81-21819

ISBN 0-8165-0741-4   AACR2
ISBN 0-8165-0758-9 (pbk.)

*To Darwin Aycock
and the Arizona State AFL–CIO,
for their support of
labor studies in Arizona.*

Contents

IV. MEXICAN LABOR, NORTH AND SOUTH OF THE BORDER

V. LABOR AND POLITICS

About the Contributing Authors

RODNEY ANDERSON has written a history of the labor movement in Mexico, *Outcasts in Their Own Land,* as well as numerous articles on the labor movement in Mexico. After receiving a Ph.D. in Latin American Studies from the American University, he joined the history faculty at Florida State University.

EDWARD D. BEECHERT is the author of *Labor Relations in Hawaii* and a number of articles on economic and labor history of the Hawaiian Islands. Coordinator of the Pacific Regional Oral History Program, he received a Ph.D. in history from the University of California at Berkeley in 1957, and later joined the faculty of the University of Hawaii.

JAMES BYRKIT has written several articles and a full-length book on the Bisbee deportation and the IWW, *Forging the Copper Collar: Arizona's Labor-Management War, 1901–1921,* a 1982 publication of the University of Arizona Press. He was awarded a Ph.D. in history by the Claremont Graduate School in 1972, and subsequently became an associate professor of history and integrated studies at Northern Arizona University.

ARTHUR CARSTENS was a founder of the Southwest Labor Conference, and was also one of the authors of California's Agricultural Labor Relations Act. At the time of his death, he was a professor of labor relations at the University of California at Los Angeles.

DAVID H. DINWOODIE has published articles on American diplomacy, international labor, and mining in the United States and Canada. After receiving a Ph.D. in history from the University of Colorado in 1966, he joined the history faculty at the University of Alberta.

GEORGE N. GREEN, as a member of the History Department at the University of Texas at Arlington, has written numerous articles on Texas politics, and a book, *The Establishment in Texas Politics.* He was granted a Ph.D. in history from Florida State University in 1966.

JOHN M. HART is the author of *Anarchism and the Mexican Working Class*, and many articles on Mexican working-class history. A member of the faculty of Houston University, he obtained a Ph.D. in Latin American History from the University of California at Los Angeles in 1970.

DAVID MACIEL, a specialist in Mexican-American history, has written prolifically about Mexican labor problems on both sides of the border. An assistant professor of history at the University of New Mexico, he received a Ph.D. from the University of California at Santa Barbara in 1978.

PAUL MANDEL, a doctoral candidate at the University of California at Los Angeles, was formerly the administrative assistant of the Arizona State University Labor Studies Program.

H. L. MITCHELL was one of the founders of the Southern Tenant Farmers Union, a predecessor of the United Farm Workers. He is the author of *Mean Things Happening in This Land*.

MONSIGNOR CHARLES O. RICE was active in the organization of several CIO unions during the 1930s, and was a close friend of CIO president, Phillip Murray. The pastor of the Church of St. Anne in Pittsburgh, Pennsylvania, Father Rice was at one time connected with the Association of Catholic Trade Unionists, an anti-Communist pressure group within the CIO.

EARL BRUCE WHITE is a specialist on the history of the IWW and has published several articles on that union, as well as on the WFM and Colorado mining labor problems. A member of the history faculty at Sterling College, Sterling, Kansas, he received a Ph.D. in history from the University of Colorado in 1980.

Abbreviations

AAA	Agricultural Adjustment Administration
ACLU	American Civil Liberties Union
AFL	American Federation of Labor
AFWU	Arizona Farm Workers Union
ALRA	Agricultural Labor Relations Act (California)
ALRB	Agricultural Labor Relations Board
ASARCO	American Smelting and Refining Company
AWO	Agricultural Workers Organization of the IWW
CGT	Confederación General de Trabajadores
CIO	Congress of Industrial Organizations
CIO-PAC	Congress of Industrial Organizations Political Action Committee
COPE	Committee on Political Education (AFL–CIO)
CP	Communist Party
CTM	Confederación de Trabajadores Mexicanos
FEPC	Fair Employment Practices Commission
FICA	Federal Insurance Contributions Act (social security)
FLSA	Fair Labor Standards Act (minimum wage law)
FSA	Farm Security Administration
GCOL	Gran Círculo de Obreros Libres
GNP	Gross National Product
ILA	International Longshoremen's Association (longshoremen's union—East Coast)
ILWU	International Longshoremen's and Warehousemen's Union (Harry Bridge's union—West Coast)
INS	Immigration Naturalization Service
IRE	Investigative Reporters and Editors (Arizona)
IUMMSW	International Union of Mine, Mill, and Smelter Workers (WFM after 1916)
IWW	Industrial Workers of the World
K of L	Knights of Labor

MOA	Mine Owners' Association
NAACP	National Association for the Advancement of Colored People
NCLB	National Civil Liberties Bureau (later, ACLU)
NFLU	National Farm Labor Union (successor to STFU and member of the AFL)
NFMC	Non-Ferrous Metals Commission of the War Labor Board
NIRA	National Industrial Recovery Act
NLRB	National Labor Relations Board
OWU	Oil Workers Union of the IWW
PAC	Political Action Committee
PLM	Partido Liberal Mexicano
SPA	Socialist Party of America
STFU	Southern Tenant Farmers Union
UCAPAWA	United Cannery, Agricultural Packing, and Allied Workers of America
UE	United Electrical Workers
UMW	United Mine Workers of America
WFM	Western Federation of Miners
WLB	War Labor Board (World War II)
WPA	Works Progress Administration

The Impact of Labor
on the Development of the West

As WESTERN HISTORY TURNS from the cowboy and Indian, a number of intriguing new groups are coming to the fore. Among these is labor: the wageworkers of the West who built the cities, mined the gold and silver, picked the crops, and brought what America called civilization to half a continent. It was a polyglot mixture, western labor. Drawn from every country of the world, every race, and both sexes, western labor was instrumental in creating the nineteenth century economic miracle which set the pattern for Germany and Japan in the twentieth century. The wageworkers may not have been as glamorous as the United States cavalry, but without them there would have been no modern metropolises in the mountains or in the deserts. The essays which follow single out the miners, the wobblies, the farm workers, and the Mexican migrants for their contributions to the growth of the nation.

In March, 1977, labor historians from around the United States and Canada gathered in Phoenix, Arizona, to explore the problems and accomplishments of the western labor movement. The essays of fourteen of these historians have been chosen to represent current scholarship in the field and together form a book that gives a distinctive view of the West—a view quite different from the silver-screen stereotype which has captivated theater audiences for half a century.

As western as John Wayne (who devoted part of his film career to the occupation of mining in such classics as Rex Beach's *The Spoilers* and the recent *North to Alaska),* the miner was the West after 1849. It was the miner who first pushed city life into the forests of Idaho and Montana. It was the miner whose lust for Black Hills gold helped start the bloodiest phase of the Indian wars. It was the miner whose toil made the great fortunes of George Hearst, Horace Tabor, and the Guggenheims. Yet, it was also the miner who demanded the eight-hour day, decent housing, and modern hospital facilities.

Modern scholarship has turned away from the glamour of the mines and toward those day-to-day problems which dominated the lives of thousands of wageworking miners. What did workers do when

[1]

the heat in the mines rose past 130 degrees and ventilation did not exist? What was life like underground where dust doomed everyone to the tortured death of "miner's tuberculosis"? One answer was unionization. Historians such as Richard Lingenfelter have done excellent work in tracing the unionization of miners back to boom times on the Comstock.[1] Others, from Vernon Jensen to George Suggs, Jr., have brought the tale of the western miner into more modern times.[2] Yet, much remains to be done in the field. Many have tried to explain the peculiar ideology which rose from the ranks of the Western Federation of Miners and was transformed into the grassroots syndicalism of the IWW. Joseph Conlin's *Bread and Roses Too* came close to the truth when it examined the seeming paradox of WFM–IWW thought.[3] Works by others have also been valuable in assessing that particularly western form of radicalism which sprang from the Rocky Mountains. Of these, J. H. M. Laslett's work on socialist ideology seems most correct.[4] The essays chosen for this book bring several new approaches to the subject, including a foray into the thirties and the mine, mill, and smelter workers. It was in the thirties that the old Western Federation of Miners (renamed the International Union of Mine, Mill and Smelter Workers in 1916) took on a new brand of leadership, which would result in a CIO expulsion during the 1940s red scare.

Although it was the miners who were most responsible for creating the Industrial Workers of the World, the IWW soon rivaled its founder as the most controversial union in the West. Nevada still remembers Goldfield as the IWW's wholly unionized town. Arizona cannot forget the IWW's role in Jerome and the unfortunate Bisbee deportation. The moving-picture industry seems continually fascinated by such IWW characters as minstrel Joe Hill. Even James Jones' classic *From Here to Eternity* paused to recall the almost inexplicable fervor which surrounded the western wobblies ("You don't remember the wobblies, but..."). For a few years, it seemed as if all the excitement of Populists, the old Western Federation, the Rocky Mountain socialists, and the single-tax movement has been condensed, mixed with a dose of Captain Daniel Shays, and labeled wobbly. Charismatic figures such as Big Bill Haywood roamed the West, preaching union and an undefined kind of revolution. Eastern clothing workers joined the western miners, the lumberjacks flocked to the cause, migrant farm workers found an ally for the very first time. All in all, it was an exciting period in the West. The wobblies may have located their headquarters in Chicago, but their soul was in the granite peaks of the Rockies.

Many writers have turned to the wobblies and their place in history. Accounts were being written while the organization still commanded respect in the lumber camps of the West, but the most comprehensive history of the IWW remains the work of Melvyn Dubofsky, whose *We Shall Be All* stands as the definitive work in the field.[5] Professor Dubofsky helped select and criticize the essays in this volume on the wobblies. They range from the familiar, James Byrkit's careful recounting of the Bisbee deportation, to the obscure, an essay dealing with wobbly activities in the oil fields. They all point to the overwhelming impact which the IWW had on a nation which had only partially committed itself to the mild reform of the progressives.

While the wobblies may have been dramatic actors on the western stage, they have been supplanted in recent years by the struggling farm workers. Strangely enough, the IWW was one of the first unions to concern itself with the plight of the unorganized migrant worker. Wobbly intervention in the fields did not bring any noted success, but the germ of migrant organization had been planted. Passing time brought new groups and new nationalities into the fields, groups that had to face the same working conditions and the same problems the wobblies had protested against before World War I. By the 1930s, several organizations were working to better the migrant's life. The southern arm of the movement was led by a group of tenant farmers who called themselves the Southern Tenant Farmers Union. Their complaint was the antitenant policies of the Agricultural Adjustment Administration, but, as the depression deepened, STFU members turned from farming to picking. The STFU was transformed from a southern farmer's union into a nationwide migrant organization.[6] The cornerstone of the modern farm-workers' union had been laid.

During the hard years of the depression, pickers in the western fields came more and more from a single nationality group, the Mexican Americans. Fleeing north from the revolution and the harsh economic reality of modern Mexico, the new migrant workers had developed their own unions by the mid-thirties. However, the decade of the thirties was one of the high points of radical control in western unions. Mexicans may have worked the fields, but the front offices of most farm unions were dominated by radical youths who learned unionism in the Trade Union Unity League and agriculture in the Bronx. Many of the leaders did not even speak Spanish.[7] Then came the war and the beginning of the farm workers' protest.

The war took 14 million men and women out of the domestic labor market. California crops which had depended upon Mexican-American and Okie labor lay rotting in the fields until the United

States Department of Agriculture solved the farm-labor crisis by instituting the Bracero Program. In essence, the statutory provisions against contract labor were waived in the case of Mexican pickers, who were welcomed north of the border for the duration of the harvest season. The Bracero Program would ultimately last for twenty-two years, years in which every effort to organize farm workers was thwarted by the use of imported hands. It was during these two decades that the entire leadership of farm-labor organizations shifted away from the thirties radicals into the hands of Mexican Americans themselves.[8] The names at the masthead were now Ernesto Galarza, Dolores Huerta, and, of course, Cesar Chávez.

Covering the last forty years of farm labor was not an easy task in three brief essays, but the papers chosen do reflect completely different segments of the farm-labor story. H. L. Mitchell, founder of the Southern Tenant Farmers Union, gives an insider's view of the STFU in the thirties. Other papers deal with both the involvement of the so-called radical unions in thirties migrant organizations (in this case the International Longshoremen's and Warehousemen's Union led by Harry Bridges) and the current problem of labor law in the fields. The three essays span not only forty years of farm-worker history, but also the geographical areas of the Southeast, the Southwest, and the Hawaiian Islands.

Dealing simply with the farm-workers' movement does not do justice to the migrant ethnic groups of the American Southwest. Mexican and Indian workers were important in the Southwest's economy from the beginning of European settlement. Moreover, American labor scholars are often unwilling to dig into the intricacies of the Mexican Revolution and its obvious impact on the American labor scene, but the presence of the Mexican border has made Mexican-born workers a decisive factor in many Southwest labor disputes. A section of this book is devoted to the particular problems of Mexican and migrant labor in the Southwest.

The origins of ethnic problems in the western United States labor market can probably be traced to the 1850s. It was during that period that mining became an occupation with monetary incentives that could lure the unsuccessful gold seekers of 1849. At the same time, the arrival of armies of Chinese to work on the railroad gave the '49 veterans keen competition for mining jobs. To make matters worse, the Chinese consistently undercut white miners' wages. Fear of the so-called "unfair" Chinese competition was one of the major reasons for the formation of the first western mining unions.[9] But, while the Chinese were the villains of the unions, other ethnic minorities, particularly Mexicans, fared quite well.

Mexican miners, miners who had worked the deep silver and gold mines of northern Mexico, were the elite of western mining towns for the first few years of the silver boom. After all, they had experience in the hard rock, while the gold seekers of America had only a rudimentary knowledge of simple placer procedures. It was not until the arrival of the Cornish in the 1880s that the Mexican miner was displaced from his privileged position. Armed with newer and more efficient European techniques, the Cornish ridiculed the Mexican methods and helped move Mexican workers from the top to the bottom ranks of mine labor. The turn of the century saw the process completed. Much of the Southwest was working under the so-called Mexican scale, a wage rate whereby Mexican workers (a term which referred also to Italian, Serbian, and Austrian miners in many camps) were paid about 30 percent less than other miners for comparable work. Management justified the differential by citing improved production with Cornish labor, production improvement which may have been explained by mid-1880s mechanization.[10]

In the modern Southwest, the ethnic labor problem is a mixture of race and economics. The demotion of the Mexican miners in the 1880s prepared the region for the wholesale reduction of all Mexican wages. The turn of the century saw a few Arizona newspapers editorializing on the virtues of the Mexican scale. One frontier editor conveniently excused exploitation implicit in the Mexican scale by inventing a pseudoeconomic rationale behind it. Allen T. Bird, editor of the Nogales (Arizona) *Oasis,* wrote in 1906:

> The crux of the difference...[between American and Mexican work is that] it is by no means the 'same work.'...It is the application of intelligence and vitality to his task which is the value of labor bought. It is universally recognized that the American miner, or the American laborer,...puts into the execution of his task far more intelligence and far more vitality than does his Mexican competitor. Consequently, on account of superior intelligence, there is less misdirected and wasteful effort and the superior vitality enables him to maintain a more intense and sustained activity.[11]

What the editor ignored was the tremendous potential such a system had for increasing the profits of copper mining. When such ethnic discrimination was finally brought to the test, it would be labor unions and not newspaper editors who challenged it on both sides of the Mexican border.

Mexican labor had existed under the Díaz regime, but it took the economic troubles of the turn of the century to give radical unions the impetus they needed to win a substantial following. The decline of the peso helped boost sales of the leftist paper, *La Regeneración,* and brought recruits to those particular Mexican wobblies, the *magonistas.* It is this latter group, the *magonistas,* that combined with American wobblies and western federationists to demand an end to the invidious double standard. It was the 1906 strike at Cananea, Sonora, led by the *magonistas,* the IWW, and the WFM which spurred Allen Bird's editorial on the Mexican scale. However, a Cananea victory for labor was not to be. Immediate reaction by management, the Arizona Rangers, and the Sonoran government brought armed forces to bear before striking miners could get control of the company's plant and equipment. Perhaps the strangest part of the affair was the use of American troops, the Arizona Rangers, to put down a strike by Mexican workers in Mexico.[12] Interestingly enough, it would be a survivor of the Cananea episode, Lazaro Gutiérrez de Lara, who would play a major part in the WFM strike in Clifton-Morenci, Arizona, in 1915–1916. As for the Mexican scale, it would take almost a decade before wages that were paid to Mexican workers in the Sonora mines equalled those paid to Americans.[13]

While the Cananea strike focused the eyes of the Southwest on the problem of ethnic differences in labor relations, the historical development of Mexican and Mexican-American labor took two different paths, following the defeat of the striking Mexican miners. On the one hand, the Mexican labor movement developed strength in its own right, as delineated by the articles of John Hart and Rodney Anderson in this volume. On the other hand, the existence of substantial numbers of Mexican immigrants in California and Arizona gave rise to a question of Mexican scale quite removed from the dual system of the early 1900s.

The essay of David Maciel analyzes American immigration from Mexico and shows how that factor influenced a new Mexican scale in the mid-twentieth century. This time, the scale was reflected in the pay of field workers and not miners. This time, the pay rates were based on the economic powerlessness and skill deficiencies of agricultural migrants rather than the ethnic background of the workers themselves. Yet, even this relatively modern Mexican scale seems destined for improvement, as alien migrants begin the difficult process of organization.

Together, the three essays on labor in the American Southwest and the Mexican Northwest show how developments on both sides of the border influenced the constantly controversial question of race and wages. The question has troubled the West for over a century and, despite important breakthroughs in agricultural industrial relations, it is a question which is still with us. The same may also be said of the final problem examined by this study, the problem of labor and politics.

The political imperative has been part of the baggage of the labor movement from the very beginning. When the first trade unionists joined into labor federations in the Jacksonian era, the prime topic of discussion was political reform and the electoral process. Labor federations of the 1860s and 1870s devoted more of their energies to politics than to collective bargaining. The same could be said of unions in the West.

David Waite, the Populist governor of Colorado, was elected with labor votes and devoted much of his administration to dealing with the problems of mine labor. The Colorado labor war of 1904 was an out-and-out battle between the Republican Party of Colorado and the Western Federation of Miners. The peculiar election of Governor Peabody in 1904 overrode the electoral mandate that voters of Colorado had given to the state's labor movement and its candidate, Alva Adams.[14] Similar tales of political battles, in which labor took an active part, could be told of Nevada, Utah, and a host of other states. Even conservative Arizona had a labor-backed governor in the person of George P. Hunt. Yet, the political problem posed by organized labor involves a great deal more than the electoral machinations of the CIO–PAC or the present-day COPE. Labor's leftward cant has always been upsetting to many westerners.

Consider for a moment the state of Utah, the state that condemned wobbly poet, Joe Hill, to death. Even before Utah had been granted statehood, the local labor movement had come under the guns of the Church of Jesus Christ of Latter-Day Saints. As J. Kenneth Davies explains in *Deseret's Sons of Toil*, Brigham Young himself saw the labor movement as a political and economic threat to the desert republic. Unions were condemned because they raised wages and rendered imported goods more attractive to the territory's inhabitants. Moreover, it was the union movement which brought many foreign, non-Mormon elements into the commonwealth; it was labor which introduced Utah to many upsetting leftist ideologies.[15] In the land of the rugged individual and the special collectivism of the Church of Jesus Christ of Latter-Day Saints, the socialist collectivism preached by much of the Rocky Mountain labor movement had a distinctly unpleasant ring.

If the radical tag was important before the turn of the century, it became increasingly useful to antilabor elements as the First World War approached. The lynching of the IWW's Frank Little was justified on the basis of his statements against the draft and the war. The deportation of wobblies at Bisbee was acceptable because mine spokesman cited radicalism and pro-German sympathies as IWW attributes.[16] Indeed, the excesses of the period seemed to harden antilabor attitudes.

The radical tag continued to haunt unions during the thirties, and it was one of the problems which plagued western unions after the Second World War. Now, radicalism was the "Communist problem." In the days of the IWW and the WFM, western unionists had slightly different views from their eastern allies, and western unions were all radical by eastern standards. Socialism was not a dirty word in western mining camps, nor was the IWW as unpopular in the West as it was on Broadway. The International Union of Mine, Mill, and Smelter Workers had turned abruptly left in the thirties, under the leadership of Reid Robinson.[17] Harry Bridges was outspokenly radical on a number of issues, and his west coast longshoremen backed him on every stand. The California CIO and its political arm, the CIO–PAC, were so radical that Richard Nixon was able to defeat Jerry Voorhis simply by linking the liberal Voorhis to the CIO–PAC name.[18] Thus, the red scare, when it hit the CIO, hit with incredible severity on the west coast. Both the International Longshoremen's and Warehousemen's Union and the International Union of Mine, Mill, and Smelter Workers were expelled from the CIO fold. At the same time, conservative elements in a number of states launched political attacks on labor and its supporters.[19] It was a bad time for the American labor movement.

The essays devoted to the troubled forties and fifties cover both sides of the political controversy plaguing organized labor. Professor Green's essay concentrates on the external threat of labor-baiting in Texas politics. Father Rice, on the other hand, approaches the red scare from inside the labor movement. As a key advisor to Phillip Murray, president of the CIO, Father Charles Owen Rice was in a position to push the wavering Murray into action against CIO radicals in such unions as the United Electrical Workers; the International Union of Mine, Mill, and Smelter Workers; and the Harry Bridges Longshoremen. Father Rice's essay is an eloquent testimonial on one man's battle to rid the CIO of its radicals.[20]

What can be said about western labor in the twentieth century? Western labor has been but an appendage of the larger American labor movement in most studies, a slightly withered branch on the tree of labor. Yet, for many years it was unique in a very special way. It was the West which bred that most atypical of miners' unions, the Western Federation of Miners. It was the West which gave America the wobblies. It was the West which kept alive the radical spark in the troubled twenties.

The West was different in other ways, too. There must have been something peculiar indeed with the sky, the air, the water—something which could produce a whole series of leaders cast in the charismatic mold of Big Bill Haywood. Maybe it was a touch of Buffalo Bill Cody, or a dash of Jim Bridger which produced that combination of con man, organizer, businessman, and zealot in the Rocky Mountains. Few eastern leaders, regardless of their accomplishments, could equal the skills of Big Bill. Few of today's labor leaders can match the loyal following of Cesar Chávez.

The West may not have been the central focus during much of the history of American labor, but it did have an important impact on certain specific fields of labor. Western mining is still shaped by the battles of the Western Federation. Chávez is still fighting the forces which the wobblies challenged at Wheatland. Western politics have only recently departed from the era of anti-Communism and labor-baiting. In short, western labor has had as much influence on the modern West as its eastern counterpart had on the country as a whole. The wageworker outlasted the cowboy.

JAMES C. FOSTER

NOTES

[1] Richard E. Lingenfelter, *The Hardrock Miners* (Berkeley: University of California Press, 1974).

[2] Vernon H. Jensen, *Heritage of Conflict* (Ithaca: Cornell University Press, 1950), a detailed study of the WFM–IUMMSW to 1920 and also his *Nonferrous Metals Industry Unionism* (Ithaca: Cornell University Press, 1954). Along a slightly different line, there is George C. Suggs, Jr., *Colorado's War on Militant Unionism* (Detroit: Wayne State University Press, 1972).

[3] Joseph Conlin, *Bread and Roses Too* (Westport, Conn: Greenwood Publishing, 1969).

[4] John H. M. Laslett, *Labor and the Left* (New York: Basic Books, 1970).

[5] Melvyn Dubofsky, *We Shall Be All* (Chicago: Quadrangle Books, 1969).

[6] A good and detailed history of the early period of agricultural unionism is Stuart Jamieson, *Labor Unionism in American Agriculture* (New York: Arno Press, 1976). This is a reprint of the 1945 Department of Agriculture Bulletin No. 836. Also, Joan London and Henry Anderson, *So Shall Ye Reap* (New York:Thomas Y. Crowell, 1970) is a biased, but well-written account of California agricultural labor.

[7] Jamieson, *Labor Unionism...*, pp. 80–129.

[8] A classic study of the Bracero Program is Ernesto Galarza. *Merchants of Labor* (San Jose: Rosicrucian Press, Ltd., 1964). Galarza was the most outspoken critic of the Bracero Program.

[9] Lingenfelter, *Hardrock Miners,* pp. 107–127.

[10] Robert L. Spude, "Mineral Frontier in Transition: Copper Mining in Arizona, 1880–1885," unpublished M.A. Thesis, Arizona State University, 1976. Also, Lingenfelter, *Hardrock Miners,* pp. 4–7.

[11] Nogales (Arizona) *Oasis,* June 9, 1906, p. 6.

[12] Lowell L. Blaisdell, *The Desert Revolution* (Madison: University of Wisconsin Press, 1962), pp. 3–20, 41–52.

[13]Migual Casillas, "Agitation or Discrimination: A Reappraisal of the Clifton-Morenci Strike" paper delivered at the Southwest Labor Studies Conference, Torrance, California, April, 1976.

[14]The complete story of this bizarre episode in western labor history is found in Suggs, *Colorado's War*....

[15]J. Kenneth Davies, *Deseret's Sons of Toil* (Salt Lake City: Olympus Publishing Company, 1977), pp. 46–48.

[16]James Byrkit, "The Infamous Bisbee Deportation," unpublished Ph.D. dissertation, Claremont Graduate School, 1972.

[17]Jensen, *Nonferrous Metals Industry Unionism*.

[18]Horace Jerome (Jerry) Voorhis, *Confessions of a Congressman* (Garden City: Doubleday, 1947).

[19]On the expulsions, see Art Preis, *Labor's Giant Step: Twenty Years of the CIO* (New York: Pioneer Publications, 1964).

[20]For the importance of Father Rice's role in the CIO Communist controversy, see Len De Caux, *Labor Radical* (Boston: Beacon Press, 1970), pp. 326–327, 427, 472–473.

I

The Western Federation of Miners

The WFM and Mine-Mill in
Historical Perspective

WHAT WAS THE WESTERN FEDERATION OF MINERS? Hated by Teddy
Roosevelt, hounded by Governor Peabody of Colorado, and hailed by
Arizona's progressive Governor Hunt, the WFM was a labor organization that drew more than its share of fire between 1893 and 1916. Just
as the United Mine Workers had tried to assemble all the eastern coal
miners under one banner at the turn of the century, the Western
Federation sought to bring the western hard-rock miners to a common
standard, whether they hailed from Canada or Arizona. Although the
union never did attract more than half the potential workforce of
100,000 to its cause, there was not a miner in the West who did not
respect the WFM and secretly cheer on its work. Yet, the WFM was
more than mere numbers. It was a political cause as well.

For a time in the American West, socialist parties were potent
third-party threats in a number of states. Colorado, Arizona, and even
the territory of Alaska would see the emergence of strong labor parties, parties whose roots could be traced to the Western Federation.
The Canadian federationists merged their efforts with like-minded
unionists in the cities of British Columbia and Alberta in a campaign
which would outlive the federation by decades. The 1970s would see
the election of a British Columbia premier whose New Democratic
Party called for the same kind of reform that was first voiced by
British Columbia federationists at the turn of the century. Carlos
Schwantes, in his 1979 study, *Radical Heritage,* clearly traces Northwest
radicalism from the New Democrats back to the Western Federation.[1]
Had he studied the rest of the West, he might have found similar
linkages with the WFM heritage. The conservative twenties would
bury that spirit for a while, but it would emerge again and again,
whether as the New Democratic Party, the Cooperative Commonwealth League, or the rudimentary Socialist Labor Party. To steal a
line from "Joe Hill": "I never died says he..."

If the Western Federation's spirit never died, its body did. By
1920, an organization which once boasted a membership of 50,000
and locals in more than 450 American and Canadian towns was left

with fewer than 10,000 dues payers and almost no power. A year later, H. L. McCluskey, its chief organizer and executive board member from Arizona, received a letter from WFM president, Charles Moyers noting, "In regard to the general condition of the organization, it daily grows worse...."[2] So bad would things get that the WFM (or IUMMSW in its post-1916 guise) would be effectively dead by the time it entered the 1930s. Yet, that death and subsequent rebirth grew out of a situation which began seventy-five years earlier in Nevada's premier silver camp, Virginia City.

As the Civil War drew to a close, Comstock Lode silver mines faced their first economic crisis. Stocks of the successful gold-silver mines in Virginia City and Gold Hill were dropping, and skeptics were predicting imminent collapse of the camp. Some owners grumbled about high costs and low profits, but others saw salvation in wage-cutting and the use of low-cost immigrant (Cornish) labor. The supposedly sacrosanct four-dollar day was sacrificed in the name of economy and survival. Unfortunately for the wage-cutting companies, such a course was not as easy as anticipated. As if by magic, the wage-cuts brought forth a labor organization whose battle cry was four dollars and whose battleground was the entire West. The Comstock miners called their organization the Storey County Miners Union; history would record it as the first mine union in the West.[3] It was from the Storey County roots of 1864 that the Western Federation would rise.

What transformed Storey County into the Western Federation? Richard Lingenfelter traces that story in his *Hardrock Miners,* noting that Comstock success was based upon two simple premises: that wages should not be cut, and that all underground workers were eligible for union membership. Over the course of the 1870s and 1880s, these ideas and the Comstock miners spread from Nevada to Montana, and eventually throughout the entire region. Wherever they traveled, the miners planted new unions and won new converts to their principles. However, mere adherence to principle did not guarantee success. The imitation Comstock locals were buffeted by adversity—from Leadville, Colorado, to the rocky canyons of Idaho's Coeur d'Alene. By 1892, the four-dollar day was a rarity, and the tiny Comstock model unions were under assault almost constantly. The time had come for action.

Action would ultimately take the form of amalgamation, amalgamation which seemed to promise some hope in the face of such industrial giants as Montana's Anaconda, or Colorado's ASARCO. A crisis had arisen during the course of a six-month Coeur d'Alene mining strike in 1892. Even with every district union backing the strike, the forces of capital had prevailed, and the losers were jailed for violating an injunction. Ruminating upon the lost strike from their Boise jail cells, a few of the strike leaders came up with the idea of a huge regional mine union, a union which would encompass the entire West. That dream became reality in 1893, when a handful of unions from Idaho, Colorado, Montana, and South Dakota met in Butte, to hammer out the constitution of the Western Federation of Miners. The principles which came out of that meeting were not new. The assembled delegates opposed the company "trucking" system, the use of Pinkertons, the lack of education in mining towns, and the lack of safety regulations; they supported the idea of "industrial," or noncraft, unionism.[4]

The WFM was not too successful at first. For a few years, it actually lost members, its list declining from about 6,000 member in 1893 to less than 5,000 in 1894–1895. Then, along came Ed Boyce. Boyce had been one of the Coeur d'Alene miners jailed in the great 1892 strike and was an avid believer in industrial unionism. As the leader of the WFM in 1896–1897, Boyce spread the federation into new areas such as British Columbia and Arizona. He also involved the federation in an interesting nonmining affiliate, the Western (later American) Labor Union, an organization that was for industrial unionism and against the American Federation of Labor. When he left the WFM in 1902, Boyce headed a union of 20,000 members which stretched from northern British Columbia to southern Arizona.[5] However, many have criticized Boyce for running a one-man show as far as organization was concerned.

The first paper in this section deals with institutional changes made in the Western Federation of Miners after the departure of Boyce, changes which facilitated nonideological organization. Entitled "The WFM Experience in Alaska and Arizona, 1902–1908," it shows how the WFM, under the direction of Charles Moyer of South Dakota, made strategic gains in Alaska and Arizona. Yet, it also questions whether such strategic gains would have made the Western Federation ultimately successful in the hostile industrial climate of 1910–1917.

Moyer's organization biases did bring some notable results. By 1912, the WFM had spread as far east as New York, and into every mining state and province on both sides of the Canadian Border. It numbered more than 50,000 miners that year, the year it tried to confront the Calumet and Hecla Mining Company of Michigan. However, that confrontation was less than successful, as were a whole string of such confrontations over the next few years: Utah Copper in 1912, Calumet and Hecla in 1913, Phelps Dodge in 1916, and

Anaconda in 1917. The federation which had risen so precipitously began to drop just as quickly. War loomed on the horizon. Membership figures never rose above 30,000 once America went "over there," although with the war came some of the highest mining wages paid in the West up to that time. (Arizona copper miners made as much as $6.75 a day during the war, a large sum even during a period of high inflation.)[6] Then came Armistice Day and, with peace, the end of the old WFM.

Just before the war, the WFM changed its name to the International Union of Mine, Mill, and Smelter Workers (1916), in a move which reflected President Moyer's increasing concern with eastern smelter workers and a possible amalgamation with the United Mineworkers of America. History would record that even as the IUMMSW, the union went down in the postwar series of strikes which marked most of American industry. The early twenties would see the pathetic Moyer letter cited earlier. Yet, a question remained unanswered...what happened?

The second essay of the section deals with that question in a quantitative manner. By creating a data bank on relevant industrial relations, ethnic groups, and strike information on 450 mining towns from Alaska to Alabama, the author tried to turn each of these variables concerning WFM failure into a quantifiable problem. If Melvyn Dubofsky, the chronicler of the IWW, viewed the WFM failure as being directly related to the rise of giant mine corporations, then WFM locals should decrease with an increase in the capitalization of mining corporations. Such a hypothesis can be tested statistically, and that is exactly what the essay does. Five different theses concerning Western Federation failure are turned into quantitative problems and then reviewed statistically in light of the WFM data bank.[7] The results are often surprising.

If the federation died an ignoble death in the twenties, the spirit of the thirties revived it, as it revived all of organized labor. New organizers headed back on paths that were beaten bare by the original WFM organizers of the 1900–1910 period. New locals sprang up in Alabama, Alaska, and Arizona. New issues arose and were exploited neatly by a new IUMMSW leadership, headed by the peculiar personage of Reid Robinson. In its second life, the Mine-Mill concentrated on many issues ignored by traditional unions. It was the Mine-Mill, for instance, which first made a concerted effort to organize minorities, particularly the Mexican minority of the Southwest. Many Mexican unionists still remember the Mine-Mill fondly as the first American institution to give them an even break.

The International Union of Mine, Mill, and Smelter Workers was also one of several unions that broke its ties with the American Federation of Labor in 1935 to back the creation of the Committee on Industrial Organization, a labor federation which favored the kind of industrial organization that was pushed by the WFM as early as the days of the Comstock. The spirit of the CIO was carried into the Southwest by the Mine-Mill, and the final paper in this section devotes itself to the organization of Southwestern copper laborers in the thirties.

However, even the strong spirit of the CIO could not bring back the glory days of the old Western Federation. In addition, the Second World War brought out a deep-rooted split within the CIO itself, a split which did not bode well for the IUMMSW.

When the CIO was sweeping into every major industry in the country from autos to steel, few cared about the politics of the organizers. After all, General Motors and United States Steel were the enemies. But in the postwar years, Russia became the enemy, and the IUMMSW was suspect because of the outspoken, leftward cant of its leadership. Reid Robinson was accused of being a red, and his locals were attacked one by one by CIO rivals. It was during the forties also that the United Steelworkers made massive inroads into the Southwest, inroads facilitated by stealing IUMMSW local unions.[8] But the Mine-Mill held on, and, throughout the fifties and sixties, it continued to bring new locals with strong Mexican membership, such as Ray, and Superior, Arizona, into the fold.

But while a few new locals did come into the Mine-Mill fold, many more left by the back door that led to the Steelworkers Union. Mine-Mill was effectively dead by the mid-sixties. Rather than let the last few locals fall completely, the IUMMSW leadership decided to call a halt to twenty years of warfare with the United Steelworkers and agreed to merge the two organizations. An agreement to that effect was drawn up and signed by both parties in 1967. The Western Federation of Miners was no more. The rugged group of individualists who had forced the four-dollar day on the Comstock Mine lost their individual identity and became nothing more than southwestern steelworkers. From start to finish, the western miners' story had taken almost a hundred years.

NOTES

[1]Carlos A. Schwantes, *Radical Heritage,* Labor Socialism, and Reform in Washington and British Columbia, 1885–1917 (Seattle: University of Washington Press, 1979).

[2]Charles A. Moyer to H. S. McCluskey, January 16, 1921, H. S. McCluskey Papers, Arizona Collection, Arizona State University Library, Tempe, Arizona.

[3]Richard E. Lingenfelter, *The Hardrock Miners* (Berkeley: University of California Press, 1974), pp. 31–38.

[4]*Proceedings* of the First Constitutional Convention of the Western Federation of Miners, Butte, Montana, May 15–19, 1893. Also, Lingenfelter, *Hardrock Miners,* pp. 196–228.

[5]Leo Wolman, *Ebb and Flow in Trade Unionism* (New York: National Bureau of Economic Research, 1936), pp. 172–173.

[6]On membership, *Ibid.* Also, Copy of Basis for Agreement submitted to United Verde Copper Company, n.d. (1917), H. S. McCluskey Papers, Tempe, Arizona.

[7]Another version of this same paper explained how the data bank was created and how various issues were dealt with quantitatively. See: James C. Foster, "Quantification and the Western Federation," *Historical Methods Newsletter,* X (Fall, 1977), pp. 141–148.

[8]For a firsthand look at the USA raid on the IUMMSW, see J. Frank Marble to Philip Murray, November 12, 1946, Box A5–11, Folder M–7, John Brophy Papers, Catholic University of America, Washington, D.C.

The WFM Experience in Alaska and Arizona, 1902–1908

James C. Foster

ON MAY 27, 1902, President Ed Boyce of the Western Federation of Miners stunned that organization's tenth convention by concluding a long and complicated annual report with the simple statement, "At this time it is my earnest desire to retire from the office of president."[1] It was the end of an era for the federation. Boyce had led the struggling union for six long years, years more often marked by frustration than celebration. Boyce himself viewed his major accomplishment during that period as merely maintaining the status quo. His union could claim only 20,000 members in a mining region which encompassed almost half of the United States. Yet, that 1902 speech was also the beginning of an era. The man whom the convention would elect to replace Boyce would, at first, prove to be a tremendously successful leader. From 1902 until 1910, that man, former General Organizer Charles A. Moyer, would double the size of the federation and make it one of the most successful unions in the West. The secret of Moyer's success could very well have been the new president's pragmatic approach to syndicalism.

Addressing the eleventh convention of the Western Federation, Moyer summed up his approach to the presidency by stating, "There is no subject of more importance...than the one of organization."[2] Although he would become deeply involved in such controversial WFM programs as political action and the formation of the IWW, Moyer would always remain the general organizer of 1902. He was obviously successful in his work. By 1907, the WFM had grown to over 40,000 members, a level that Moyer would maintain until 1913. The number of local affiliates also expanded dramatically, from Boyce's high of 160 locals to a 1907–1910 level of over 260 local unions. During the same eight-year period, a number of new mining districts also entered into the federation. The WFM of 1910 counted members in Alaska, the Yukon, Minnesota, and Michigan—all areas outside the pale of Western Federation membership in 1902. Yet, Moyer did not neglect the traditional heartland of the federation. The eight years of WFM dynamism also saw organizers bringing new locals into the fold in such old federation strongholds as Arizona, Colorado, and Nevada. The Moyer years would remain the WFM's proudest.[3]

Much has been written about the failures of the Western Federation, the headline-making defeats in Idaho in the nineties, in Colorado and Nevada in the succeeding decade, and of Michigan's Copper Range in the teens. Analysts have examined and reexamined the motives and tactics of the twenty-year corporate open-shop movement in mining. Yet, few have noted that during half of the antiunion period, the Western Federation continued to grow at an almost geometric rate. This organizational phenomenon, occurring under the inspirational leadership of Charles Moyer, may have been just as important as the more publicized efforts of the antiunion corporations. Today, most of western mining has been unionized, and the ultimate success of the mine-union drive could well be traced to the methods and inspiration of Charles Moyer's dedicated band of mine-union organizers.[4]

With the retirement of Boyce in 1902, an immediate change took place in the WFM's emphasis on organization. The old policy of entrusting organization to the six executive board members (who tried to organize their regions as well as minister to the needs of the existing locals) and one full-time organizer was abandoned by Moyer in favor of a more flexible policy of hiring part-time organizers for three- to six-month tours of duty. The president had noticed that board members tended to be ineffective when operating out of their home districts. Why not, he reasoned, supplement their efforts with part-time men whose familiarity with the home ground made them better organizers? By 1907, Moyer's success with this system could be seen in the federation payroll, which was loaded with part-time help. The nine-fold increase in organizers was fully supported by the Western Federation membership. At the 1903 convention, when Moyer asked for suggestions on general federation policy from the floor, the overwhelming response was best stated by member Mike Connors. "Cut out politics and organize," he said.[5]

One of the keys to Moyer's organizational success was his utilization of the new part-time organizers in districts which had been all but ignored by the federation during Boyce's tenure. As important as any of the new areas was what Charles Moyer termed the "northern mineral states." Originally, this had referred only to the midwestern mining areas of Minnesota, Wisconsin, Michigan, Illinois, and Missouri, but, as the organizers went farther and farther afield, the area was broadened to include Alaska, the Yukon, Ontario, and

Quebec.[6] The WFM's greatest success in the early part of the decade was in Alaska, a district which clearly demonstrated Moyer's part-time organizers in action.

Alaska and the Yukon had been ripe for unionization ever since the glitter had worn off the gold rush at the turn of the century. As early as 1900, WFM members who had been lured north to Dawson and Nome had written the *Miners Magazine* that the two gold rush camps were far from ideal for wageworking miners. The labor glut which accompanied the gold rush pushed wages down to such a low level that autonomous local unions sprang up in almost every camp.[7] Still, the Western Federation, concerned with its Colorado fight, ignored the most northern frontier. It took a request from Nome for a charter, in 1905, to alert Moyer, the organizer, to this northern opportunity. He sent Marion W. Moor, an executive board member from the first district (Arizona, California, and Nevada) and a proven organizer, to Nome, with charter No. 240 and instructions to explore the region with unionization in mind.[8]

Moor's experiences during his month in Alaska illustrate the federation's pragmatic approach to organization. In Denver, Moor had been told to expect a mining district which supported 15,000 people and a 1,500-man union. He did not know that his 1,500 unionists would be spread over 300 square miles of the Seward Peninsula. From the very start, traditional forms of organizing were ruled out, as it would have been impossible to cover the district thoroughly in the allotted time. The average organizer would have given Nome its charter and returned, frustrated, to the lower states—but not Moor. Noting that Nome's new Local No. 240 would be a great deal weaker than its high membership would indicate, Moor spent his month finding allies for No. 240. Even though the national WFM was in its anti-AFL phase, Moor worked for weeks to cement an alliance between the new local and an AFL federal labor union which controlled the Nome waterfront. Strategic gifts of cash and public support won the infant WFM local a strong ally in an ideological quarter which might have been ignored by less pragmatic organizers. The WFM–FLU (AFL) alliance founded by Moor would be the basis for the ultimate success of Local No. 240.[9]

Moyer followed the Moor trip with another Alaskan organizing expedition a year later. This time the man selected to court the Alaskan miners was Joel Nelson, a part-time organizer and president of the Western Federation's famous Local No. 220, the Goldfield, Nevada, union. Nelson's trip was similar to Moor's in several ways. Again, the purpose of the trip was to deliver a charter to a self-organized Alaskan local (No. 104 of Ellamar). Once again, the original object was set aside when local conditions turned out to be different than promised. Local No. 104 was holding a strike against Ellamar Copper Company and was hopelessly pitted against the three intransigent Meenach brothers, owners of the company and the company town of Ellamar. Rather than try to break what amounted to a lockout, Nelson took the bulk of No. 104's members and found them jobs in several nearby mines. Then he peacefully organized the new mines into Local No. 134, dubbed the Prince William Sound local.[10] Part of Moyer's success in using part-time organizers had been the utilization of local talent. Since neither Moor nor Nelson were Alaskan, they could not operate as Moyer did, and many of their troubles stemmed from that simple fact. In the meantime, Moyer's attention had been captured by organizing efforts in some of the older federation districts and he was unable to devote much time to Alaska.

Arizona, having been partially organized before the turn of the century, presented a different situation. Indeed, Ed Boyce himself had added a local in the state in 1900, when he helped bring Local No. 17, at Helvetia, into the fold. Admittedly, his concern with Helvetian ideological purity (he spent a great deal of time condemning them for the "unpardonable crime" of reading the *Los Angeles Times*) took precedence over organization, but Arizona did have thirteen WFM locals when Moyer took over the presidency in 1903. Arizona, although one of the older areas in the federation, was not important to the WFM in terms of membership. There were more federationists in Butte, Montana, than in the entire state of Arizona.[11] However, Arizona copper mining was booming, and Moyer was well aware of Arizona's potential; he had helped organize many of the state locals during the 1901–1902 period. Unfortunately, Moyer's first organizer in Arizona, J. T. Lewis of Globe, had none of the skill of the federation president. Although he and part-time organizer C. A. Parisia brought three small locals into the WFM in 1902–1903, and made substantial gains in bringing Mexican Americans into exisiting unions, he missed a major opportunity by not taking advantage of the Morenci eight-hour-day strike. Even appeals made at the eleventh WFM convention failed to interest Lewis in the Morenci union, and the federation watched from the sidelines as the Arizona Rangers drove 3,000 strikers back to work.[12]

Lewis was replaced at the twelfth WFM convention in 1904, and organization in Arizona improved immediately. Interestingly enough, the man who replaced Lewis was the same Marion Moor of McCabe, Arizona, who would take the federation to Alaska in 1905. Moor's first official duty was to preside over a Prescott, Arizona, convention which created Arizona State Union No. 3. This body would be particularly important in the future when, at the urging of Moor and others, it would take up the task of Arizona organization (supplementing national organizers). In the meantime, Moor traveled throughout the state and organized, or revived, a half-dozen locals.[13] It was under Moor that the federation (aided by State Union No. 3) again tried to crack the notorious camp at Bisbee. Moor and John B. Clark, of the state union, worked in Bisbee almost five months, trying to get enough WFM members into the Phelps Dodge mine to risk a shutdown. Hounded constantly by the Arizona Rangers and company spies, they give up in February, 1906, after every WFM convert was fired from the mines. State federation leaders made it clear, however, that their retreat was only temporary; a new approach would be made the following year.[14]

As an Arizona organizer, Marion Moor used his knowledge of local conditions either to win the organizing fight or to cut federation losses during retreats. In 1904, Moor succeeded in reviving the long dormant Gold Road Union (No. 34) by a rather interesting two-step process. He cut off all WFM aid to the aging local leadership, which had presided over the gradual dissolution of No. 34, and encouraged new, nonunion men to come into the camp. Knowing that the poor ventilation and heat of the mines would soon drive away all but the determined (it was called a "ten-day camp"), he then organized the new miners and reported to the 1906 WFM convention that his revived, more active Local No. 34 had won union hours and union wages. He tried similar tactics against the "card system" which was instituted in Snow Ball, Arizona (Local No. 124). However, this time intransigent management overcame guile. Although new miners quickly turned to the union for relief from bad working conditions, management was more willing to accept the problems of a revolving labor force (Snow Ball became a true ten-day camp) than it was to accept the WFM. Holding a WFM card meant permanent surrender of one's work card.[15]

The tactics and organizational tricks which made Moor successful both in Alaska and Arizona were repeated a hundred times by a score of other organizers, as Moyer desperately worked to overcome the losses in Colorado. Organizers such as Joy Pollard, Olinto Marcolina, and James Peretto worked camps from Lake Superior to south of the border. Their efforts kept WFM membership relatively constant all through the Colorado debacle and, by 1907, had actually increased federation support. The next few years would mark the peak of their efforts. Alaska and Arizona both reflected the national situation.

By the spring of 1907, the Alaska WFM was still restricted to the areas immediately surrounding the pioneer locals at Nome and Prince William Sound. Non-WFM mine union activity was not so restricted.

Strong self-organized locals in Juneau and Fairbanks were on the verge of major strikes, strikes which would ultimately involve the Western Federation. In Juneau, a miner named Yanco Terzich was having his first taste of unionism. Two years later, he would be on the WFM's executive board.

Juneau, Alaska, had many of the hallmarks of mining camps far to the south. Although it had several mines, Juneau was dominated by the wealth and wishes of the Treadwell mining group, a London-based corporation which operated in Alaska through a martinet manager named Robert Allen Kinzie. Treadwell had gone to great lengths to keep its labor force docile and nonunion. Kinzie and his predecessors had even made a point of recruiting Serbians and Montenegrans for underground work; both were considered antiunion. Kinzie went one step further in 1907, when he began to stir Japanese and Hindu miners into Treadwell's racial mix,[16] but that turned out to be an error.

In late March, 1907, a Montenegran miner shot a Japanese cook in a Treadwell boardinghouse. The incident was transparently racial, but two very skilled WFM members (from Jerome, Arizona) used it as a foundation upon which to build WFM Local No. 109. Writing to Albert Ryan, secretary of Arizona State Union No. 3, one of the WFM's opportunists noted that all that had been needed was an "incident." Given an opportunity to get all of Treadwell's miners together, he wrote, any good federationist could have convinced the crowd that the enemy was the company, not the Japanese or Hindus. The two WFM men turned a potential race riot into an anti-boardinghouse strike. Two men in the crowd, harangued by the federationists, went even further. Yanco Terzich and Thomas Steffensen became organizers that night.[17]

Terzich proved to be instrumental in the founding of Local No. 109. A Montenegran, he transformed a group of Slavic miners into the nucleus of No. 109 and was responsible for carrying the Juneau WFM into the World War I era. As he told the federation's 1907 convention, Serbs and Montenegrans were natural unionists, if only the WFM's message could be carried in the Slavic languages. This was just the kind of practical advice the WFM sought. An hour later, the federation had a slavic organizer name Terzich; that summer, Treadwell miners were paid a Terzich-negotiated wage.[18]

Tom Steffensen's appeal was not his linguistic ability, but rather his talent for organizational improvisation. The same convention which designated Terzich an organizer gave Steffensen a similar commission for the great un-unionized Alaskan interior. From the outset, Steffensen realized that the key to many camps would be the small businessman as well as the miner. Only if the two were joined could any headway be made against mine management. That was the basic strategy used by the WFM in organizing Alaska's third major camp, Fairbanks.[19]

Fairbanks had an autonomous, but moribund, union when Steffensen arrived in September, 1907. He immediately set about reconstructing it. First, he went to each small town in the district (there were nine) and, using Denver money, began to contract for a union hall on every creek. Each hall would be built out of local materials purchased from local businessmen. It was a bad year in the district, so every dollar was doubly welcome. Within a month, most businesses were sporting WFM banners, and one local newspaper was even editorializing about the beneficent influence of the federation. Second, he talked to miners wherever he went, trying to discover their common grievances. When he discovered that the one solid issue was the desire for an eight-hour day, he began to campaign for just that. He next organized his local (WFM No. 193), which acquired 2,000 card-carrying members within weeks, all publicly committed to the eight-hour day. Finally, he convinced Local No. 193 to pledge itself to a January 1, 1908, strike in favor of the common goal. The carefully organized business-labor coalition did the rest. The editor of the *Tanana Miner* (who had been promised WFM help in organizing a labor paper) formed a group of businessmen who went to both management and local government, insisting that the miners' demand be met. By mid-December, an arbitration panel settled the dispute by granting the eight-hour work day to the miners. Pragmatic organization had won in Alaska.[20]

The same methods and approach to organization were also used in Arizona, but in this instance the results proved that there were limits to pragmatism. The limits were not obvious at first. Federation success with Mexican workers, due to the special efforts of James Peretto's Union at Large (an organizational concept similar to the AFL's Federal Labor Unions) and the IWW local at Phoenix, began to buoy the spirits of the Arizona WFM in early 1907. Also, state organizers Frank Little and Fernando Velardo finally managed to plant two small locals (No. 158 and No. 159) in the Clifton-Morenci district,[21] and State Union No. 3 was able to circulate three organizers through the territory, due to the ten cents per capita organizational tax.[22] Arizona's WFM had become the kind of organization-conscious body that Moyer seemed to want, but neither the new locals, new members, nor the new organizers could disguise the fact that the

Arizona Federation was still not successful. There were few wage agreements in Arizona which could compare with the WFM settlement in Alaska.[23]

William Field Staunton was an admitted enemy of the federation in Arizona, but his comments about the WFM strike in Congress during March and April, 1902, pointed up some important shortcomings of the Arizona Federation. Local No. 155, he noted, was more interested in recognition than in such substantive economic issues as wages and working conditions. Moreover, the WFM demanded recognition when it had only about twenty percent of the camp's workers in the union; something as esoteric as recognition would not keep the other 80 percent committed to a long strike. Staunton's observations proved correct and, with a little manipulation on his part, the strike and Local No. 155 died quickly.[24] An intelligent and active management could beat the tricks of organization anytime.

Five years after the Congress affair, the up-and-coming Arizona State Union No. 3 proved at Bisbee that five years had not made the Arizona WFM wiser. Bisbee had resisted the Western Federation in two previous organizational outings (1903 and 1906), and the management of the Phelps Dodge Company had proven itself capable of matching every federation organizational trick with a union-busting trick of its own. In 1903, the company had persuaded Bisbee's fraternal organizations to condemn the WFM (which resulted in a 90 percent drop in attendance at the union's meetings) and, three years later, it sent spies into union circles (who were able to help the company fire every union member).[25] Regardless, the WFM's 1907 effort utilized more money and more organizers for but one purpose—organization. Management privately admitted that mine conditions were bad enough to have justified a strike on that ground, but the union struck to the discredited Arizona pattern—recognition rather than economics.[26]

The Bisbee affair of 1907 went almost as management would have desired. State and national federation officials began their campaign in February. Two local organizers, Joseph Cannon and Percy Rawlings, set up WFM No. 106 in Bisbee and made a concerted attempt to interest the town's miners in the new organization. Nationally, the WFM was able to bring in such stars as "Mother" Mary Jones to harangue the new members and, incidentally, to visit nearby El Paso and make certain that Bisbee owners would not be able to hire scabs there. The immediate effects of the WFM's work were promising. Over 1,200 men joined Local 106 in two months. However, Phelps Dodge and the other companies were not caught unprepared. As in 1906, union men were fired wholesale. The justification for some 1,600 layoffs (the companies apparently believed in overkill) was due to "repairs" and a "shortage of fuel" which miraculously affected only those companies most heavily unionized.[27] When the union replied by calling a strike on April 10 management retaliated with a classic, union-busting technique; it surreptitiously created a "patriotic" (or company) union.[28] Local No. 106 gave up in December.[29]

The pragmatic Alaskan locals soon followed Bisbee in decline. All WFM efforts seemed to go for naught in 1908. Spurning an excellent settlement in January, Fairbanks Federation No. 193 found that it had misjudged the temper of the Tanana district. The allies that Steffensen had won deserted the union when Local No. 193 began talking strike. The antiunion federal judge, James Wickersham, was then able to assemble a strong anti-WFM coalition which broke the strike, enabling him to jail Steffensen and to get himself elected to Congress.[30] Terzich's Juneau local called a strike in the spring of 1908, for no apparent economic reason, and began a long period of decline which it would never reverse.[31] Only Nome, the original Alaskan local, survived 1908 unscathed. The Nomeites continued to work under a favorable 1907 wage agreement and almost succeeded in electing one of their own members to Congress. Until World War I, Nome would continue to support a strong WFM local.[32]

Nationally, the Western Federation seemed to be in good health in 1908. To the outsider, the WFM's bulging membership rolls more than offset the small setbacks in Arizona and Alaska. Yet, those setbacks would prove to be accurate forecasts of the fate of the entire Western Federation of Miners in coming years. Membership declined drastically in 1909 and, by 1915, the once proud federation was barely as strong as it was in 1902. The brilliant Moyer could only wonder what had gone wrong.

What most hurt Moyer's WFM was an unconscious emphasis on pragmatic but superficial organization. Moyer's fine tuning of the organizational structure did indeed bring the best men to the fore, but it did nothing to ensure the continuing existence of the new locals when the high-powered organizer left. Because of this, the WFM lost almost twenty locals a year. In 1907, Alaska had six locals with 5,000 members; a year later, there were but 2,000 members in three locals. The old locals in Butte and Globe had survived over the years due to the organizational abilities and interests of a large percentage of the membership,[33] but the boom locals of the 1906–1913 period were like sinners at a tent meeting; the effect was amazing as long as the preacher was there, but when he left they returned to business as usual. The new locals were not noted for longevity.

If superficial organization was the first of the federation's problems, a better prepared opponent was a close second. By 1910, a well-read mine owner could use the examples of Colorado, the Coeur d'Alene, or Goldfield miners in mounting an antiunion drive in his district. Strikebreakers, Pinkertons, back-to-work movements, and injunctions had all been perfected as antiunion tools. Men like William Staunton in Arizona and Judge Wickersham in Alaska fully understood the uses of each. Moreover, a new generation of college-educated mine engineers (like Kinzie in Juneau) realized that machinery and new mining techniques had minimized the WFM's vaunted monopoly of mining skills.[34] Yet, there was more.

As important a shortcoming as either of the above was a WFM ideology which equated industrial unionism with radical-sounding politics. The WFM refused to sanction contracts, but contracts could have worked to the federation's advantage. The WFM embraced Socialism, but Socialists were suspect and the SPA was weak. The Western Federation retained a democratic, decentralized administration, but more centralization might have kept the faltering locals intact. Interestingly enough, an equally industrial United Mine Workers was able to thrive in the same era by keeping economics and politics apart.[35]

In the long run, the federation failed. The country averted its eyes when management brutally dismembered the WFM during the period 1914–1920. After all, the WFM—unlike the UMW—was "radical" and expendable. It was not really as radical as its opponents portrayed (it had only a few Haywoods), but it would not be until the 1935 enactment of the Wagner Act that the radical tag (management's most effective anti-WFM weapon) would lose most of its importance.[36] What Moyer really needed in 1910 was section 8(a)5 of the Wagner Act, a law which would have transformed pragmatic organization into effective collective bargaining.

NOTES

[1]Report of President Edward Boyce to the tenth convention of the Western Federation of Miners in *Proceedings of the Tenth Annual Convention of the Western Federation of Miners of America,* May 26–June 7, 1902, Denver, Colorado, p. 14.

[2]Report of President Charles Moyer to the eleventh convention of the Western Federation of Miners in *Proceedings of the Eleventh Annual Convention of the Western Federation of Miners of America,* May 25–June 10, 1903, Denver, Colorado, p. 32.

[3]Statistics on WFM membership, numbers of locals, and areas of organization came from various annual reports of WFM secretary-treasurers. For example, see *Report of Secretary-Treasurer Ernest Mills to the Western Federation of Miners on the Fiscal Year Ending June 30, 1913* (an almost complete set of these can be found at the Wisconsin State Historical Society, Madison, Wisconsin).

[4]Several excellent studies have recently been done on this negative side of the Western Federation experience. See George G. Suggs, Jr., *Colorado's War on Militant Unionism* (Detroit: Wayne State University Press, 1972) or James W. Byrkit, "Life and Labor in Arizona, 1901–1921: With Particular Reference to the Deportations of 1917," unpublished Ph.D. dissertation, Claremont Graduate School, 1972. A different approach to the WFM can be found in John Ervin Brinley, Jr., "The Western Federation of Miners," unpublished Ph.D. dissertation, University of Utah, 1972.

In Arizona alone, the twenty-three mine unions presently associated with the United Steelworkers of America can usually be traced back to WFM unions first organized in the period under study (only four or five were originally organized by the USA). Interview with Dudley Killingsworth, District 38, Subdistrict 8, United Steelworkers of America, Tempe, Arizona, February 20, 1975.

[5]*Proceedings of the Eleventh Annual Convention...*, p. 261. Moyer's increased emphasis on organization could be seen in a variety of ways. In his annual report of 1903 (eleventh convention), he mentioned both the idea of using part-time organizers and the names of five men hired in that capacity during 1902–1903 (including Marion Moor of Arizona). See pp. 25–33 of the above proceedings.

The response can be gauged by reading pp. 261–265 of the eleventh convention's proceedings.

[6]Report of President Charles Moyer to the thirteenth convention of the Western Federation of Miners in *Proceedings of the Thirteenth Annual Convention of the Western Federation of Miners of America*, May 22–June 9, 1905, Salt Lake City, Utah, p. 31. By 1906, Alaska, Quebec, and Ontario had become items on the WFM's convention agenda: see *Proceedings of the Fourteenth Annual Convention of the Western Federation of Miners*, May 28–June 13, 1906, Denver, Colorado, pp. 154–155.

[7]Walter Carter to Ed Boyce, February 28, 1900 reprinted in *Miners Magazine*, April, 1900, p. 24; W. R. Goldsmith to Ed Boyce, March 12, 1900, reprinted in *Miners Magazine*, May 1900, pp. 27–29; and "Stay Away from Nome," *Miners Magazine*, August 1900, p. 1. The gist of the three reports was that Alaska and the Yukon were crowded with wageworking miners and wages were dropping rapidly.

[8]Report of Marion W. Moor to the fourteenth convention of the Western Federation of Miners in *Proceedings of the Fourteenth Annual Convention...*, pp. 218–222. Also, *Miners Magazine*, August 3, 1905, p. 3.

[9]"Some History of the Nome, Alaska, Strike," *Miners Magazine*, January 11, 1906, p. 5. Also *Nome Nugget*, August 16, 1905, p. 1; October 14, 1905, p. 1. The Nome local even won the political support of major Nome businessmen: see, for example, Entry for March 2, 1906, Carl Lomen Diary, Box 13, Lomen Family Collection, University of Alaska Archives, Fairbanks, Alaska. For a brief history of Nome Local No. 240, see James C. Foster, "AFL, IWW, and Nome," *Alaska Journal*, Spring, 1975.

[10]*Miners Magazine*, April, 1900, p. 11.

[11]*Ibid.* Comparison of membership can be found in *Proceedings of the Eleventh Annual Convention...*, pp. 86–89. Boyce's ideological bias can easily been seen by comparing his address to the tenth convention with Moyer's address to the eleventh convention. The first was filled with calls for cooperative ownership, socialist political action, and war against capitalism. The latter concentrated solely upon strikes and organization.

[12]The Mexican-American question proved to be most controversial in the WFM's Arizona operation. Locals in Kofa, Jerome, and Clifton-Morenci incorporated Mexican workers, but the other locals resisted Mexican unionization and were often broken by the use of Mexican scabs. Moyer did his utmost to get Arizona to organize Mexican Americans and he had some success. In 1903, J. T. Lewis called for Mexican organization in Arizona for "the best interests of the federation." Report of J. T. Lewis to the eleventh convention of the Western Federation of Miners in *Proceedings of the Eleventh Annual Convention...*, pp. 95–96. On Clifton-Morenci, see W. M. Murphy and Albert Ryan to Charles Moyer, n.d. (June, 1903) in *Proceedings of the Eleventh Annual Convention...*, p. 224. Also, an account of unofficial WFM action can be seen in James S. Douglas to Phelps Dodge Corporation, June 11, 1903, Box 42, Folder 5 (Phelps Dodge Corporation), Lewis W. Douglas Papers, University of Arizona Library Special Collections, Tucson, Arizona.

[13]Report of Marion Moor to the thirteenth convention of the Western Federation of Miners in *Proceedings of the Thirteenth Annual Convention* ..., pp. 252–255.

[14]Report of Marion Moor to the fourteenth convention of the Western Federation of Miners in *Proceedings of the Fourteenth Annual Convention* ...,pp. 218–222. A good secondary source on the conflict in Bisbee during 1906 can be found in Vernon Jensen, *Heritage of Conflict* (Ithaca: Cornell University Press, 1950), pp. 357–358. A previous attempt had been made in 1903 by J. T. Lewis and an organizer named Hugh Kennedy. See Report of J. T. Lewis to the twelfth convention of the Western Federation of Miners in *Proceedings of the Twelfth Annual Convention of the Western Federation of Miners of America*, May 23–June 8, 1904, Denver, Colorado, p.25; also, Percy Rawlings, "Organizing Bibee," *Miners Magazine*, March 7, 1907, p. 9.

[15]"Arizona Labor Conditions," *Miners Magazine*, February 21, 1907, p. 8. Also, Report of Marion Moor to the thirteenth convention of the Western Federation of Miners in the *Proceedings of the Thirteenth Annual Convention* ..., pp. 252–255.

[16]"The Treadwell Mines," *Alaska-Yukon Magazine*, September, 1907, pp. 73–81, 91. Also, *Daily Alaska Dispatch*, March 29, 1907, p. 4.

[17]Charles Burke to Albert Ryan, April 14, 1907, reprinted in *Miners Magazine*, April 18, 1907, p. 14. The two WFM men were Burke and Casey Thorpe.

[18]Report of Yanco Terzich to the fifteenth convention of the Western Federation of Miners in *Proceedings of the Fifteenth Annual Convention of the Western Federation of Miners*, June 10–July 3, 1907, Denver, Colorado, pp. 356–364.

The wage settlement negotiated by Terzich called for an extra dollar per day in lieu of use of the company boardinghouses (the very demand the union had made before the start of a successful nineteen day strike). *Daily Alaska Dispatch*, April 19, 1907, p. 1, and Sewald Torkelson to *Miners Magazine*, June 7, 1907, reprinted in *Miners Magazine*, July 11, 1907, p. 14.

[19]For Steffensen's methods, see *Tanana Miner*, October 14, 1907, p. 1; October 28, 1907, p. 1; and November 3, 1907, p. 1. The newspaper which was won over was the *Tanana Miner*, edited by W. F. Thompson. See Thompson's pro-WFM editorial in *Tanana Miner*, November 10, 1907, p. 2.

[20]The full report of the arbitration panel (composed of equal numbers of business, labor, and mining leaders) can be found in the diary of District Judge James Wickersham. Wickersham was the head of the arbitration panel. Entries for December 6, 1907 and December 11, 1907, James A. Wickersham Diary, Roll 3, James A. Wickersham Diaries (film), University of Alaska Archives, Fairbanks, Alaska.

The settlement called for an eight-hour day with pay of $5.00 (the union's demand) which would be in effect from April 1 to October 1, 1908 (the working season). It also included nondiscriminatory rehire of all union men, but did not include recognition of the WFM.

[21]The Union at Large is explained in John Ervin Brinley, "The Western Federation of Miners," unpublished Ph.D. dissertation, University of Utah, 1972, pp. 61–62.

In Arizona, the Union at Large seemed to be particularly interested in organizing Italian unionists (Clifton-Morenci had a large number).

[22]Report of Marion Moor to the fourteenth convention of the Western Federation of Miners in *Proceedings of the Fourteenth Convention* ..., p. 222. Also, "Arizona Labor Conditions," *Miners Magazine*, February 21, 1907, p. 8.

[23]The Alaskan locals did fairly well in getting wage increases. Nome miners raised their daily pay by $1.00 while lowering the hours of labor from ten to eight. The Arizona locals were constantly on the defensive. Only Globe's Local No. 60 was able to maintain a respectable union scale for more than a short time. On Globe, see *Proceedings of the Eleventh Convention* ..., pp. 230–232 (complaints about an agreement signed by the local), and *Miners Magazine*, April 14, 1907, p. 4. On Nome's rich settlement of 1907, see *Fairbanks Daily Times*, April 7, 1907, p. 4.

[24]Entries of March 8, 10, 19, 20, 29, 1902 in William Field Staunton Diary, Box 1, Diary of July 12, 1901, to March 28, 1903; William Field Staunton Memoirs, Vol. I, Box 1, Memoirs; and Congress Gold Company Release, March 15, 1902, Box 5, Folder 4; all in William Field Staunton Papers, University of Arizona Library Special Collections, Tucson, Arizona.

Staunton did quite a bit of manipulation in the 1902 strike. He brought in Mexican scabs from Phoenix, deputized several dozen sympathizers with the law's cooperation, and hired a Pinkerton operative to infiltrate the WFM (Local No. 155). When this did not stop the strike, he tapped the union's phone and all the telegraph lines in a ten-mile radius of Congress. For the other side of the strike, see "Congress Miners Locked Out," *Miners Magazine*, May, 1902, pp. 9–10. The union claimed that Staunton had even hired the town's two clergymen to start a back-to-work movement.

[25]On the 1903 and 1906 attempts, see Jensen, *Heritage*, pp. 357–358. Also, J. Albert Mallory, "The Class Struggle in Bisbee," *Common Sense*, (March 1906), reprinted in *Miners Magazine*, April 5, 1906, p. 14; and the *Bisbee Daily Review*, December 25, 1907, p. 1, and December 27, 1907, p. 1.

[26]Percy Rawlings, "Organizing Bisbee," *Miners Magazine*, March 7, 1907, p. 9. Also, the famous debate over Bisbee at the 1907 convention, *Proceedings of the Fifteenth Convention...*, pp. 193–203. On the strike's end see *Miners Magazine*, August 27, 1908, p. 7. *Arizona Labor Journal*, August 21, 1913, p. 46.

James B. Douglas privately admitted as early as 1903 that working conditions in the Bisbee mines were so bad that they would have justified a strike. James S. Douglas to Phelps Dodge Corporation, June 11, 1903, Box 42, Folder 5, Lewis W. Douglas Papers, University of Arizona Library Special Collections, Tucson, Arizona.

[27]*Arizona Journal-Miner*, February 17, 1907, p. 6 and February 28, 1907, p. 8. Also, Dale Fetherling, *Mother Jones, the Miners' Angel* (Carbondale: Southern Illinois University Press, 1974), p. 79, and Byrkit, pp. 93–96.

[28]The organization was dubbed the Bisbee Industrial Association, and every member was given a "working card" in return for the $1.00 membership fee. *Arizona Journal-Miner*, March 8, 1907, p. 5.

A similar tactic was tried the following year in Alaska, where the Treadwell mines organized a "white man's union" (most WFM members were Montenegrans and were not "white" by the group's standards), which was given free use of Treadwell facilities and broke a 1908 strike: *Daily Alaska Dispatch*, February 15, 1908, p. 3, and March 20, 1908, p. 1.

[29]*Miners Magazine*, August 23, 1908, p. 7.

[30]Entries of December 15, 1907, March 15, March 18, 1908, James Wickersham Diary, Roll 3, James A. Wickersham Diaries (film), University of Alaska Archives, Fairbanks, Alaska. Also, *Nome Industrial Worker* (publication of Local No. 240) August 10, 1908, pp.1–4; and Jeanette Paddock Nichols, *Alaska* (Cleveland: Arthur Clark, 1924), pp. 309–317. For views of a man soliciting the Alaska WFM vote, see "Scrapbook," Box 2, John P. Clum Papers, University of Arizona Library Special Collections, Tucson, Arizona.

[31]Report of President Charles Moyer to the seventeenth convention of the Western Federation of Miners in *Proceedings of the Seventeenth Convention of the Western Federation of Miners*, July 12–August 3, 1909, Denver, Colorado, pp. 25–26; and *Daily Alaska Dispatch*, June 25, 1908, p. 4.

[32]The union was still strong enough to challenge Judge G. J. Lomen's appointment as a federal judge in 1918. See Resolution by Local No. 240, IUMMSW, July 30, 1918 in Box 6, Folder I, Lomen Family Papers, University of Alaska Archives, Fairbanks, Alaska.

[33]Brinley, pp. 174–183. A simple observation of the activities of the Butte and Glove unions at conventions and in the *Miners Magazine* shows that both had an uncommon number of skilled union men who were able to both organize at the local level (many of the boom locals were founded by organizers from the two) and negotiate successful labor contracts (although the WFM did not like the idea of contracts).

[34]An important conclusion of Brinley, pp. 190–195. This was particularly true in Arizona and Alaska: See Byrkit, pp. 92–93. Wherever profit per unit was low, skilled labor lost its edge, due to the utilization of machinery to make up for low-profit margins with high production. Skilled labor was at its best when miners had to follow a meandering, but highly concentrated ore body underground.

[35]An excellent comparison of the two industrial mining unions can be found in the conclusion of Brinley, pp., 174–196. It should be noted that two WFM locals did use contracts (Butte and Globe), and both were unusually successful.

In both Arizona and Alaska, the WFM was by definition radical and violent. Some of the WFM's enemies accepted such a definition quite uncritically: see Will L. Clark (supervisor of United Verde Copper Co.) to Charles W. Clark, April 24, 1909, History Drawer 10, Correspondence 1898–1917 Folder, United Verde Copper Company, Jerome, Arizona.

[36]Section 8(a)5 of the amended Wagner Act simply stated that management had to bargain collectively with its employees if they so desired. A similar law existed during the WFM period in Canada (the Canadian Industrial Disputes Acts of 1907), and it materially aided WFM locals in British Columbia and Ontario: see Harry A. Millis and Royal E. Montgomery, *Organized Labor* (New York: McGraw-Hill, 1945), pp. 783–793.

The definitive work to date on the WFM in Canada (British Columbia) is Martin Robin, *Radical Politics and Canadian Labour, 1880–1930* (Kingston: Industrial Relations Centre of Queens University, 1968).

An Inquiry into the Fall of the WFM, and Summary of the WFM Codebook

James C. Foster

As SAMUEL GOMPERS PAUSED IN 1919 to write his last testament to the labor movement, he could not resist the temptation to hurl one final rebuke at a hated adversary. "The Western Federation of Miners," wrote Gompers, " ... was so determined to subordinate the labor movement to Socialism that reason could not prevail." There was nothing but venom in the words as the AFL president described the WFM and its one-time president Ed Boyce. "It is easy to teach revolutionary doctrine, but very difficult to remove the stigma of revolutionary tactics. The WFM is still suffering from its chosen course."[1]

With the merger of the IUMMSW and the United Steelworkers in the late 1960s, the "suffering" of the Western Federation ended once and for all, but the interest the organization held for historians had hardly begun. The Western Federation of Miners has, in recent years, emerged as the most intriguing, yet most frustrating, union for labor historians to study. Its key role in the creation of the Industrial Workers of the World in the United States and in the organization of the One Big Union in Canada marked the WFM as a leader in the synthesis of Rocky Mountain syndicalism. Its adventures in Coeur d'Alene, Colorado, and British Columbia intrigued scholars and storytellers alike. Its leadership from Boyce and Haywood to Moyer generated decades of debate and controversy. Its violent tactics fascinated that new breed of mobility-conscious social historians. Yet, the Western Federation also proved overwhelmingly frustrating to historians who probed its past. The Western Federation left little behind in the way of manuscript sources. Member miners apparently kept few diaries and even fewer correspondence collections. The Denver headquarters, which did compile careful records at one time, burned most of its material during the dark days of the twenties. State and district offices either kept no records or lost them to time and the decline of the WFM. As far as primary sources were concerned, only two bright spots appeared on an otherwise drab horizon. The federationists of

[33]

Canada's District 6 had preserved scrupulous records, which were passed on to the International Union of Mine, Mill, and Smelter Workers and, eventually, to the University of British Columbia Library. Mine owners, as concerned about the WFM as latter-day historians, also kept careful tabs on the Western Federation opposition. A few creative historians, following the lead of George Suggs, discovered that companies from Phelps Dodge to Homestake had maintained excellent, if biased, records of WFM activity.[2] Regardless, the task of the Western Federation historian is not an easy one. With traditional primary sources in such short supply, the historian has to depend more and more upon quantifiable, ecological data and the statistical methodology of the social sciences. Surprisingly, closer examination of such data has yielded a number of new insights into the union.

Traditional WFM histories, limited in scope due to the source problem, have revolved around the activities of the large and important locals. Newspaper and limited manuscript material were available for Butte, Bisbee, Globe, and other large WFM operations; consequently work in such material resulted in a rather thorough understanding of the battles and internal affairs of the "super-locals" of the federation. But the Western Federation was much more than a mere alliance of large locals.[3] In its twenty-odd years under the WFM title, the federation brought over 577 local unions into the fold, local unions which ranged geographically from Alabama to Alaska. A majority of these were not in the immediate environs of Butte, Cripple Creek, or Globe, but were in Kentucky, Tennessee, New Jersey, and Illinois—there was even a local in Brooklyn. As a result, there are whole districts within the federation which American historians have never described. Indeed, there is not so much as a mention of District 6 (Canada), with its 6,000 members, in Vernon Jensen's classic, *Heritage of Conflict.*[4] Obviously, when quantification takes the activities of all 577 locals into its calculations, it will provide a much more accurate picture of the Western Federation than the Butte-Cripple Creek approach.

The key to quantifying the Western Federation has been the WFM record itself. While good manuscript sources were not left behind, excellent printed sources did survive. Vernon Jensen's pioneering work in the field was based upon just such sources, such as the *Miners Magazine*, convention proceedings, and local union newspapers. The magazine, for instance, was published between 1900 and 1921 as first a monthly and then a weekly record of WFM activities. More contemporary correspondence concerning the Western Federation appeared in the various columns of the magazine than in all other sources combined. If a strike was called or an internal union fight was brewing, specific and unexpurgated letters explaining the situation soon found their way into the correspondence columns of the *Miners Magazine*. When the magazine failed to reveal a story, WFM convention proceedings could always be depended upon to bring it to light. Not only were these proceedings accurate reflections of the condition of the union (including membership), but they were also useful in revealing how various locals stood on the issues of the day. The questions of socialism, the IWW, the AFL, and the controversial WFM contract policy were all brought before the convention on an almost yearly basis.

The proceedings and the magazine composed the bulk of published sources on the WFM, but regional and local labor newspapers often filled in the details that were ignored by these national publications. To complete the story, company records and company-owned newspapers gave accurate renditions of company policy concerning the Western Federation.[5] All of this, combined with existing manuscript sources, could well produce an accurate portrait of the WFM.[6] However, until the advent of computer-assisted research, the sheer size of the task has discouraged most researchers. In the meantime, quantification has come to labor history.

Computer research in labor history has not been a recent development. Stephen Thernstrom's mobility studies have been available for more than a decade, and census-based social history has been around since Merle Curti's Trempealeau work. However, few scholars, until recently, have applied computer research to the traditional branches of labor history. Few have used computers to explain the vagaries of union growth, failure, and death. The pioneering work in this phase of labor history was the crude evaluation of the union movement made by Leo Wolman in his 1936 study, *Ebb and Flow in Trade Unionism*. That work, funded by the National Bureau of Economic Research, used quantitative methods (but not a computer) to ascertain the relation between union membership and union strength.[7] More recently, Jonathan Garlock applied computer techniques to assemble an extensive data bank on the Knights of Labor. Although the WFM project required different kinds of data, its approach was similar to the Garlock study.[8]

Wolman's first problem was to compile a machine-readable archive, based upon the WFM sources previously mentioned. Unlike the Garlock study, the WFM study demanded far more than mere research into membership, occupational patterns, and ethnic identification; Wolman devoted a great deal of time to ascertaining exactly what data could be used to check the veracity of various theses concerning the Western Federation. This led to the definition of fifty-seven variables ranging from membership to migration,[9] and information on each of these was compiled for the 577 locals listed by John Brinley in his 1972 WFM dissertation as well as 40 additional local unions uncovered by the author.[10] When the data bank was completed, it contained details on every WFM strike, wage settlement, local leader, employing company, local political posture, and violent incident between 1893 and 1920. It also listed every local by state, town, membership size, community size, and company size. Thus, locals could be grouped in a variety of ways, which would facilitate interstate (were Colorado locals more successful than British Columbia ones), intercity (were small town locals different from large community ones), and intercompany comparisons (were locals dealing with small companies more successful than those dealing with large corporations).[11] The data bank completed, the next task was one of definition.

Over the past eighty years, unionists, scholars, and others have put forth a variety of reasons for the eventual failure of the Western Federation of Miners. For the sake of simplicity, these reasons are being summarized in six theses. First, Vernon Jensen's classic explanation of WFM failure revolves around the violent climate of Rocky Mountain mining camps. His *Heritage of Conflict* blames that milieu of violence and counter-violence for creating an industrial relations system based upon confrontation rather than cooperation. While the United Mine Workers were working within the peaceful framework of the National Civic Federation, where such great capitalists as J. P. Morgan discussed labor issues with the likes of the UMWA's John Mitchell, the Western Federation condemned the ideological errors of such a course.[12]

A second thesis concerning Rocky Mountain violence and, indirectly, the Western Federation has recently emerged in the works of quantitative social historians. Based upon the disappearance of large numbers of working-class people from the census rolls (a fact which Thernstrom discovered as early as his Newburyport study), this thesis contends that Rocky Mountain violence (and particularly strike violence) was engendered by a floating class of dropouts, whose lowly social position gave them nothing to lose and a great deal of satisfaction to gain through what Haywood would describe as "direct action." Such social historians blame this floating group, not mining-camp confrontation, for WFM failure.[13]

A third thesis, one used more by corporate than labor historians, blames WFM "radicalism" for the union's failure. These historians argue that the radical rhetoric of the WFM was out of step both with the times and the region, an argument which is similar to that used by both Gompers and a number of conservatives within the WFM itself.

Having accepted such rhetoric, they argue, the WFM could expect no aid either from local politicians or from more conservative elements within the labor movement.[14]

A fourth thesis, one perfectly summarized by Melvyn Dubofsky in *We Shall Be All,* places WFM failure in the context of a small and fragmented union trying to face an increasingly unified corporate structure. A union which could succeed in the Cripple Creek of the 1890s would not necessarily be successful against such corporate giants as ASARCO, Phelps Dodge, and Anaconda in the early 1900s. Mine ownership became increasingly concentrated between 1890 and 1900, and the Western Federation could not muster the men to face such consolidated wealth and power.[15]

A fifth thesis blames Western Federation failure on the decreasing economic worth of the federation's skilled miners. Their stranglehold on skill made them indispensable in the 1890s, but new mining techniques and low grade ores found them mechanized out of their jobs and position of power.[16]

Finally, the most intriguing thesis of all blames America's antiquated labor laws for the failure of the federation and notes the relative success of Canadian locals under the 1907 Industrial Disputes Act. The act, with a few features that would emerge under the 1935 Wagner Act (particularly the 8[a] 5 requirement that management bargain collectively), provided a legal umbrella which protected Canadian federationists from the kinds of tactics which purged the WFM from Colorado and Arizona.[17] All of these theses can be examined quantitatively.

To cope adequately with Jensen's emphasis on violence, the WFM codebook has classified violence according to number of outbreaks (VIONUM), duration (VIOLEN), type (VIOTYPE), apparent cause (VIOCAUSE), and apparent perpetrator (VIOLATE). On the basis of locals already coded, violence was neither as pervasive nor as union-inspired as Jensen concluded.[18] The average union experienced no more than 0.829 violent incidents in its lifetime (7.2 years). Most of the coded unions experienced no violence of any kind. Only the exceptional Cripple Creek local in Colorado had more than eight such incidents in its history, and most of the troubles stemmed from management's carefully orchestrated Colorado labor war of 1903–1904. Strangely enough, there was a positive correlation between a local's success and the amount of violence associated with the local (Pearson's r of .5647 with a significance level of .001). On the surface at least, Jensen's conclusions seem to be in error.

The migrant violence thesis is almost as easily dismissed. In the entire study, only eight locals reported that violence involved migrant miners. However, the study did reveal that there was more migration among miners than the social historians had anticipated. The average WFM local experienced a turnover of about 45 percent of its membership during its existence. Many small locals experienced an even higher turnover (about 10 percent of the cases showed turnover in excess of 80 percent). Yet, correlating turnover with violence (MEMTURN with VIONUM) resulted in a Pearson's r of only .2194, hardly worthy of mention. A few loose ends were left with this rough procedure, and these were handled by additional features of the codebook. For instance, many WFM locals experienced an influx of massive numbers of Yugoslavian, Italian, or Mexican contract laborers. None of these could be considered "migrant" under the definition of the American social historians. Thus, a second correlation was run, taking into consideration the source of migration (MEMMIG), and the partial coefficient showed even less association between membership turnover and violence (with most of the violence occurring in locals with significant numbers of contract laborers).[19]

The problem of equating failure with the advent of large mining corporations was quantified by comparing local success (SUCNO) with the capitalized size of the employing corporation (COCAP).[20] Again, the anticipated high negative correlation did not show up. Although the coefficient was negative, the size of that coefficient (–.0497) did not warrant an assumption that success decreased rapidly as company size increased. Other parameters of success also declined slightly as capitalization increased. Correlations between length of existence, strikes won, and other indicators of success, with company size were slightly negative. A final factor was introduced into the equation by separating out the effects of the very large corporations (those with capitalization exceeding $50 million) on success. Even then, a partial correlation coefficient differed only slightly from the uncompensated r (partial r = –.0749). While there was no doubt of the hostility of such giants as Phelps Dodge, that hostility was not everywhere translated into successful union purges. Indeed, the other large corporations seemed to have shown a rather enlightened attitude in the labor relations sector. The federation's failure was not brought about by the advent of the industrial giants.

Was the WFM radical? While its writings condemned it in many eyes, its labor relations policies seemed anything but radical. Quantifiably, there was little or no violence in the camps. Observation of the five tenets of radical behavior (support of the socialist party = SOCISM, support of the IWW = IWW, support of syndical violence = SYNDVIO, and opposition to the AFL = AFL and UMWA = UMW) showed little support for radicalism in most camps.[21] Although the WFM founded the IWW, most locals supported the federation's stance when it severed its ties with the wobblies in 1907–1908. Only four locals admitted to supporting the concept of syndical violence, even in theory. A majority of the unions supported mergers with the AFL and United Mine Workers. Creating a composite variable called RADICAL (a dummy interval variable of views on the five radical positions), correlations were run between radicalism and success. There was no significant correlation between the two. In fact, there were almost too few radical locals to compute a meaningful statistic. If radicalism felled the federation, it was a radicalism by reputation rather than fact.

The thesis put forward by western historians explaining WFM defeat in terms of the decreasing worth of the skilled miner required a bit of explanation before it could be reduced to quantitative terms. In the early West, a miner who could follow the intricate meanderings of a valuable gold or silver vein was indispensable to mine owners and was usually paid accordingly. However, the turn of the century and consequent increased importance of low-grade copper ore brought an end to such happy days. Copper ores were usually found in huge deposits, where the only underground skill needed was a strong back; there was no need to pay $5.00 per day for a skilled miner whose skill was unnecessary. The change from skilled to nonskilled labor was expressed quantifiably in two areas. First, locals were classed according to the metal that was mined (METAL). If this thesis was valid, gold and silver miners should have done better than copper or iron miners. Secondly, mine companies were classified according to placer, lode, or open-pit operations (COTYPE).[22] Correlation coefficients were then computed for success with each of the two variables. Results again cast doubts on the accepted thesis. A coefficient of only .3476 was computed between SUCNO and METAL and a coefficient of but .2427 was found between SUCNO and COTYPE. Neither showed a significant correlation between skill and success.[23]

The last thesis, the one dealing with the enlightened labor policy of Canada, was tested by comparing the success, term of existence, and strikes won by American unions as compared to Canadian (in this case British Columbia) unions. On the whole, the Canadian unions had only a slightly larger average membership (about 178 to 157), a slightly longer lifespan (8.897 to 7.212 years), and were involved in fewer strikes (.487 to 1.805). Being involved in fewer labor disputes, they won fewer than the American locals and therefore showed a lower number of absolute successes, but this was offset by a strike success ratio of .790 for Canadians as compared to .366 for Americans. Other comparisons showed no major differences. The fewer number of strikes and the almost incredible lack of violence (mean

Canadian violence = .032 cases per local lifetime) did show that something was working well in Canada. It is very possible that the Industrial Disputes Act, which forced both parties to bargain face-to-face, negated the value of violence and a hard-line industrial stance; even when violence was introduced into a situation, the company still had to meet with the union. In the United States, on the other hand, a little judiciously prescribed violence could easily chase the union right out of the county.

One last statistical procedure was tried to ascertain whether a combination of factors could have indeed defeated the WFM as predicted. A multiple regression problem was set up comparing success with company size (COCAP), amount of violence (VIONUM), a dummy version of the variable (METAL), and membership turnover (MEMTURN). Surprisingly enough, the sum of the factors—working in conjunction—did produce an interesting effect on success. Company capitalization, membership turnover, and the metal being mined had no effect, but violence, taken in conjunction with the dummy variable US (non-Canadian locals) produced a multiple r of .58905 (r squared .34698). Examination of beta weights showed that the strongest influence on success was violence (.5822)—quite the opposite of the Jensen thesis.

An alternative thesis, based upon personal observation of the Western Federation, credited union size, existence, and violence with success. Regressing the three variables, plus US, against success created a multiple r of .72789 (r squared .52982). All three variables seemed to contribute equally to the final figure (beta weights of .3214, .3898, .2738 respectively for MEMBERS, EXIST, AND VIONUM). The simplest explanation of WFM success (or, conversely, failure) was that the largest locals with the most aggressive industrial relations policies lasted longest and had the most success. In the dog-eat-dog world of the early twentieth century West, law and order simply did not exist. Only the large and tough unions proved too difficult for the mine corporations to break. In such cases, a detente was apparently reached between labor and management. Minor wage increases and hour reductions would be granted as long as the union had the power to threaten the continued well-being of a company's plant and operation.

In the end, Vernon Jensen was correct when he termed western industrial relations a "heritage of conflict." What he missed was the fact that conflict brought success.

NOTES

[1]Samuel Gompers, *Seventy Years of Life and Labor,* Vol. 1 (New York: E. P. Dutton, 1925), p. 421. Written in 1919, this was Gompers last shot at the WFM. It is interesting to note the lack of negative comments about Moyer.

[2]George G. Suggs, Jr., *Colorado's War on Militant Unionism* (Detroit: Wayne State University Press, 1972). Another work which was based upon similar company records was James W. Byrkit, "Life and Labor in Arizona, 1901–1921," unpublished Ph.D. dissertation, Claremont Graduate School, 1972. Byrkit used both Phelps Dodge and United Verde records.

[3]The classic example was Vernon Jensen, *Heritage of Conflict* (Ithaca: Cornell University Press, 1950). The Jensen work was—necessarily—based upon large locals in Butte, Colorado, and Arizona.

[4]The Figure of 577 comes from John Ervin Brinley, "The Western Federation of Miners," unpublished Ph.D. dissertation, University of Utah, 1972. Brinley does not take into account some forty-plus locals founded after 1916. Membership of District 7 comes from James C. Foster, "The Western Federation Comes to Alaska," *Pacific Northwest Quarterly*, October, 1975, pp. 161–173.

[5]One of the best collections of company records which pertain to the Western Federation can be found at the University of Arizona Library in Tucson. The star collection is that of Lewis Douglas, which includes the complete correspondence of the founder and first president of Phelps Dodge.

[6]A complete record of existing manuscript sources pertaining to the WFM can be found in Brinley, "The Western Federation of Miners," pp. 247–249. However, Brinley missed the two best collections which relate to the WFM: the Mine-Mill Collection of the University of British Columbia and the various manuscript collections (particularly Mackenzie King) of the Canadian Public Archives (Labour Section). He also overlooked the papers assembled by Vernon Jensen in writing *Heritage of Conflict,* which are housed at Cornell's Labor Management Documentation Center.

[7]Leo Wolman, *Ebb and Flow in Trade Unionism* (New York: National Bureau of Economic Research, 1936).

[8]Jonathan Garlock, "The Knights of Labor Data-Bank," *Historical Methods Newsletter,* 4 (September, 1973), pp. 149–160.

[9]For the complete list of variables and their coding see Appendix A, The WFM Codebook: A Summary.

[10]As mentioned above, the forty additional locals were formed in the years 1916–1920 and come from yearly reports of the WFM secretary-treasurer.

[11]The codebook defines companies through a variety of means including capitalization, number of employees, types of operation, and location of corporate offices.

[12]Jensen, *Heritage of Conflict,* vii–x.

[13]The best statement of this came in an unpublished paper delivered at the Southwest Labor History Conference of 1975: Charles Stephenson, "Workers and Mobility: Studies of a Class in Motion."

[14]This is partly the thesis of Brinley, "The Western Federation of Miners" and was a very common belief even in the WFM. See for instance the long debate over even the use of the word "dynamite" at the 1907 convention. Western Federation of Miners, *Proceedings of the 15th Annual Convention,* June 10–July 3, 1907, Denver, Colorado, pp. 350–370.

[15]Melvyn Dubofsky, *We Shall Be All* (Chicago: Quadrangle Press, 1969), pp. 19–35.

[16]This was mentioned by Brinley, but major emphasis came in James Brykit, "Life and Labor in Arizona," pp. 92–93. Of course, this was particularly true in copper areas where low grade ore became the rule after 1917–1918.

[17]Brinley, "Western Federation of Miners," p. 181. Also, a description of the law can be found in Harry A. Millis and Royal Montgomery, *Organized Labor,* Vol.3 (New York: McGraw-Hill, 1945), pp. 783–793. Its effects are detailed in Martin Robin, *Radical Politics and Canadian Labour* (Kingston: Industrial Relations Centre of Queens University, 1968).

[18]The mean value of VIONUM (number of violent incidents) was .905 for locals coded.

[19]The source of migration was the subject of variable MEMMIG which identified migrants as local, same state, same region, or alien immigrants.

[20]See codebook for various variables dealing with the employing company. The constituent elements of success as identified by computer are given in the derived variable SUCCESS.

[21]See codebook definitions of POLACT, SOCISM, IWW, CONTRACT, SYNDVIO, and inversely, AFL and UMW.

[22]So far only the variable COTYPE exists, but a future codebook will include variables on both wage scales (the variance in rates of pay) and kind of mineral mined.

[23]Two computer-derived variables which were not included in the original codebook dealt with the composite questions of skill and radicalism. They were:

SKILL (relative skill of local)	RADICAL (composite radicalism)
1 placer or open-pit mining	1 one or more violent incidents caused by union
2 lode mining	
3 smelter or mill work	2 strong support of a labor party
4 engineer or mechanic local	3 strong support of IWW, an SPA–WFM alliance, and opposition to contracts—or—strong opposition to AFL and UMW
	4 active users of violence as a political tool

APPENDIX A
THE WFM CODEBOOK: A SUMMARY

Variable Name	Explanation	Details
STATE	Location: State or Province	Coded Variable w/32 Codes (nominal)
MEMBERS	Membership of Local	Actual Mean Membership
ETHNIC	Major Ethnic Group	Coded Variable w/9 Codes (nominal)
ETHPER	Percent of Major Ethnic Group	Actual Percentage
STRIKES	Number of Strikes	Actual Number
STRIWON	Number of Strikes Won	Actual Number
STRILEN	Strike Length in days	Actual Number
STRICAUS	Strike Cause	Coded Variable w/8 Codes (nominal)
WAGEINC	Number of Wage Increases	Actual Number
WAGSIZE	Size of Increase in cents/day	
SUCNO	Number of Successes	Actual Number
SUCTYPE	Types of Success	Coded Variable w/8 Codes
SUCSIZE	Size of Success	Actual Cents/Day
EXIST	Years of Existence	Actual Number
FSTYR	First Year of Existence	Actual Number (i.e.– 899 = 1899)
UNAFF	Years of Existence before WFM Affiliation	Actual Number
ENTPR	Union Enterprise	Coded Variable (hospital, etc.) w/8 codes
ORGANI	Name of Organizer	Coded Variable w/35 Codes
LEADERS	Type of Leadership	Coded Ordinal from Creative to Company Controlled w/5 Codes
LEADNAT	Number of Leaders Who Reached District Prominence	Actual Number
CORRUPT	Union Corruption	Coded Ordinal from None to Serious Corruption w/7 Codes
UNITYPE	Type of Local: Mining Specialty	Coded Variable w/9 Codes
COCAP	Company Capitalization (highest in period)	Actual Number in Thousands of Dollars

APPENDIX A *(Continued)*

Variable Name	Explanation	Details
COOWN	Company Ownership	Coded Ordinal from Local to Absentee Foreign w/6 Codes
LABPOL	Company Labor Policy	Coded Ordinal from Anti- to Prounion w/5 Codes
SCABS	Company Strikebreaker Policy	Coded Ordinal w/3 Codes
COUNION	Type of Company Union	Coded Variable w/4 Codes
COUNMEM	Membership of Company Union	Actual Number
COEMPLOY	Number in Company Workforce	Actual Number
CONAME	Company Name	Coded Variable w/100 Codes
COWFM	Company Attitude Toward WFM	Coded Ordinal w/5 Codes
COMA	Company Membership in Mine Owners Association	Coded Variable w/4 Codes
COTYPE	Type of Company Specialty	Coded Variable w/9 Codes
VIONUM	Number of Violent Incidents	Actual Number
VIOTYPEL	Most Common Form of Violence	Coded Variable w/9 Codes
VIOLATEL	Most Common Precipitator of Violence (party)	Coded Variable w/3 Codes
VIOTYPE2	Second Most Common Form of Violence	Coded Variable
VIOLATE2	Perpetrator of the Second Most Common Kind of Violence	Coded Variable
VIOCAUSE	Reason for Violence	Coded Variable w/9 Codes
VIOLEN	Length of Violent Outbreak	Actual Days
MEMIG	Source of Membership Migration	Coded Variable w/6 Codes
MEMTURN	Mean Yearly Membership Turnover	Actual Percentage
MIGVIO	Violence Associated with Migrants	Coded Variable w/4 Codes
POLACT	Local's Position of Political Action	Coded Ordinal w/6 Codes
SOCISM	Local's Position on Socialism	Coded Ordinal w/3 Values

APPENDIX A *(Continued)*

Variable Name	Explanation	Details
IWW	Local's Position on the IWW	Coded Ordinal w/3 Values
CONTRACT	Local's Position on Contracts	Coded Ordinal w/4 Values
SYNDVIO	Local's Position on Syndical Violence	Coded Ordinal w/3 Values
AFL	Local's Position on the AFL	Coded Ordinal w/3 Values
UMW	Local's Position on the United Mine Workers	Coded Ordinal w/3 Values
TOWORK	Total Workforce	Actual Number
EXVIOL	Number of Violent Incidents If It Exceeds 9	Actual Number
POPULA	Town's Population	Actual Number
END	WFM's Statement on Local's Demise	Coded Variable w/7 Values
METAL	Metal Mined by Local	Coded Variable w/9 Values

The Rise of the Mine-Mill Union in Southwestern Copper

D. H. Dinwoodie

THE MINE, MILL, AND SMELTER WORKERS UNION in the Southwest developed from a skeleton organization in the 1930s to a position by the end of World War II as the major collective bargaining agent for production workers in the copper industry. A study of this change calls on propositions of movement and political theory focusing on the structural setting in which the labor movement mobilization occurred.[1] The character and social position of the work force, with its large Chicano component, held implications for cohesion, leadership, and associational ties. The public policy sector, particularly as affected by the forces of depression and war, provided a range of institutional and economic resources. The union offered an organizational framework to bridge these arenas of social coalescence and public resources. Consolidating this interaction provided rewards for the workers and strength for the union, though aspects of the setting foreshadowed future problems for Mine-Mill.

For most of the depression years, the state of these categories offered little ground for optimism that a successful labor movement could soon arise in the southwestern copper industry. The work force was dispersed over a wide area in Arizona, New Mexico, and west Texas; was insulated from other labor groups and employment opportunities; and was subordinate in an entrepreneurial milieu to agrarian and business classes.[2] The copper interests varied from the small family extractive operation to highly capitalized and integrated mining-processing-marketing systems. Many of the 15,000 workers in the industry were employed by the corporate giants—Phelps Dodge, Nevada Consolidated, Anaconda, American Smelting and Refining —that dominated life in the mining camps and smelter towns. Mexican immigrants and Spanish Americans formed a high proportion (50 or 60 percent) of this industrial labor. These Chicanos were subjected to pervasive social and economic discrimination. Housing, education, and recreation typically were segregated. On the job, Chicanos were restricted to common labor positions, featuring substandard job classifications and pay scales and lacking standard seniority provisions. The moribund state of the metal industry augmented social dislocation. Low copper prices and high production costs caused cutbacks in operations and work forces. Severe unemployment and economic deprivation now overshadowed long-standing wage discrepancies between the Southwest and other mining regions.

Social divisions and associated opportunities for manipulation were accompanied during the depression years by close relationships in the public arena between business and government. Their mutual support had been traditional. As Governor Sidney Osborn of Arizona described it to a constituent during the war years: "The story of corporation control over government in Arizona goes back so far and has so many angles, mostly vicious, that it would be impossible for me adequately to paint a picture of the situation within the limits of a short letter."[3] This connection was reinforced by the economic malaise. Business-oriented legislatures and corporate executives serving on government boards developed tax, welfare, and law enforcement policies protecting enterprise and its political supporters.[4] Labor unrest, immigration problems, and allegations of radical activities were repeatedly handled by public agencies responding to private purposes, such as sheriff's departments, state motor patrols, and the Immigration Service. New Deal welfare programs—normally decentralized in administration—featured adjustment of aid levels to industry's labor requirements, discrimination in work relief and family support rates, and favoritism in project contracts. A counterforce to economic manipulation in the public arena as well as the work place was offered during the New Deal years by the expanding federal role in labor relations.[5] Yet, for the metal workers in the Southwest, this potential was frustrated at first by the ambivalent federal commitment both to promoting collective bargaining and preserving entrepreneurial prerogative. Until late in the 1930s, government response to widespread antiunion discrimination in the metal industries rested more on democratic rhetoric than on forceful legislation or administration.

The dismal social and political outlook was matched for most of the 1930s by the state of the International Union of Mine, Mill, and Smelter Workers.[6] Its tradition of miner militancy had withered in the open-shop atmosphere of the 1920s; membership strength had collapsed along with metal markets. There was organizational promise in the anger that accompanied the depression and in Washington's labor relations initiatives. Indeed, the collective bargaining provisions of the NIRA and the short-lived copper code encouraged Mine-Mill organizers, AFL representatives, and workers to reestablish ephemeral local unions at a number of southwest mines and plants. But the locals could not counter varied repressive techniques by themselves, and the national organization was occupied with personal infighting, the dispute within the AFL over industrial unionism, and a search for financial solvency. Expansion from its base in the northern Rocky Mountain region to other mining and processing centers came slowly in the uncongenial depression years and in no place faced a more hostile environment than in the home of the southwestern copper kings.

The New Deal promise that changing social, public, and organizational relationships could foster successful labor mobilization moved toward fulfillment in the later 1930s. Ethnic and working-class isolation generated cohesiveness and activism even as it facilitated social control. This is implicit in the fact that there were local unions available for suppression. Broader linkages in the movement toward social coalescence were evident as time went on. A smeltermen's union at Laredo, Texas, composed of Mexican Americans and Mexican nationals, grew out of tenacious organizing efforts of farm laborers, led by Juan Pena, from the coal mining town of Darwin, Texas.[7] The formation by this group, in the late 1930s, of a UCAPAWA farmworkers local union encouraged the establishment of the industrial local, into which Pena and other activists moved. For a time, the Laredo workers received support from the Mexican consul and, after the rise under Lázaro Cárdenas of the Mexican labor federation, the CTM, they formed connections with the body in Nuevo Laredo.

Similar manifestations of ethnic and labor ties developed in El Paso.[8] The cross-border links were more substantial in this location because of the complex urban and industrial makeup of the sister cities at the Paso del Norte. AFL organizations existed for some time among Spanish-speaking workers, including bakers from El Paso's many shops and laborers at the Asarco smelter. But activists like Humberto Sílex, a Nicaraguan immigrant and smelter worker, were questioning the craft-union connection and seeking broader bases of support. Labor protests in 1939 on each side of the river were aided by workers on the other side. The CTM in Ciudad Juárez encouraged this, as did the Mexican consul in El Paso, an army officer strongly committed to President Cárdenas' labor reform policies. Though Sílex and the president of the AFL laborers' local he had recruited to industrial unionism soon were fired by Asarco, a base for labor mobilization was developing within a wide network of social relationships.

Even in areas more remote from the cross-border linkages, or more subject to company domination, a degree of worker cohesiveness was maintained in the 1930s.[9] A core of activism at Silver City, New Mexico, later tapped by Mine-Mill, formed around elements in the Spanish-speaking labor force associated with a defunct union local and resentful of social and economic discrimination. A similar ethnic foundation at the Clifton-Morenci, Arizona, operations of Phelps Dodge may have received stimulus from recollections of the World War I strike repression as well as from continuing discriminatory treatment of Chicano workers. Copper Queen Mine activists, including Verne Curtis, subsequently a Mine-Mill representative, maintained the identity and commitments of the Bisbee Miners Union. In several locations in the Southwest, some degree of cohesion and mutual support among exminers was present in the New Deal work projects and the so-called unemployed unions. Orville Larson, later Mine-Mill vice president, recalls the vigorous protests of Miami, Arizona, Workers Alliance members to relief practices and malpractices. They demonstrated pointedly their view of relief administration by delivering a decayed ham from a spoiled food shipment to the desk of the state welfare board chairman, who doubled as a copper company executive. For Spanish-speaking miners and exminers other opportunities for association came through fraternal societies that voiced grievances to business and government authorities.

The political pattern of government-business integration continued to reinforce corporate paternalism. Yet, certain federal agencies challenged the local power configuration. After the constitutionality of the Wagner Act was established in 1937, the National Labor Relations Board began actively to support democratic industrial relations in the Southwest. Agency edicts and supportive court decisions protected union organizing, which, in turn, provided the basis for NLRB-supervised representation elections. Several prominent antiunion discrimination cases in the late 1930s and early 1940s—including those of forty blacklisted Bisbee Miners Union members and of Humberto Sílex—returned activists to the work place and alerted the labor force to its organizing and voting rights.[10] Once a collective bargaining agent had been determined through an NLRB election, Conciliation Service commissioners could mediate a negotiating breakdown as they had for years in other regions and industries. Both bodies opened channels of access to management and, in a broader political sense, legitimized workers' coalescence and the union role in an environment traditionally closed to these features.

The American response to the war in Europe accelerated this penetration by national public policy. Burgeoning defense production boosted copper prices, labor demands, and, belatedly, wage levels.[11] A connection between national defense efforts and the institutional role may be demonstrated by the large number of NLRB decisions in 1940 and 1941 favorable to organizing labor forces. New mechanisms were introduced to regulate manpower requirements and to settle union-management disputes threatening essential war production. The War Manpower Commission responded to the first purpose and, as well, spawned local committees giving voice to workers' concerns.[12] To resolve labor conflicts, the National Defense Mediation Board was established in 1941 and was replaced in early 1942 by the much stronger National War Labor Board and its subsidiary agency, the Denver-based Non-Ferrous Metals Commission.[13] While the commission operated within federal guidelines for economic stabilization and labor-management peace, it possessed extraordinary authority to adjudicate wage, union security, and fringe issues. NFMC settlements followed the War Labor Board's "Little Steel" decision of mid-1942 by applying the maintenance of membership formula to the fractious union security question. Yet, the commission often awarded copper industry pay raises that exceeded the WLB's 15 percent ceiling on wage compensation for wartime price inflation. These increases were permitted under provisos for correcting intraindustry wage inequalities.

The International Union of Mine, Mill, and Smelter Workers, now headquartered in Denver, served as the essential link between agency power and worker demands. Along with public ambience, the union's character had changed. Organizing vigor and administrative expansion had been encouraged by the young president, Reid Robinson, and by energetic radicals added from various sectors of mobilizing labor including the CIO and the Communist Party.[14] An improved financial condition came at first from CIO contributions and then from lengthening membership rolls, as defense-related production began to expand in key western mining areas and eastern fabricating centers. Responding to the activity within industry and government, Mine-Mill, in 1941, took aim at several targets of expansion, including southwestern copper.

About a dozen organizers were assigned there under the leadership of International Representative Orville Larson, a big, able, and outgoing man. He and organizers like Verne Curtis, Howard Goddard, and George Knott were fully experienced in metal-industry unionism. Several spoke Spanish: Harry Hafner, a Spanish Civil War veteran, Leo Ortiz, and Arturo Mata, among the fulltime staff; and volunteer organizers like Humberto Sílex, Ceferino Anchando, and Joe Chávez in El Paso, J. E. Vásquez in Douglas, Juan Pena in Laredo, and Emilio Villegas in Morenci.[15] Many of them, radicalized in the Chicano labor market, favored a combined assault on the issues of membership, wages, and ethnic discrimination. Mata, for example, had been deported as a child from Morenci, Arizona, where his father was a leader in the World War I strikes. Returning to the United States in the 1920s, he had been active in farm- and metal-workers' organizations and civil rights activities. Ortiz was well acquainted with wage inequities in the California hard-rock mining industry. And Sílex in various industrial centers around the country had encountered discrimination in assignment and promotion. At Asarco, his superior was a young Anglo who was so new to the job that Sílex was cautioned: "Don't let the boy get hurt."

It was not the policy of Mine-Mill to ignore ethnic discrimination. The widespread nature of the practice in the industry served throughout as an inherent organizational weapon among Chicanos. Yet, there were limited external leverages that could be used to resolve the problem and large numbers of Anglo workers to recruit, many of them new arrivals from the Texas segregation belt. The union consequently concentrated basically on broad membership, economic benefits, and industry-wide organization, rather than ethnic issues. A range of methods was used in membership drives.[16] The core of former union men was sought out; there was contact between activists and recruits on the job, in their homes, or in recreation halls; and officers of an AFL laborer's union were convinced to defect on occasion, and funds were transferred into friendly hands. Support for attacking a company stronghold was sometimes given from a squad of union organizers. In the case of the classic capture of the Clifton-Morenci cul-de-sac, for example, Knott, Leo Ortiz and Larson, holed up in the farm town of Safford, Arizona, entered the Clifton-Morenci company zone at night, arranged surreptitious meetings with local contacts (meetings held even in the graveyard), and soon secured key men in all the Phelps Dodge departments. Once an organization had developed and an NLRB election had been scheduled, Larson and the district staff arranged concentrated campaigning. Publicity techniques such as parades and appearances by Mine-Mill executives brought out the crowds; fundamental organizing groundwork by rank and file committees in mine or plant departments insured the votes.

Though Mine-Mill seldom secured exclusive bargaining rights, by 1943 it had made major election inroads into craft- and company-union territory.[17] In the Silver City area, it shared representation of the production workers in Nevada Consolidated's open-pit mine with AFL unions and held sole bargaining rights in most of that area's smaller mining and smelting operations. At El Paso, it had won victories at the Phelps Dodge refinery and at Asarco, where the nine-year AFL domination was eliminated. In Bisbee-Douglas, Arizona, the union had been certified for several years at the small Shattuck-Denn Corporation and the Douglas smelter of Phelps Dodge, though that company's mines at Bisbee were held for another year by the AFL. At Morenci, Mine-Mill had just secured representation rights for the 2,000 workers in the giant Phelps Dodge open-pit mining and smelting operation. Bargaining rights had been won in various units of the three major copper companies operating around Miami, Arizona. At Laredo, Juan Pena's group had even obtained a closed-shop contract.

The number of signed contracts lagged considerably behind NLRB certifications. Corporation antagonism toward the replacement of traditional management prerogative with collective bargaining remained strong. Organized labor's no-strike pledge removed a major source of union power, but a negotiating impasse brought the hearing and arbitral powers of the Non-Ferrous Metals Commission into play.[18] Public and labor representatives on the commission found the Mine-Mill arguments on the copper industry's wartime profit position persuasive, on the one hand, and its wage inequities intolerable, on the other.[19] Beginning with the Douglas smelter case in June, 1942, the union received favorable contract awards from the NFMC at most of the above locations where it held bargaining rights. The settlements normally provided substantial wage increases, maintenance of union membership for the life of the contract, grievance mechanisms, and paid vacations. Even while decisions lagged, Mine-Mill could induce pay raised from a recalcitrant company anxious to forestall further union growth.

Despite the stablization in labor relations, certain industry features remained worrisome to Mine-Mill. Copper producers in central and southwestern Arizona continued to resist unionization. Ethnic discrimination through economic devices remained common. In the Miami area, three major companies were dragging their feet on contract negotiations involving this issue. And an exodus of Spanish-speaking miners for west coast defense industries contributed to a manpower shortage threatening war production. In many ways, these factors hung together on the discrimination problem, which affected company attitudes of union and government strength and influenced the metal workers' commitment to the union and the work place.

Stressing economic issues in the early wartime organizational push, Mine-Mill had not shelved the ethnic concern. Members and staffers had consistently sought contract arrangements prohibiting discrimination on the basis "of race, creed, color or national origin...," and had attained some early success at the Douglas smelter and at two locations near Silver City.[20] But such provisions were open to interpretation, and, in any case, dual wage rates and misclassifications, failure to upgrade, and segregated employment in "Mexican gangs" remained widespread throughout the copper zone. So, the union had turned to public points of focus. One of these was the President's Committee on Fair Employment Practice established in mid-1941 to respond to Black demands for equity and to defense requirements for full manpower utilization. In the spring of 1942, Mine-Mill and several other CIO unions actively interested in protecting Chicano labor—notably the National Maritime Union, the Oil Workers Union, and UCAPAWA—convinced FEPC officials that the extent of ethnic discrimination in the Southwest justified a public hearing, exposing the problem.[21] Government and union sectors actively prepared for the hearings.[22] FEPC officials set up temporary field offices in El Paso from which to promote compliance with Roosevelt's executive order and to prepare evidence. Mine-Mill organizers were instructed to verify instances of discrimination. Contacts were made with civil rights groups, churches, and fraternal bodies. Union membership came forward with descriptions and protests of common industry practices.

These activities proved to be too flamboyant for government bureaus concerned with the international role of the United States. The hearings were cancelled, apparently on the grounds that public revelations would damage the nation's posture in Latin America. The FEPC and Mine-Mill interchange did produce some positive effects, however.[23] A number of Chicano employees of the copper companies were promoted immediately after the men had filed complaints of discrimination with the El Paso FEPC office. One of the offending companies eliminated its dual wage scale for Chicano and Anglo laborers by abolishing the below average rates. The FEPC commitment to equal employment opportunities for Chicanos was maintained by a special representative in the Southwest, Carlos E. Castaneda, though the agency's legal weakness hampered his continuing negotiations to remedy conditions in the metal industries.

Faced then, at the midpoint in the war, with continuing discriminatory practices and lagging membership campaigns, Mine-Mill moved "to force" intervention by the NFMC.[24] Aware of the extent of discrimination, the commission had been apprehensive of airing an issue that might disrupt labor-management relations in a critical defense industry. But now the union was able to point to manpower problems that compelled NFMC action. At hearings called by the commission in the fall of 1943,[25] Larson gave a blunt description of the conditions he and other activists had long fought, and union attorneys presented evidence assembled by rank and file members and the research department. Company representatives countered by explaining pay-scale differentials and work-place segregation in terms of cultural tradition, skill variations, and jurisdiction conflicts between craft and industrial unions. The most telling kinds of evidence were the detailed payroll lists, which the companies were required to submit, revealing innumerable wage discrepancies unrelated to educational levels or length of service. Basing its ruling on presidential fair-employment orders, the commission directed an end to what it called "a consistent pattern of discriminatory rates" at Miami Copper Company, the International Smelting and Refining Company, and Inspiration Consolidated. The commission directed that the dual-wage system be abolished, by eliminating all substandard rates. Eventually, the wage equalization principle was extended to additional major sites in the region.[26]

By the end of the war, Mine-Mill represented about three-fourths of the copper production workers in the Southwest and had negotiated contracts providing major wage and working condition improvements over prewar patterns. Base rates had more than doubled, and grievance procedures and seniority provisions were well established. Ethnic antagonism and segregation were still widespread in the Southwest, but the most blatant examples of job discrimination in the copper industry had been ended. In this instance, the union had strongly supported the efforts of workers and the involvement of government agencies. The status of the union in the area contrasted markedly with the feeble organization of early depression years. In Mine-Mill District No. 2, Utah's concentrated mining zone showed the greatest organizational vigor. But in the border states of Arizona, New Mexico, and Texas, membership had grown to about 3,000, distributed among twenty locals.[27] Beyond the changed system of industrial decision-making, the growing exercise of open collective expression was demonstrated in the broad cooperation of organized labor, church, and ethnic groups in Arizona during four successful electoral campaigns of liberal governor, Sid Osborn.

The rise of Mine-Mill in the Southwest was a product of the dynamics of interaction among the social, public, and organizational sectors. Coalescence within the working class and the formation of internal associations were fostered by oppressive conditions, social isolation, and ethnic relationships. Mobilization was then vitalized by broadening linkages provided by the federal government role and a strengthening union movement. Agency intervention responded to industrial dysfunction in a time of first domestic and later international crisis,[28] as well as to labor constituency's demand and its provision of client organizations. And the growth of a vigorous Mine-Mill union, while impelled by CIO connections, leadership energies, and Chicano commitment, depended on the utilization of a range of resources—human, institutional, and financial—available only in the large social and public arenas.[29] The gains of Mine-Mill and the copper industry workers proceeded from an extended interplay of forces. With deepening ideological conflicts and shifting public priorities, this supportive fabric would become gravely weakened during the Cold War years.

NOTES

[1]Anthony Oberschall presents well the dimensions of social movements in *Social Conflict and Social Movements* (Englewood Cliffs, N. J.: Prentice-Hall, Inc., 1973). Richard Gillam reviews a portion of the diverse writings on political structure in *Power in Postwar America* (Boston: Little, Brown, and Co., 1971). Harald Mey discusses the "field" concept of interacting social forces in *Field Theory: a Study of its Application in the Social Sciences* (London: Routledge and Kegan Paul, 1972).

[2]Reports by investigators Ernest G. Trimble (n.d.), D. R. Donovan and G. J. Fleming (August 10–13, 1942), and Barron Beshoar (August 13, 1942), Fair Employment Practice Committee Records, Southwestern Hearing Series, Record Group 228, National Archives.

[3]Osborn to Ernest Angell, May 16, 1942, Governor Osborn Files, Wartime Conditions, Arizona State Library and Archives.

[4]Particularly revealing of the indistinct line between public policy and private interests are the Federal Emergency Relief Administration Files, Field Reports, Arizona, New Mexico, Record Group 69, National Archives.

[5]National Labor Relations Board, Regional Administrative Series, Los Angeles, Denver, RG 25, National Archives.

[6]Vernon H. Jensen, *Nonferrous Metals Industry Unionism, 1932–1954* (Ithaca: Cornell University Press, 1954).

[7]Minute Book, 1937–38, Laredo Smelter Workers Union, and Pedro Rodríguez oral history interview transcript, Texas Labor Archives, University of Texas, Arlington.

[8]Department of State files 812.5043/21 and 812.5043/86, RG 59, National Archives; Sílex Defense Committee File, International Union of Mine, Mill and Smelter Workers Papers, Western Historical Collections, University of Colorado; *El Paso Herald Post,* March 7–22, 1940, passim; interview with Humberto Sílex, El Paso, Texas, May 12, 1976.

[9]Interviews with Orville Larson, Tucson, Arizona, May 10, 1976, and J. M. Graham, Los Angeles, California, April 30, 1976; organizers' files, IUMMSW Papers, President Reid Robinson correspondence; and United States Conciliation Service File 196–596, RG 280, National Archives, regarding Latin American Club of Arizona.

[10]6 NLRB 624, 7 NLRB 862, 15 NLRB 732, 19 NLRB 547, 28 NLRB 442, 34 NLRB 968, 37 NLRB 1059, 38 NLRB 555, 40 NLRB 180 and 986. The connection between NLRB decisions and Mine-Mill organizing efforts is shown in *CIO News, MMSW edition,* July 22, 1940, p. 1; Aug. 19, 1940, p. 1; Jan. 6, 1941, p. 1; Feb. 10, 1941, p. 8.

[11]Robert F. Campbell, *The History of Basic Metals Price Control in World War II* (N.Y.: Columbia University Press, 1948), pp. 27–81. Jensen, p. 49, notes the correlation between the defense program and NLRB role after mid-1940.

[12]Local Union No. 509, IUMMSW Papers.

[13]Records of the National War Labor Board, Non-Ferrous Metals Commission, RG 202, National Archives. Joel Seidman, *American Labor from Defense to Reconversion* (Chicago: The University of Chicago Press, 1953), summarizes the government's labor relations policy during the war.

[14]Jensen stresses ideological divisions within Mine-Mill.

[15]Organizers' files, IUMMSW Papers; Larson and Sílex interviews.

[16]Organizers' files, particularly Larson, Curtis, Mata, Hafner, IUMMSW Papers; Larson, Sílex, and Graham interviews.

[17]Larson to Ralph H. Rasmussen (executive board member), August 13, 1943, IUMMSW Papers, Reid Robinson correspondence.

[18]Certification to the NFMC came after Conciliation Service mediation efforts. USCS files 196/8118 and 196/7613.

[19]Industrial mobilization assured the corporations of capacity production, low-interest loans, and premium prices for the high-cost producers. Larson and attorney Nathan Witt often presented the union case at these hearings.

[20]USCS file 196/8118; and Trimble report, cited above in FEPC records.

[21]Allan D. McNeil (assistant to president) to Larson, May 7, 1942, IUMMSW Papers, Groups of Organizers.

[22]Trimble, Donovan-Fleming, and Beshoar reports, FEPC records.

[23]Trimble report, and Carlos E. Castaneda correspondence, FEPC records.

[24]McNeil to Larson, Sílex, Curtis, and Knott, December 4, 1942, IUMMSW Papers, Groups of Organizers; and Larson to Robinson, Aug. 9, 1943, and Robinson reply, Aug. 12, IUMMSW Papers, Larson file.

[25]Case No. 111–718–D Non-Ferrous Metals Commission Files. Also 14 War Labor Reports 146, and 18 War Labor Reports 591.

[26]3 Labor Arbitration Reports 41; *The Union,* May 30, 1945, p. 3, and August 8, 1945, p. 3.

[27]Notes on membership figures, CIO Secretary-Treasurer's Office Collection, Box 111 (IUMMSW), Archives of Labor History and Urban Affairs, Wayne State University.

[28]Recent examinations of the internal impact of the war are: David Brody, "The New Deal and World War II," in *The New Deal,* 2 vols., eds. John Braeman, Robert H. Bremner, and David Brody (Columbus: Ohio State University Press, 1975), 1:267–309; Richard Polenberg, *War and Society* (New York: J. B. Lippincott Company, 1972); and John Morton Blum, *"V" was for Victory* (New York: Harcourt Brace Jovanovich, 1976).

[29]The connection between movement success and the management of societal resources is implicit or explicit in the writings cited at the beginning of the essay.

II

The Industrial Workers of the World

The Western Wobblies

THERE WAS A CHARACTER in James Jones's *From Here to Eternity* who spoke occasionally of the long-dead IWW, the union which transformed the West in that period before 1920.

You don't remember the Wobblies. You were too young. Or else not even born yet. There was never anything like them, before or since. They called themselves materialist-economists, but what they really were was a religion. They were workstiffs and bindlebums like you and me, but they were welded together by a vision we don't possess. It was their vision that made them great.

That vision began amidst the wreckage of the Western Federation's first great strike, the so-called Colorado Labor War. Beginning in 1903, the WFM had set out to make Colorado smelters into union shops, just as three out of every four Colorado mining towns had already become WFM towns. However, the federation had not counted upon the power of the statewide Mine Owners Association, which soon made common cause with Republican Governor James Peabody. The WFM had assumed that the combined economic might of the mines could force the mills into the union fold. Such was not the case.

In a two-year battle, the WFM was not only defeated but was driven completely out of the state as an industrial relations power. The state militia used martial law as a skilled conductor uses his baton. The militia's expenses in the affair were neatly paid by MOA bonds, and the governor presided over it all as if he were doing the state a favor. Scores of WFM activists were seized in both Cripple Creek and Telluride and were deported from Colorado as unceremoniously as cattle. When the electorate protested in the 1904 election, a lame-duck legislature set aside the voter's mandate by reversing votes that came from the mine counties. Obviously, a new tack was needed. The Industrial Workers of the World would be that tack.

What was the IWW? Born out of the frustrations of Colorado labor unionists, the IWW was the WFM's attempt to form a nationwide "industrial" union, whose economic power could come to the aid of the federation in future confrontations with capital. A planning session was held in Chicago in 1905 and a general convention would

meet in the same city in June. From all over the country came the
left-leaning unionists of the day, unionists who would join under the
red banner of the Industrial Workers of the World. They held only
two beliefs in common: that unions should be "industrial" (and thus
avoid the elitist sins of the American "separation" of Labor) and that
politics should be revolutionary. For the wobblies, America was a vast
land of unorganized and unskilled labor in need of organization, a
land of unfettered capital in need of confrontation. The IWW provided both organization and confrontation in a most creative manner.

Between 1905 and 1910, the new union confined its class struggle
to internal affairs. The Western Federation leadership which had
given birth to the IWW was eased out of power within two years, its
place being temporarily taken by the dilettante of the left, Daniel
DeLeon, a college professor with a penchant for causing instant disorder. There was a great deal of talk about organizing the salmon
canneries of Alaska and the fruit harvesters of California, but few
were brought into the fold during those first years. However, several
top organizers did pledge themselves to the IWW during that time of
confusion. Frank Little, the WFM organizer who had first brought the
Arizona miners of Clifton-Morenci into the Western Federation, came
over to the IWW and brought Goldfield, Nevada's, Vincent St. John
with him. Goldfield itself became the legendary IWW town in those
years, the only town in the world completely organized by the IWW. It
was also in those years that the world heard its first wobbly song:
"Hallelujah, I'm a Bum" was supposedly written by Spokane
(Washington) IWW member Harry McClintock in the 1890s and was
first printed on the IWW song card in 1908 along with three other
tunes. During 1908–1909, fellow Spokane wobbly, J. H. Walsh, compiled the song card and, then, the first edition of the famed *Little Red
Songbook*. Not content with this, Walsh next organized some musi-
cians, dressed them in a red version of the Salvation Army uniform,
and took them on a tour of the Northwest as the IWW Band.[1] The
wobbly legend was just beginning.

With neither the numbers nor the skill to mount a serious threat
to American industry, the IWW depended upon style from the very
beginning. Walsh's IWW Band may have been a traveling joke in
the Northwest, but the catchy lyrics of wobbly songs won many a
drawing-room convert to the cause. In time, the public pressure
created by the drawing-room wobblies would materially aid the IWW
in its more serious industrial activities. A case in point was the free
speech fight.

The IWW's goal of organizing the unskilled lumberjacks of the
Pacific Northwest and the migrant workers of California depended

upon ready access to those workers in the recruitment centers of Stockton, Fresno, and Spokane. Yet, wobbly spokesmen were constantly harassed by law enforcement officials who drove the labor organizers out of town before a union drive could begin. On the other hand, spokesmen for the Jehovah's Witnesses and other fundamentalist groups were given the run of the labor districts. To the IWW, it was an issue of free speech.

When the authorities refused to see the issue in quite the same light, Spokane IWW leaders sent out a call to the entire Northwest to come and protest the violation of fundamental liberties. Wobblies responded by the hundreds, riding the rails to Spokane where they preached unionism on every street corner. Authorities responded by throwing every last agitator in jail, only to discover that the jailing of hundreds of wobblies was very serious business. To begin with, wobbly prisoners never acted like traditional criminals. They sang and lectured and seemed bent upon converting their very jailers to the cause. There was something infectious about a band of men and women who could sing in such a time of stress. Besides, there was the cost. Feeding hundreds of prisoners cost the taxpayers thousands of dollars. Finally, there was Elizabeth Gurley Flynn, a teenage wobbly descended from generations of Irish rebels. During her jail stint, she found that the Spokane police used one women's jail as a brothel, and she circulated this information to the garden clubs of the Washington city. With budgets unbalanced and wives on the warpath, the city fathers of Spokane capitulated. Free speech had been won.[2]

This was a typical wobbly fight. They won not with massive picket lines or perfect organization, but rather with a creative touch which turned the unemployed of the region into a public relations asset. By 1912, there was hardly an American who had not heard a wobbly song or read of a wobbly strike. That was quite a record for an organization which had not organized a single industry. Significantly, it was a group with a strong western bias.

The glory years of the IWW were 1912–1917, a period which corresponds to the leadership of western-oriented "Big Bill" Haywood. Big Bill had begun his union life under the banner of the Western Federation of Miners and, when the WFM sent out the call for the founding meeting of the IWW, he chaired the session which he described as the "Continental Congress of the Working Class." It was Haywood who materially assisted Moyer in pushing the WFM toward a greater reliance on organization. As IWW secretary-treasurer, it would be Haywood who would send wobbly troops into the mills of Lawrence, Massachusetts, the mines of Butte and Bisbee, and the oil fields of the Southwest. His emphasis would be the same as it had been in his WFM days—organize the despised ethnics, the low wage workers, and the forgotten, and give them a union home.

The western wobblies fit the Haywood picture perfectly. While other organizations ignored the new ethnic workers, the IWW opened a branch office in Los Angeles which tried desperately to reach northward migrating Mexicans. A few yellowing copies of *El Rebelde* and *Huelga General* are all that remain of that effort today, but, at one time, Frank Little and others (Fernando Vellardo for example) carried on an appeal to Mexican workers which reached from the fields of California to the barrios of Texas. This, of course, tied in nicely with the efforts of the Magón brothers and other Mexican wobblies, who had carried their version of the revolution to the northern borders of the United States. Joe Hill, the wobbly bard, reportedly worked with the *magonistas* in the abortive Baja revolution of the teens. In fact, WFM strikers at Clifton-Morenci, Arizona, in 1915–1916 credited part of their strike to the efforts of dedicated *magonistas* and other members of the wobblies' Mexican band.[3] However, western wobblyism was not limited to southwestern Mexicans and Spokane lumberjacks.

It was the Haywood IWW which first tried to give some form of organization to the dispossessed migrant pickers. Officially, the IWW's Agricultural Workers Organization was the vehicle for this drive, a drive which began in 1914 after the wobblies concluded that free speech won public relations battles but not many new members. Yet, the agricultural fight had begun with the free speech campaign and had first seen some organizational success in the Wheatland, California, hop riot of 1913. Wheatland would be the inspiration for one of Zane Grey's lesser works, *Desert of Wheat,* and would long be remembered as California's first farm-worker's strike. But as far as an industrial relations success, Wheatland paled in comparison to the IWW's major agricultural effort, the great midwest organizing drive of 1915–1916. Historians have long marveled over the varied success of the AWO in its effort to set up a 400-mile picket line in the wheat fields,[4] but few have realized that the AWO involved itself in a lot more than wheat.The first essay in this section explores other AWO involvement in the Midwest.

Earl Bruce White concentrates his attention on that aspect of the IWW which would inspire labor radicals for decades—long after the demise of the active IWW. Only the wobblies had tried to organize all workers in those first desperate years of the twentieth century; Samuel Gompers had refused to waste AFL efforts on the unskilled. Indeed, the only serious AFL attempt to break into the unorganized ranks of mass industry came under the leadership of exwobbly William Z. Foster, during the 1919 steel strike. Professor White shows that the IWW had quite an opposite view on organization. Expanding on an incident only briefly mentioned by most IWW historians, he examines the wobblies' efforts to organize the Mid-Continent Oil Field and the substantial reaction which that organizing drive spurred. It is interesting to note that an AFL drive which focused on the army cantonments and the shipyards during the same period had the *de facto* backing of the Wilson administration; such was not the case with the wobblies' efforts in oil. Organizing carpenters and ship workers was almost patriotic; working with pipeline operatives was not.

As Professor White points out in his essay, the oil-organizing drive was really a by-product of the IWW's attempt to organize the midwest's migrant farm workers. Many men who worked the great wheat harvests also worked on pipeline projects and in the oil fields themselves. The work, which would bring upwards of $30,000 per year to Alaskan pipeline workers, brought a barely adequate wage to the midwest migrants who spent their off-seasons working for Sinclair, Pew, or the forerunners of Cities Service. It was a job category in which the AFL's professional organizers did not display the slightest interest. Yet, when the IWW briefly succeeded in bringing a few oil-field workers into the fold, they deemed the wobbly organizers who performed the feat as the most dangerous men in the midwest.

Throughout his essay, Professor White utilizes a number of sources which other IWW historians have failed to use. He makes good use of both the Kansas City court transcript and various federal records pertaining to the trial and the IWW defendants. Professor White has also ferreted out the records of the ACLU, which detail the experiences of witnesses to the Tulsa Outrage. All in all, the White essay is an excellent exploration of a previously obscure IWW tale, which may be of much greater significance than historians have realized.

It did not take long for the brave days of 1915–1916 to turn into the dark days of 1917. The darkest of those days for the IWW came in mid-July, 1917. The location was Arizona.

While Professor White wrestles with the problem of oil-field organization, James Byrkit devotes his essay to the most spectacular event in the IWW purges of the First World War. That event was the so-called Bisbee Deportation. As Professor Byrkit's essay reveals, Bisbee was not an isolated instance of vigilante justice. Quite to the contrary, Bisbee was but one in a series of events which would eventually wipe the wobblies from the western map.

Prior to the war years, the IWW had won several important battles. The free speech fights in California and Washington had been propaganda victories of major porportions. The titanic struggle at Lawrence had proven even more satisfying to the wobblies' media masters. Even during the losing strike at Paterson, IWW publicity efforts had kept management from using all the weapons in its arsenal. The war changed all that.

With the coming of the war, production for victory became the cause of most Americans. Owners and managers, chained to the IWW for years, could now cast off their burdens in the name of patriotism. After all, management was fighting "Imperial Wilhelm's Warriors," not a legitimate labor organization. Tactics which IWW propagandists would have depicted as brutal in prewar days became a justifiable means of maintaining war production. Strikes were antiwar by definition. Unions were generally suspect. The IWW was an easy target. Thus, wartime industry managed to use copper, timber, and oil strikes as convenient means of ending the wobblies' western hegemony. Professor Byrkit shows how a company in Bisbee, Arizona, rid itself of wobblies.

The wartime raids killed the IWW. The organization which had started as the WFM's answer to the American Federation of Labor died when most Americans followed Wilson into war. It was buried when America found itself believing the propaganda of George Creel.

NOTES

[1] Joyce L. Kornbluh, *Rebel Voices: An IWW Anthology* (Ann Arbor: University of Michigan Press, 1964), pp. 65–66.

[2] Elizabeth Gurley Flynn, *I Speak My Own Piece* (New York: Masses and Mainstream, 1955), pp. 95–100.

[3] Lowell C. Blaisdell, *The Desert Revolution* (Madison: University of Wisconsin Press, 1962).

[4] Melvyn Dubofsky, *We Shall Be All* (Chicago: Quadrangle Press, 1969), pp. 294–318.

The IWW and the Mid-Continent Oil Field

Earl Bruce White

A FEW YEARS AGO, the Chicago IWW published a small pamphlet that included a list of topics neglected by historians. One was the IWW in the oil fields and another the Wichita Case. Indeed, these topics have been ignored by historians, but the two incidents are inextricably woven together in a web that almost defies a solution. In 1917, the IWW was accused of dynamiting the Tulsa home of prominent oil man, J. Edgar Pew. Next, seventeen IWW oil workers were tarred and feathered at Tulsa. Finally, the most dangerous man in the IWW, Phineas M. Eastman, resigned his post in Augusta, Kansas, and oil-field organizer, Frank J. Gallagher, took over IWW operations in the Mid-Continent Oil Field. These incidents became known as the Krieger Case, the Tulsa Outrage, and the Wichita Case.

The Mid-Continent Oil Field is a series of oil pools located in southeastern Kansas and central Oklahoma. The Kansas field is centered in Butler County around the towns of Augusta and El Dorado: the Glenn and Cushing pools take in the Tulsa area. These three pools form a narrow, ellipse-shaped area, running from south of Tulsa, Oklahoma, to south of Wichita, Kansas, and this was the main location of IWW activity in 1917. The Healdton pool in southern Oklahoma, only some fifty miles from the Texas border, was also part of the same area. The field was discovered in the early part of the century but was not developed to any extent until 1915 and 1916; by 1919, it was producing 51 percent of the domestic oil in the United States and was the largest producing area in the country.[1] More important than this was the fact that this area, along with Texas and Louisiana oil fields, produced over 60 percent of the nation's crude oil during World War I.[2] It now becomes apparent why the IWW's 1917 activity in the Mid-Continent Field takes on new meaning.

The IWW had struggled for existence since its birth in 1905. Industrial strikes at Goldfield, Nevada, McKeesport Rock, Pennsylvania, and Paterson, New Jersey, had not brought the IWW a large membership or treasury. The free speech fights in San Diego, California, Butte, Montana, and other locations, had fared little better. Therefore, by 1914, the IWW was desperately in need of finances and members. The annual IWW convention of 1914 saw Vincent St. John, incumbent secretary-treasurer, decline to run for renomination to the highest post the IWW had to offer. Cyclopean Frank Little came to the rescue at that moment with a new tactical proposal.

Little's plan was to organize the country's migratory agricultural workers by the next harvest season. He envisioned using union locals that bordered on the harvest fields to form an organizational meeting for that purpose. Bill Haywood, newly elected secretary-treasurer, announced the establishment of a Bureau of Migratory Workers shortly after the adjournment of the 1914 convention. Haywood's term better defined the scope of IWW activity, as migratory workers were not exclusively agricultural; the oil field pipeliner of Oklahoma and Kansas worked seasonally in both the harvest and oil fields.[3] Therefore, from its inception, the migratory union included oil workers. Butler County, Kansas, for example, site of the Kansas pool of the Mid-Continent Field, was not one of the biggest wheat-producing counties in Kansas, but it was far from the smallest. In 1915, it produced 26,593 acres, and in 1916, 20,211 acres.[4] Migratory workers harvested the Butler County wheat and then stayed on to work as pipeliners in the new oil field. Much the same pattern was followed in Oklahoma, where the migrant IWWs followed the wheat harvest and then went into the oil areas.

A former secretary-treasurer of the IWW and the main Wichita IWW defendant, Charles W. Anderson, wrote his account in 1918 of the birth of the migrant's union. Anderson related that a call went out from general headquarters for members to assemble in Kansas City, Missouri, on April 15, 1915. Headquarters had already agreed on two guiding principles for that meeting. One was that every effort be made on the part of the total IWW membership to insure that only one union covered the entire harvest country, and the other that a universal initiation fee be adopted throughout the IWW to end competition for membership among the various locals. Only nine delegates went to Kansas City but they met for two days, elected Walter T. Nef as secretary-treasurer, and launched the Agricultural Workers Organization No. 400 (AWO 400). Initially, an organization committee of five members was elected, and Kansas City was designated as the union's headquarters. However, there was a uniqueness to AWO 400. Job delegates would be used to initiate and recruit members; that is, those members actually working in a given area would have credentials identifying them as organizers who were authorized to initiate new members, issue membership cards, and place dues stamps on outstanding cards. The scheme bore fruit by the middle of June, 1915, and, from that point on, AWO 400 was a viable force within the IWW.[5]

Membership increased so rapidly that another meeting was held in Kansas City in August, 1914, and the decision was made to move the AWO 400 headquarters to Minneapolis, Minnesota. Four new office employees had to be added at Minneapolis to handle the increase in membership. To facilitate recruiting, Minneapolis placed stationary delegates at important geographical points to supply the job delegates. The results of this new strategy were the addition of approximately 2,300 new members in 1915. Expansion improved in 1916, with over 700 members initiated by AWO 400 in the month of July alone. Minneapolis now had to have a staff of fifteen to handle the increased membership, and also created four separate departments. Success also brought dissension, as not all IWW members agreed with the policy of paying job delegates a commission for each recruit, feeling this led to a certain amount of force and violence rather than to a true conversion. But the AWO 400 convention of 1916 endorsed the job delegate system by electing Forrest Edwards, a staunch supporter of recruiting tactics, as its new secretary-treasurer. The fiscal year 1916 saw the AWO 400 become the mainstay of the IWW, with an income of $49,114.84. The AWO 400 contributed fifteen cents of each member's dues to the general treasury, and gave twenty-five cents for each initiation fee to the IWW newspaper, *Solidarity,* to cover an automatic subscription for each new member. This prosperity enabled the general headquarters to occupy four floors of a building at 1001 West Madison, Chicago.[6]

The Oil Workers Union No. 450 (OWU 450) was established on January 1, 1917, with its affairs to be handled by AWO 400 in Minneapolis until such time as it became large enough to become an independent union. The addition of OWU 450 caused another surge of membership, which made the Minneapolis headquarters the largest complex within the IWW outside of the Chicago headquarters. The AWO 400 occupied most of the third floor of the Kasota Building at Fourth and Hennepin in downtown Minneapolis, where it installed a power multigraph and became one of the best business offices in the nation.[7] However, not all of this growth and progress took place without some sacrifice. Auguries of what would come in the fall of 1917 occurred during the previous summer, when hundreds of active delegates were jailed for organizational work for both AWO 400 and OWU 450.[8]

This background information then should place a new perspective on federal and state prosecutions of the IWW during the World War I period. First, it is impossible to separate the oil workers from the harvest workers, as they shared the same headquarters at Minneapolis and often the same locals, and could work within either union, depending upon the season. Secondly, an understanding of events that led up to it should give a new significance to the so-called Wichita Case. Previous historical writing on the Wichita Case has rated it as a minor or secondary cause; however, the facts do not fully bear out that contention.Wichita was an oil case, and the individuals involved were important for that reason. Take Phineas Madison Eastman, for example, the secretary-treasurer at the Augusta, Kansas, local of AWO 400–OWU 450 from February until September 1, 1917. Eastman was considered the most dangerous man of over 200 IWWs prosecuted by the federal government at Chicago, Sacramento, and Wichita between 1917 and 1919.[9] His main crime appears to have been an anonymous letter to the Augusta Chamber of Commerce, threatening destruction of oil tanks and pipelines.[10] Then there was Frank J. Gallagher, a Wichita defendant, who was exclusively an oil-field worker and organizer for the IWW. When presidential commutations were initially offered to the IWW political prisoners in 1923, Gallagher was not considered because he had perpetrated oil-field strikes in Oklahoma during 1917.[11]

Wichita, however, is but the culmination of the reaction of the federal and state governments to IWW activity in the Mid-Continent Oil Field. The critical period for the IWW began on September 1, 1917, with the resignation of Phineas Eastman at Augusta. This was followed by the appointment by Minneapolis headquarters of Gallagher as a traveling delegate for the Mid-Continent Oil Field, the October 25th dynamiting of Pew's Tulsa home, the Tulsa Outrage in early November, and, finally, the federal raids on the Augusta local on November 20–21, 1917. All these incidents were related in such a way that the total became greater than the sum of its parts.

Available evidence does not indicate when union locals of AWO 400–OWU 450 were established in Augusta, Kansas, and Tulsa, Oklahoma. Therefore, the historian can only gather impressions from the available documentation. The impression is that neither local was flourishing. Many of the Wichita defendants had been short-term secretaries of the Tulsa local, but hostility in the area seemed to warrant organizers with greater ability.[12] It appears that Tulsa was not a safe place for the IWWs, particularly after the tar and feathering, but also before that incident. Likewise, Augusta, although a refuge where oil-field workers and organizers fled to, held meetings, and planned strategy, was, at best, a pitiful example of an IWW stronghold, as the headquarters consisted merely of a tent.[13] Three IWW German aliens owned a small home there, which they opened for the storage of individual member's property and IWW literature.[14] Yet, this humble local was the focal point for the organization of the Mid-Continent Oil Field and the haven for Oklahoma members who bore psychological and physical scars. Phineas M. Eastman brought a militancy to Augusta in early 1917 that influenced the town during the union's entire existence.

Phineas M. Eastman was a mature man of forty-six, with approximately a decade of IWW organizational work behind him when he solicited the secretary-treasurer's position at Augusta from Bill Haywood. Eastman's background lay in the South, where he was born and had worked all his life.[15] He had first come to the attention of Haywood and the IWW during the protracted Texas-Louisiana lumber wars of 1911–13. Haywood went to Louisiana to solidify the amalgamation of the Brotherhood of Timber Workers and the IWW in 1911 during a particularly bitter strike there. Available evidence does not indicate a meeting or friendship between Haywood and Eastman;[16] however, Eastman was well enough known to be elected to the general executive board of the IWW in 1913, and was so deeply involved in the Maryville, Louisiana, lumber strike of that year that he was physically abused and deported by the local citizenry.[17] By early 1917, he was again ready for the challenge of IWW organizational work. Apparently, Haywood had asked him to take another position in the South, but Eastman refused as he saw no future there.[18] He then countered and asked Haywood for the Augusta position, in a series of letters in which he bragged about his sabotage in Louisiana for the IWW, his courage, and his dedication to the IWW. Haywood appointed him to the post in February or March, 1917.[19] Eastman's militancy came out in a very vicious letter he wrote anonymously and in a disguised hand to the Augusta Chamber of Commerce on May 27, 1917, that was later identified by a government handwriting expert.

Sir: Your damned speaker from Missouri in a speech to you and your members advised you to take steps to unlawfully suppress the W.C.U. [Working Class Union] and all organized workers, who are against your blood sucking, cowardly conscription. We warn you that the first dirty move that you make against the workers, whether they be organized or unorganized, we will reply with a handful of matches and numerous sticks of dynamite and nitro.

At your first move up go your homes and pipelines and tanks. One box of matches can whip the whole country.

Take notice and do not start anything with the worker. Just leave us alone and everything will be fine and dandy.[20]

He also signed and sent an antidraft resolution from the Augusta membership to Haywood the same month, which would be considered an overt act in all three federal indictments of the IWW. Eastman was apparently also involved in some kind of conflict with traveling delegate Frank J. Gallagher over strategy in the oil fields.[21] However, he was successful enough in all his endeavors that IWW activities worried both Butler County officials and the United States district attorney for Kansas.

Eastman resigned on September 1, 1917, and left Kansas on September 11th. He remained a fugitive until his arrest in Colorado in June, 1919, where he was living under an assumed name.[22]

Several questions can be raised about Eastman's tenure and resignation at Augusta. Was he Haywood's choice at Augusta because of his militancy and loyalty alone? Apparently this was the case, as Eastman's background in southern agriculture was not of a migratory nature; he had worked in plantation stores and was familiar with the more sedentary plantation workers and sharecroppers. Much the same was true of his experience in the lumber industry, where the laboring force was provided with company housing, a hospital, a store, etc.[23] Therefore, the conclusion can only be that Eastman was brought to the oil fields for his ability and not his past experience with either migratory agricultural or oil workers. However, his lack of experience could have led to the conflict with Gallagher, an experienced oil-field worker. Finally, why did Eastman resign at Augusta? There is no simple answer to that question. Eastman later claimed that he quit and moved to Colorado because of his wife's health,[24] and a case can certainly be made for that contention. But some IWW members claimed that he was forced to resign because of the antidraft resolution. There is not enough available evidence to determine the truth of that allegation, but Eastman vehemently denied it.[25] The final possibility is that he feared arrest by the federal government. A circumstantial case can be made for this possibility. Eastman was indicted in Chicago on September 26, 1917, and apparently could have known, through Haywood, that raids would be conducted.[26] Whatever the reason, Eastman's resignation was the beginning of a new phase in the Mid-Continent Oil Field.

The Minneapolis headquarters and not Haywood now directed the operations in the area. The Chicago indictment had resulted in the jailing of Haywood and Forrest Edwards of AWO 400, and shipping clerk Charles W. Anderson became the new secretary-treasurer of AWO 400.[27] Anderson turned to the vast experience of Frank J. Gallagher, variously known as John Shannon and John King, urging upon him the necessity of organizing the Mid-Continent Oil Field by the spring of 1918. Gallagher's letters to Anderson during this period showed a marked reticence on his part to take on the responsibility, but he finally accepted the challenge and was ordered to use the newly elected organizing committee of AWO 400. The committee consisted of Oscar E. Gordon, a tough, tattooed, ex-Army sergeant, a good soapbox orator with a great deal of IWW organizational experience in the midwestern harvest fields, and acting secretary of the Augusta local; Wencil Francik, lately from the mines of Bisbee, Arizona, but with an Iowa farm background, and a member of the IWW since 1909; and Michael Sapper, a Russian immigrant with a mixed work record.[28] Gallagher wrote the following letter on October 31, 1917, to Anderson, which showed his doubts about the committeemen and his general attitude toward the IWW and the Mid-Continent Oil Field.

> ...Now, I hope you will not misunderstand me and think I have cold feet. That is not a complaint I was ever troubled with, but this is the way I feel about the oil fields. As you know, I have spent lots of time trying to organize the oil workers and this has turned out to be a personal matter with me. In fact, my greatest ambition is to see the oil fields line up solid in the IWW and would like to be in at the finish, that is, active until the last man is lined up. Now, if I go into the oil fields, I know I am flirting with my liberty, and I am willing to take a chance, but I want to know I have accomplished something; otherwise it would be foolish to take a chance on a long jolt without the satisfaction of knowing it was worthwhile. I am willing to do anything at any time for the organization, and do not understand the position taken by the three committeemen. Gordon also informs me that some of the committeemen are oil workers. I don't know anything about Sapper, but I do know that Francik and Gordon are not, and I have my doubts Sapper being an oil worker. I know every one of the oil slaves, but never knew of Sapper working in the oil fields. He may have worked in the oil fields one winter, but that does not say he understands the industry. Well, to sum up, if they will meet me, I will be foolish and go down there and will work for a master. With best wishes, I am, Yours for the IWW.
>
> *John Shannon, Box 1074 Omaha, Nebraska.*[29]

The date of this letter is very interesting, as it was written only two days after the commencement of pressure on the IWW at Tulsa.

Sometime on the morning of October 29, 1917, the home of Carter Oil official and stock holder, J. Edgar Pew, was dynamited.[30] Eugene Lyons, then a young Socialist newspaper reporter, assisted the IWW defense in 1919 when Charles Krieger was finally tried for the dynamiting. Some years later, Mr. Lyons summed up the situation in Tulsa at the time of the incident.

The dynamiting charge against 'Big Boy' Krieger, a tall, raw-boned Pennsylvania Dutchman, was so palpably a frame-up that no one even pretended it was anything else. The average citizen of Tulsa, which was then ruled by a vigilante Committee of One Hundred, merely had a sporting interest in whether the Standard Oil crowd could make their fantastic invention stick. The case was the last stage of a determined effort of the oil interests to drive IWW union agitation, which had been making considerable headway, out of the state. Organizers had been beaten, tarred and feathered, ridden out on rails. But they kept coming back like so many pesky flies. One night someone set off dynamite under the Pew porch, where Mrs. Pew normally slept. She wasn't there, it happened, and not much harm was done. But the press promptly headlined it as Red Terror and the authorities proceeded to round up every suspected IWW in Oklahoma.[31]

Michael Sapper, a member of the AWO 400 organizing committee, summed up the situation in Oklahoma a few days later, on November 10th, in a letter to C. W. Anderson at the Minneapolis AWO 400 headquarters, and it confirmed all that Eugene Lyons had stated.

Cushing, Okla. 11–10–17

C. W. Anderson,
Fellow Worker:

Met J. Shannon [Alias of Frank Gallagher] on the 8th in Arkansas City and held the meeting. And was decided on lots of publicity job bulletins and oilworks leaflets which the 3 of us already had decided to do. J. Shannon went to the Ardmore fields. I then decided to come down to Drumright to Francik in Tulsa....On Wednesday the 7th the law and order of Drumright came down to the hall and smashed the windows and furniture and took with them some literature and arrested one fellow worker by the name of George Wilson....Chester Mackben was arrested at Skidder and taken to Pawnee County jail. He is held on a charge of va-grancy....The supplies in Drumright is safe and will be sent to Minneapolis....I had to leave Drumright on the threats of death if I didn't leave before sundown. Cushing is just as bad the cops went in one of the boarding houses where all the floaters stop and search for IWW cards....They are very hostile through here. In Yale they pick you up as soon as you light in and frisk for a card. The papers through here are full of threats and advocating vio-lence and the masters tools are sure practicing it. Nearly every job is some gunmen. So you see it is impossible to do any active work for a traveling delegate. The country through here is flooded with work, and our only way to get back at the barbarians is on the job. Fellow workers coming through here wants to plant their cards.

Yours for Industrial Freedom,
MICHAEL SAPPER
Augusta, Kansas.[32]

Two days later another member of the organizing committee, Wencil Francik, painted a similar picture for Anderson.

Tulsa, Okla. 11–12–17

C. W. Anderson

I have wired you for $100.00 as to have some money to pay rent in a couple of days to have the lease good. I just sent a letter to O. E. Gordon asking him to come here and meet me around the post office. Some member like Gordon should have charge of this place. The Hall does not stay open as yet as the Fellow Workers think best not to open it for a few days. Just seen Boyd at Sand Springs going to Augusta for a couple of days. [Boyd also became a Wichita defendant]…I was going to sell out but will not as I saw the boss at Sand Springs and they told me not to. So I'll keep it a going as they want to push this case through and not to lay down now. Your for O.B.U.

WENCIL FRANCIK, Tulsa Okla.[33]

These, then, were the words of a contemporary newspaper man and three of the four IWWs that were going to organize the Mid-Continent Oil Field. Lyons stated that the Pew dynamiting was the excuse to round up the IWW in Oklahoma; Gallagher wrote of flirting with his liberty by going there; Sapper had to leave Drumright, Oklahoma, under the threat of death; and Francik was so discouraged that he wanted to quit trying to organize in the Tulsa area. Again, the available evidence does not indicate whether any of these men were aware of the impact the Pew dynamiting was to have on the IWW in Oklahoma, but their letters indicate that they were fully aware that Oklahoma was hostile to IWW oil workers. Evidence does show that they were probably aware of another incident that took place on November 9th. Twelve IWW prisoners were being tried for vagrancy in the Tulsa City Police Court on the night of November 9, 1917. These men had been arrested on November 4th at the IWW hall in Tulsa and were oil-field workers. Nothing of significance was found in the IWW hall, and subsequently, the men were charged with vagrancy; they then demanded a trial. Five men testified on the IWW's behalf, but the prisoners were still found guilty and fined $100.00. Police officers then arrested the five defense witnesses and took all seventeen men away from the courtroom in three large touring cars at approximately 11:15 P.M., ostensibly for safekeeping at the county courthouse. However, a few blocks from the police court, the touring cars were stopped by a dozen men in flowing black coats with attached capes and cowls over their faces. This group, calling itself the Knights of Liberty, ordered the police away from the cars and took charge of the IWW prisoners. These vigilantes then drove northward to the vicinity of Convention Hall, where they were met by ten or twelve more cars. This small caravan proceeded to just outside the city limits of Tulsa and disgorged its IWW victims, who were ordered to strip to the waist. All seventeen of the prisoners were then whipped with a rope until blood was drawn in most instances. Next, tar and feathers were applied, the men's clothing was set on fire, and the prisoners were ordered to go and keep going. To emphasize their orders, the Knights of Liberty fired dozens of shots over the heads of their victims, who ran into the darkness of the chilly morning.[34] This affront to decency and civil liberty was dubbed by the National Civil Liberties Bureau (NCLB) as an outrage and later became known as the Tulsa Outrage.

Among the seventeen victims was Edward M. Boyd, a fifty-three year old IWW and subsequent Wichita defendant. The historian is indeed fortunate that Ed Boyd was present, for he began a correspondence with the National Civil Liberties Bureau and its successor organization, the American Civil Liberties Union (ACLU), that lasted into the year 1921. Boyd related his account of the Tulsa Outrage to the NCLB, wrote incessantly about the Wichita Case, jail conditions in Kansas, IWW defense strategy, and finally, his impressions of Leavenworth Federal Penitentiary. Edward M. Boyd was the chronicler of the Mid-Continent Oil Field organizational efforts by the IWW. Boyd was secretary of the Tulsa local at the time of the outrage, which further illustrates the hostile attitude toward IWW oil workers in that city.[35] Nothing was ever done to apprehend those responsible for the outrage.

The NCLB became involved almost immediately and contacted a local attorney, the Tulsa mayor, and the Oklahoma governor, R. L. Williams.[36] When these efforts did not meet with any immediate success, the NCLB then hired a private investigator, Mr. L. A. Brown of Kansas City.[37] Mr. Brown went to Tulsa and uncovered some interesting facts. One report from him is a letter, dated December 29, 1917, and addressed to Roger Baldwin of the NCLB.

> ...Your lawyers report from this state was correct. No investigation could be made here if it were known that such investigation was being attempted. The town was placarded with bills afterwards stating that any atty. who attempted to defend would receive the same treatment etc.
>
> But I am making some progress and the Dept. U.S. Marshall in charge here told me today he had two trunks full of their literature and letters and there was not one word of disloyalty in it and they had nothing on them and couldn't get it. He also stated, the two reports of the affair sent out by the organization were

absolutely correct as far as they went. His name is John Morgan. He also said he did not approve of such methods and tried to get them not to do it....[38]

Brown also sent a report that specifically named Tulsa officials he felt were involved in the outrage.

(1) Patten, Policeman; Carmicle, Policeman.
(2) Regardless of just how much active part the police took in the donning the black masks and becoming leaders of the mob, there is a preponderence of evidence to show that the city officials including the Police Judge, City Attorney, as well as the Police are *partecep criminus* to the outrage....[39]

Apparently local attitudes and the important positions held by those responsible for the Tulsa affair prevented any attempts at criminal prosecution, but Ed Boyd got his revenge two years later when he testified for the defense in the Krieger trial at Tulsa. Boyd related that he was not able to give the names of those responsible but still was satisfied that he had exposed them.[40] However, this was of little comfort to OWU 450 at the time, as they were about to launch their organizational campaign of the Mid-Continent Oil Field.

Frank Gallagher's hesitancy in the matter has already been noted, but Minneapolis pressed the issue. C. W. Anderson closed the subject by instructing Gallagher to go to the oil fields.

Nov. 2nd. 1917

C. E. Gordon:—

Fellow Workers:—

The unexpected has again happened. The federal authorities has visited us and took all the membership, delegate accts, delegate financial reports files and in fact all the index records in the office. We are still doing business. The books are still here.

I am this day instructing Shannon to proceed to the Oil fields and I want you committee members to get together with him at some convenient point and outline plan of action for organizing the oil fields. This has got to be done immediately. Gordon will without a doubt be the point for this meeting and you have got to get busy down there now as no one can tell what will happen. Shannon knows the oil fields and is an oil worker and knows the men there, and thats what counts now. He will probably be leaving the Omaha district immediately. You will have to get together as soon as possible, as now is the time for action. The organization has got to be kept going even if the records are gone temporarily. Hoping you get together immediately and wishing success remain

Yours for One Big Union.
C. W. Anderson[41]

In another letter to Gordon a week later, Anderson wrote that he was aware of some raids in the Tulsa and Drumright oil areas but had no definite details.[42] Anderson had set the wheels in motion for the Wichita case and sealed the fate of himself, Gallagher, and the organizing committee.

Gallagher responded to Anderson's instructions and set up the organizational meeting for November 8th.

> K. C. Mo. Nov. 6th, 1917
>
> C. E. Gordon,
> Augusta, Kans.
> Fellow Worker:
> Please meet me in Ark. City Kans. Thurs. Nov. 8th for a conference. I have wired Francik and Sapper....[43]

This meeting was to become the famous or infamous Arkansas City Conspiracy and the basis for the Wichita Case. It would be thought that such a group of conspirators had planned rampant destruction in the Mid-Continent Oil Field, mob violence, and numerous oil strikes. However, Oscar R. Gordon's account of the Arkansas City meeting has a pale resemblance to such a conspiracy.

> Augusta, Kans., 11–8–17
>
> C. W. Anderson,
> Fellow Worker:
> Arrived at Augusta at 9:20 P.M. from meeting in Arkansas City was informed of nature of wire for me as a F.W. took it to El dorado hoping to meet me there and expedite matters.
> Sapper left Ark City at 5:25 P.M. for Drumright, and Francik for Tulsa. I think they will be on the job in the morning down there and will wire Sapper to get Lawyer for their cases.
> Shannon went to Healton fields. In our meeting we decided to give lots of publicity to papers, get out some new leaflets one after the other and try and have job # Del on every job and have job bulletin exclusively for oil workers....[44]

Looking back nearly sixty years with historical perspective, it can readily be discerned that Anderson had either selected the worst time to go into the Mid-Continent Field, or he was acting out of desperation. The pressures on the IWW in Oklahoma were tremendous within that ten-day period from the Pew dynamiting on October 29th to the Tulsa Outrage on November 7th, and yet, on the very next day, November 8th, the organizing committee went into Oklahoma. The letters of both Sapper and Francik have already noted the wall of hostility they encountered in their organizational efforts. The question then remains as to why Anderson selected this particular time to step up unionization of the Mid-Continent Field.

There are several possibilities. The entire IWW organization was under attack by the federal government as a subversive organization, once the nation entered World War I. Anderson's letter of November 2nd illustrates this, as he urged action and the necessity of keeping the union going even if federal raids were occurring. He obviously considered the IWW to have been in a life and death struggle for existence. If this was true, then Anderson was not wrong in going into the Mid-Continent Oil Field when he did. Another explanation concerns the change of leadership, both in Minneapolis and Augusta. Eastman had left Augusta about the same time that Anderson became head of AWO 400. Still another explanation involves the federal government that, through its Wichita prosecutor, Fred Robertson, contended that the IWW had conspired to tie up oil production and thus hinder the war effort.[45] A look at events in the Wichita drama may help to illuminate these possibilities.

Historians have provided various interpretations of the Wichita Case and its relationship to other federal prosecutions of the IWW, the Mid-Continent Oil Field, and the State of Kansas. The published scholarship in this area goes back to at least 1962 and Philip Taft's excellent article on the federal trials of the IWW.[46] Taft was only interested in Wichita as part of that era of federal prosecution and gave Wichita a minor role. The classical work came the next year from William Preston, Jr., who analyzed the total suppression of radicals but again assigned Wichita a minor role while at the same time discussing Oklahoma.[47] Preston discussed the Mid-Continent Oil Field but saw the Wichita Case as one handled according to the whim of the local United States district attorney.

> When IWW organizers increased their activity in the mid-continent oil fields during the fall of 1917, the oil interests sought their suppression.... They turned for aid to the federal attorneys whose districts embraced the mid-continent field, one at Tulsa, Oklahoma, and the other at Kansas City, Kansas. The results were strikingly different.
>
> United States Attorney W. P. McGinnis at Tulsa quietly rebuffed the corporate invitation for an anti-Wobbly round-up....He refused to arrest IWWs in anticipation of what they might do.
>
> In the eastern part of the oil field, situated in southern Kansas, a most dissimilar solution prevailed. Compared with the Oklahoma areas, the IWW, its agitation, and the calls for its suppression were all the same. The United States attorney, on the other hand, had a broad view of the law. While there had been no

strike, but only a concerted membership drive, the local Department of Justice office in conjunction with state authorities apprehended some one hundred Wobblies on November 17, 1917....[48]

It appears from this statement that Preston somewhat misinterpreted
the IWW's role in the Mid-Continent Oil Field. He has failed to take
into consideration the legal maneuvering of the Pew dynamiting incident, which subsequently turned into the Krieger Case and the Tulsa
Outrage. There was no need for the United States district attorney, W.
P. McGinnis, to act in Tulsa at all. Witness the letters from the Tulsa
area of Sapper and Francik, who were leaving town under the threat
of death; there was so much hostility and violence that the IWW hall
in Tulsa could not stay open, and IWW oil workers were being tarred
and feathered. It should also be remembered that the headquarters
for the Oil Workers Union was not in Tulsa but in Augusta, Kansas.
Even with three out of four members of the organizing committee
of AWO 400–OWU 450 actively working in Oklahoma, Oscar E.
Gordon, the fourth member, stayed at Augusta. Gordon was an ex-
army sergeant, a leader of men, and he was needed in Augusta. Even
Francik stressed this point in his letter of November 12th when he
wrote, "I just sent a letter to O. E. Gordon asking him to come here
and meet me around the post office. Some member like Gordon
should have charge of this place." But, Gordon did not go to Tulsa;
rather he stayed in Augusta where he was needed for important
union work. Consequently, the pressure applied on the IWW oil
workers in Oklahoma forced them out like animals fleeing a forest
fire, back to the refuge at Augusta and the Kansas pool.
    The most recently published scholarship on Wichita was by
Clayton R. Koppes in 1975.[49] Koppes generally agreed with Preston's
quotation and took the viewpoint that Wichita was a Kansas case, with
much of the responsibility for its initiation lying with United States
district attorney for Kansas, Fred Robertson. Koppes based his conclusions upon two standard pieces of research used by most historians
dealing with the Wichita Case. The first is the trial testimony of Butler
district attorney, Robert McCluggage, in which he admitted, under
cross-examination, that the local oil companies were interested in the
prosecution of the IWW oil workers in the Augusta-El Dorado area.
McCluggage's testimony, in turn, was partially read by former Wichita
IWW co-defense attorney, Caroline Ann Lowe, before a congressional
committee in 1922. Miss Lowe concluded from the McCluggage testimony that the local Kansas oil companies were behind the prosecution of the Wichita IWW.[50] Koppes strengthened that point
from a United States Department of Justice file by using the following telegram:

Kansas City, Kans., August 17, 1917.

Attorney General,
  Washington, D.C.

County attorney at El Dorado, Kansas, makes alarming claim that over three thousand industrial workers of world are assembled in oil field threatening riots and pillage as soon as soldiers stationed there leave for training at Fort Sill. I suggest special agent be ordered there immediately.

Robertson,
U.S. Attorney.[51]

U.S. Attorney General Gregory replied to Robertson the next day.

August 18, 1917.

United States Attorney,
  Kansas City, Kansas.

Stunned. Have instructed Bagley send agent immediately to oil field and to make use such other assistance as may be necessary to cover situation insofar as practicable for Federal Government. You should call Governor's and other proper state officials attention to county attorney's statement.

Gregory (signed)[52]

This is irrefutable evidence of Robertson's culpability in listening to the Butler County district attorney, Robert McCluggage. It also supports Preston's interpretation. However, both scholars have failed to take into account the "Eastman thesis."

A better name might be the "Howe-Eastman thesis," as federal agent Thomas J. Howe was inextricably tied to any evaluation of Phineas M. Eastman. It was Thomas J. Howe who considered Eastman the most dangerous man in the entire IWW, but note his own words from a 1923 letter to United States Pardon Attorney James A. Finch.

...I prepared all of the documentary evidence in the Chicago case, and participated in the trial of the case, ... I then, in company with Assistant Attorney General Porter, proceeded to Kansas City and was then assigned to assist the United States Attorney in the preparation of the Kansas case....

After my first visit to Kansas I returned to Chicago and gathered from the material on hand everything of any interest bearing on the activities of the defendants in the Kansas case. I also took with me all the material used in the Chicago case showing a general conspiracy.

...On my arrival in Kansas (1923) I found that the defendant Phineas Eastman was pardoned. In my opinion he was the most vitriolic and vicious of all the defendants in the three cases, being well educated and a forceful talker. He was very bitter against the war program, conscription and service in the military forces....[53]

The thesis hinges partially on contemporary newspaper accounts of the Wichita defendant's trail and on federal records. Howe's importance in the totality of the federal prosecutions of the IWW still remains somewhat unclear, with a distinct possibility that he gathered evidence against the IWW as far back as 1916. Newspaper accounts credited him with covert activity among the Wichita IWW, as many of them knew him from his days when he posed as an IWW member. If this information is accepted as generally true, then it sheds new light on the Wichita Case.

If a careful comparison of the *Kansas City Times* and *Star* (morning edition of the former and evening coverage of the latter) is made with the trial transcript of the Wichita Case, some interesting conclusions can be made. First, the testimony of witnesses and recording of government exhibits were accurately reported by both newspapers; a day-by-day comparison of the two records readily bears out this contention. Given the accuracy, then, of the Kansas City newspapers on these counts, the following report should be generally true.

> Eastman, a former member of the IWW executive committee, the controlling council, was regarded by the government as the guiding hand of the organization in the Midcontinent oil fields and the Western agricultural regions. Thomas Howe, agent for the department of justice, was dispatched from Washington, and for more than twenty months he followed the case.
>
> There were times when Howe appeared as a 'wobbly,' mixing with other members in the oil fields, hearing their threats and joining in the conferences. When he learned of letters they disappeared but afterward Fred Robertson, United States district attorney, would receive them by registered mail.
>
> Howe followed Eastman's letters to Chicago and Haywood's and Edward's letters to Augusta, Kans., Tulsa, Okla., and other southwestern points. He conducted forty-eight raids, which resulted in the seizure of all of the government's documentary evidence in this case. In the courtroom Howe sits on the side of the government, quiet and unpretentious, but the defendants know him, and some of them call him 'Tommy' and others by other names.
>
> As Col. S. B. Amidon, special prosecutor, sat last night reading through the letters of the defendants, he stumbled occasionally over the nearly illegible handwriting. From across the room where he sat, Howe prompted him. He knows the contents of the documents nearly word for word.
>
> Howe's efforts focused on Eastman and his activities, and after Eastman's arrest the secret service agent toured the country trailing his letters....[54]

This newspaper account indicates to me then that Eastman was the focal point for governmental surveillance, particularly since he was named and indicted in the Chicago Case on September 28, 1917. In other words, Eastman was a Chicago defendant originally because of his importance in the total alleged IWW conspiracy. He was also a fugitive, as he left the Augusta IWW local approximately September 11, 1917, and went into hiding under an assumed name. The Kansas raids of IWW locals do not coincide with the other forty-eight federal raids throughout the nation in September. Rather, the Augusta local was raided almost three months later, on November 20 and 21, 1917, and this has possibly misled historians in their evaluation of the Wichita Case.[55] Government records clearly indicate that the search warrant issued on November 19, 1917, for purposes of raiding the Augusta IWW local, was captioned "U.S. vs. Phineas Eastman."[56] This would be very unusual if Eastman was not the important defendant, since he had left Augusta nearly three months before the warrant was issued. Also, the warrant listed the names of other known IWW residents such as Oscar E. Gordon, a very important man in the organizational efforts in the Mid-Continent Field, as previously noted.[57] Yet, the warrant is for Eastman and not Gordon, Gallagher, Sapper, or Francik. Since government records also bear out the Koppes' contention that the Augusta raid occurred because of pressure from the Butler County district attorney, how can the Koppes' and Howe-Eastman thesis be reconciled?

The answer is that two distinct investigations of the IWW local in the Mid-Continent Oil Field were conducted. The initial probe must have been undertaken by Thomas J. Howe and probably went back to 1916, when he began to gather evidence for all the IWW prosecutions. The secondary investigation was carried out, as Koppes stated, because of pressure from Kansas oil companies. In other words, the federal government was working on two investigative levels, and apparently the investigators were unaware of each other's work. Then, probes made by a local department of justice agent, Oscar Schmitz, as a result of complaints made by the Butler County district attorney, revealed that the government was already interested in Eastman, and the search warrant was issued.

There is still some question as to why Eastman was considered such a dangerous character. The answer is that Eastman's activities were readily proven and were the hard, almost irrefutable acts the government needed for IWW convictions. Two or three examples should suffice. First was the antidraft resolution sent from the Augusta local to IWW headquarters on May 21, 1917.[58] That resolution was used as an example of an overt act in the indictments of all three federal prosecutions of the IWW. The claim could be made that the resolution was never acted upon, and indeed that defense was made.[59] However, the most damning evidence was Eastman's threatening letter to the Augusta Chamber of Commerce, which has already been quoted. Even worse than threats of violence and destruction was another alleged Eastman letter of March 8, 1917, in which he bragged of past sabotage:

> The sabotage done at Maryville was done by Bill Baker, Charles Kline and myself. Could not get them to even sand some cars. No, Charley, Baker and I did it all. Been no risk for them, but was considerable one for us....[60]

Eastman was referring here to Maryville, Louisiana, and the lumber strike of 1912–13. It was Eastman's pen that betrayed the IWW at Chicago, Sacramento, and Wichita. He was the important man at the Wichita defendants' trial.

The purpose of this essay is not to examine the Wichita Case in any detail, but rather to show its greater importance to the IWW in the Mid-Continent Oil Field. However, the Howe-Eastman thesis of two investigative levels prior to the arrest of the Wichita defendants also leads to the trial itself, which was held in Kansas City, Kansas, December 1 to 19, 1919. The federal prosecutors were trying the case on the basis of a general antidraft conspiracy and a conspiracy to hinder oil production in the Mid-Continent field. Eastman was the focus of the former and Gallagher and the AWO 400 organizing committee were the focus of the latter.

It took state and federal authorities two years to perfect their cases, and it fell to the star-crossed Fred H. Moore and his co-counsel, Caroline Ann Lowe, to defend the IWW in that area. Charles Krieger went to trial in October, 1919, for the Pew dynamiting. Moore and Lowe were able to get a hung jury in his first trial, which ended November 10, 1919.[61] Then they had to rush into the Wichita Case at Kansas City on December 1st. They lost the Wichita Case just as the IWW lost in the other two federal prosecutions at Chicago and Sacramento. The Wichita defendants were sentenced from three to nine years in Leavenworth Federal Penitentiary,[62] and, when the prison gates shut on them, it ended the IWW efforts in the Mid-Continent Oil Field.

NOTES

[1]Harold F. Williamson et al., *The American Petroleum Industry: The Age of Energy 1899–1959* (Evanston, Illinois: Northwestern University Press, 1963), pp. 21–24.

[2]Carl Coke Rister, *Oil! Titan of the Southwest* (Norman, Oklahoma: University of Oklahoma Press, 1949), p. 344.

[3]Philip Taft, "The IWW in the Grain Belt," (*Labor History*) (No. 1, Winter 1960):56.

[4]Kansas, *Combined Thirty-first and Thirty-second Annual Report of the Department of Labor and Industry for 1915 and 1916* (Topeka: Kansas State Printing Plant, 1916), pp. 217–218.

[5]C. W. Anderson, *Defense News Bulletin* (IWW), June 1, 1918. Hereafter cited as DNB.

[6]Philip S. Foner, *The Industrial Workers of the World, 1905–1917,* Vol. IV of the *History of the Labor Movement in the United States,* 4 Vols. (New York: International Publishers, 1965), pp. 477 and 484 and Taft, "The IWW in the Grain Belt," p. 62

[7]Anderson, DNB, June 1, 1918.

[8]Anderson, DNB, June 1, 1918 and *Industrial Solidarity* (IWW), June 10, 1922. Hereafter cited as *Solidarity.*

[9]Letter, April 16, 1923, Special Assistant U.S. Attorney Thomas J. Howe to U.S. Pardon Attorney James A. Finch. Record Group 204, Pardon Attorney File 39–242. National Archives, Washington, D. C. Hereafter cited as PA 39-242.

[10]*Kansas City Times,* December 13, 1919. In most instances, evidence used at the trial of the Wichita IWW will be taken from the Kansas City newspapers, as it is easier to locate than in the trial transcript which runs over 1100 pages.

[11]*Report,* June 19, 1923, U.S. Attorney General to President Harding. PA 39–242.

[12]*James Hamilton Lewis Letter and Exhibits. Exhibit "H" a brief summary of the nationality, history and other pertinent matters bearing upon each individual* defendant, Federal Records Center, Kansas City, Missouri, and letter from Wencil Francik to C. W. Anderson, November 11, 1917. Indictment Criminal Case 763 United States v. C. W. Anderson, et al, filed June 7, 1919, pp. 29 and 30, Federal Records Center, Kansas City, Missouri. Sources hereafter cited as Lewis Letter Exhibit "H" and Third Wichita Indictment. *The James Hamilton Lewis Letter and Exhibits* are a source of controversy between the author and Dr. Clayton R. Koppes. Koppes attributed the *Letter and Exhibits* to Kansas U.S. District Attorney Fred Robertson, and the author attributes it to IWW defense attorney, Fred H. Moore. The reason the authorship is important is because it is the only known document that has any background information about the Wichita defendants, such as birth, years in the IWW, age, IWW positions held, etc. This author has proven, to his satisfaction, that the document was written by Fred H. Moore, and the eight page typewritten proof has been submitted to *Labor History* for publication.

[13]*Testimony* of United States Deputy Marshal Sam P. Hill. Trial Transcript, *United States* v. C. W. Anderson et al, December 1–19, Kansas City, Kansas, pp. 130–159 passim, PA 39–242. Hereafter cited as *Trial Transcript.* Mr. Hill conducted the government raid on the Augusta IWW local and described the tent and private lodging where he seized evidence used in the subsequent trial.

[14]*Ibid.*

[15]*Phineas Eastman Pardon File,* Record Group 204, Pardon Attorney, National Archives, Washington, D. C. Hereafter cited as Eastman Pardon File. This file contains between 150 and 200 items on legal-sized pages of letters, petitions, and documents, many of which were written in Eastman's own handwriting. The file gives a complete history of Eastman's work record and background up to the year 1919.

[16]James E. Fickle, "Louisiana-Texas Lumber War of 1911–12, "*Louisiana History* 16 (Winter, 1975):59–85; Merl E. Reed, "The IWW and Individual Freedom in Western Louisiana, 1913," *Louisiana History* 10 (No. 1 Winter, 1969):61–69; and Merl E. Reed, "Lumberjacks and Longshoremen; The IWW in Louisiana," *Labor History* 13 (Winter, 1972):41–59.

[17]*Eastman Pardon File,* and Reed, "IWW in Western Louisiana." p. 64.

[18]*Trial Transcript,* pp. 1000–1001.

[19]*Kansas City Star,* December 13, 1919. The newspaper was quoting evidence presented in the Wichita Case.

[20]*Kansas City Star,* December 12, 1919.

[21]*Letter* June 8, 1921, Frank Gallagher to John Downs, PA 39–242. Gallagher was writing from Levenworth Penitentiary, complaining about some of his fellow Wichita IWW prisoners' former tactics.

[22]Eastman Pardon File.

[23]*Ibid.*

[24]*Ibid.*

[25]*Ibid.*

[26]Harrison George, *The IWW Trial* (Chicago: Industrial Workers of the World, n. d.; reprint ed., New York: Arno Press, 1969), p. 11. George listed the men indicted at Chicago on September 26, 1917, and Eastman is on that list.

[27]Anderson, DNB, June 1, 1918.

[28]*Oscar E. Gordon File.* Record group 94, General Records of the Adjutant General's Office, National Archives, Washington, D.C.; *Oscar E. Gordon Prison File* Leavenworth Federal Penitentiary; and Lewis Letter Exhibit "H."

[29]Letter, Gallagher to Anderson, October 31, 1917. Third Wichita Indictment.

[30]*Information, Oklahoma v. Charles Krieger* No. 1576. Tulsa County Court, Tulsa, Oklahoma and *Solidarity,* March 8, 1919. Hereafter cited as Krieger Case.

[31]Eugene Lyons, *Assignment in Utopia* (New York: Harcourt, Brace and Co., 1937), p. 14.

[32]Letter, November 10, 1917, Sapper to Anderson. Third Wichita Indictment.

[33]Letter, November 12, 1917, Francik to Anderson. Third Wichita Indictment.

[34]Bigelow Letter, December 21, 1917, addressed to Mr. Bigelow but unsigned, and Letter, undated, Ed. M. Boyd to Roger Baldwin. *American Civil Liberties Union Papers,* vol. 35. Hereafter cited as *ACLU Papers*. The Bigelow letter is from an eyewitness to the Tulsa outrage, and of course, Ed Boyd was one of the abused IWWs.

[35]Letters, Ed. M. Boyd to ACLU, *ACLU Papers*, Volumes 35, 86, 89, and 136 passim.

[36]Letters, National Civil Liberties Bureau to Attorney J. J. Carney, November 12, 1917; Oklahoma Governor R. L. Williams, November 14, 1917; and Telegram, NCLB to Tulsa Mayor, November 12, 1917, *ACLU Papers*, Vol. 35.

[37]Letter, L. A. Halbert to Roger Baldwin, December 20, 1917, *ACLU Papers*, Vol. 35.

[38]Letter, Investigator Brown to Baldwin, December 29, 1917, *ACLU Papers*, Vol. 35.

[39]Report, Investigator Brown to Baldwin, undated, *ACLU Papers*, Vol. 35.

[40]Letter, Ed. Boyd to Ella Bloor, October 14, 1919, *ACLU Papers*, Vol. 86.

[41]Letter, Anderson to Gordon, November 2, 1917, Third Wichita Indictment.

[42]Letter, Anderson to Gordon, November 9, 1917, Third Wichita Indictment.

[43]Letter, Gallagher to Gordon, November 6, 1917, Third Wichita Indictment.

[44]Letter, Gordon to Anderson, November 8, 1917, Third Wichita Indictment.

[45]Third Wichita Indictment.

[46]Philip Taft "The Federal Trials of the IWW," *Labor History* 3 (Winter, 1962):57–91.

[47]William Preston, Jr. *Aliens and Dissenters: Federal Suppression of Radicals, 1903–1933* (Cambridge: Harvard University Press, 1963), pp. 118–151, passim.

[48]Preston, *Aliens and Dissenters,* pp. 130–1.

[49]Clayton R. Koppes, "The Kansas Trial of the IWW, 1917–1919," *Labor History* 16 (No. 3 Summer, 1975):338–358.

[50]Testimony, Butler District Attorney Robert McCluggage, Trial Transcript, pp. 411–13; and Testimony, Caroline Ann Lowe. *Amnesty for Political Prisoners,* hearings before the Committee on the Judiciary, House of Representatives, 67th Congress 2nd Session, March 16, 1922 (Washington: Government Printing Office, 1922), p. 32.

[51]Telegram, Kansas U.S. District Attorney Fred Robertson to U.S. Attorney General, August 17, 1917. Record Group 60, General Records of the Department of Justice, File No. 189152, National Archives, Washington, D. C. Hereafter cited as DJ 189152.

[52]Letter, U. S. Attorney General to Robertson, August 18, 1917. DJ 189152.

[53]Letter, Special Assistant, U.S. Attorney Thomas J. Howe to U.S. Pardon Attorney James A. Finch, April 16, 1923, PA 39–242.

[54]*Kansas City Star,* December 13, 1919.

[55]Testimony of U.S. Deputy Marshal Sam P. Hill, Trial Transcript, p. 49.
[56]Search warrant, United States v. Eastman, November 19, 1917, DJ 189152.
[57]*Ibid.*
[58]Third Wichita Indictment.
[59]Fred H. Moore to jury, Trial Transcript, pp. 995–1001; and Eastman Pardon File.
[60]Letter, Eastman to Haywood March 8, 1917, Third Wichita Indictment.
[61]Docket Entries, Krieger Case.
[62]*Kansas City Times,* December 19, 1919.

The Bisbee Deportation

James Byrkit

EARLY IN 1916, Walter Douglas, son of Dr. James Douglas, the illustrious developer of Bisbee's Copper Queen mine, was named vice president and member, board of directors, of the Phelps Dodge Corporation. Douglas had visited Morenci in 1915 during the historic Morenci-Clifton strike. He was indignant with what he saw there: a strike at an impasse, a governor sympathetic with working men, the prohibition of strikebreakers and, later, national guardsmen who were not conspicuously siding with management.[1]

His anger was intensified by a January, 1916, article in the liberal journal, *The New Republic,* which praised the strikers' peaceful nature. He wrote a long letter to the editor, refuting the article, and then went on to praise the copper companies and denounce the workers, Arizona Governor George W. P. Hunt, and the liberal press. He called the description of the Ludlow Massacre "fabled," and then reminded *The New Republic* and its readers that "an Arizona vigilance committee commands instant attention and respect."[2]

This letter, apparently, was Douglas' declaration of war against a labor movement that had become too powerful for him to tolerate any longer. Mine operators around the state organized behind Douglas' leadership. Arizona's liberal constitution, written by representatives of labor, had angered him enough. The tax laws, corporation laws, labor laws and workingman's compensation laws passed by the first and second state legislatures were too much. He had to fight back. Douglas became a national antiunion leader. In November, 1916, in Chicago, he was elected president of the American Mining Congress.[3]

In the same town—Chicago—and in the same month and year—November, 1916—that Douglas was elected president, the Industrial Workers of the World held their annual convention. On

James Byrkit's full-length volume on the history and events surrounding the Bisbee Deportation, *Forging the Copper Collar: Arizona's Labor-Management War, 1901–1921,* is a 1982 publication of the University of Arizona Press.

November 25, the IWW Committee on Organization and Constitution passed a proposal authorizing $2,000 to organize the miners in the West. Late in January, 1917, IWW Organizer Grover H. Perry left Chicago to found an Arizona state chapter in Phoenix, where he was met by J. L. Donnelly, the state leader of the International Union of Mine, Mill, and Smelter Workers. Donnelly asked for Perry's support in rebelling against the national IUMMSW and its president, Charles Moyer. Perry refused, and he set about to organize the state IWW. In February, Moyer revoked the Arizona IUMMSW charter, saying that the district's attitudes were too radical and independent. Within two months, solid IUMMSW members in Bisbee were paying for their little red cards, the membership books of the IWW. On April 10, four days after President Wilson had signed a declaration of war against the Central Powers, Stuart W. French, general manager of the Bisbee branch of Phelps Dodge, purchased four machine guns with accessories and ammunition from the Marlin Arms Corporation of New Haven, Connecticut.[4]

By the middle of May, 1917, the IWW had captured the Bisbee IUMMSW local. At a statewide conference in Bisbee on June 15, despite the objections of organizers Frank Little and Grover Perry, strike fever was strong and the membership drew up some standard demands:

1. abolition of the physical exam
2. two men to work on machines
3. two men to work in raises
4. discontinuing of all blasting during shift
5. abolition of all bonus and contract work
6. abolition of the sliding scale of wages with a flat daily rate of $6.00 for all men working underground
7. no discrimination against the members of any organization[5]

The items were voted on and approved, but the miners decided to claim that the demands represented the thinking of the IUMMSW membership—not that of the IWW.[6]

After leaving the meeting, Perry called IWW president, Big Bill Haywood, in Chicago to ask the wobbly chief to come to Arizona and talk the workers out of striking. Both men believed that the time was not right for such drastic action. On June 26, Gerald Sherman, mine superintendent at the Copper Queen, tore up the written list of demands. Infuriated, the local union leaders immediately called a strike without benefit of a general strike vote. All union leaders then openly identified with the IWW. However, little evidence exists to show that more than four hundred Bisbee miners at the most, out of a total of more than 4,700 mine workers employed in Bisbee, even paid their dues to the IWW. Regardless, on June 27, more than 3,000 miners walked out.[7]

For two weeks, the strike crippled Bisbee. On July 10, vigilantes in Jerome, Arizona, almost 300 miles north of Bisbee, rounded up and deported, via railroad from Jerome, sixty-seven "troublemakers," all purported to be members of the IWW.[8]

Early in the morning on Thursday, July 12, 1917, a *posse comitatus,* two thousand strong, swept through the streets of Bisbee, Arizona, and arrested more than 2,000 people. Led by Cochise County Sheriff Harry Wheeler, armed vigilantes composed of members of the Bisbee Workman's Loyalty League and the Bisbee Citizens' Protective League picked up anyone they deemed "undesirable." The deputies herded their prisoners into Bisbee's downtown plaza, while two machine guns commanded the scene. Included among the captives were numerous Bisbee business and professional people who supported or sympathized with the strikers.[9]

From the plaza, the deputies marched the arrested men to the local ball park. There, mine managers offered those workers on strike one last chance to return to work; many men agreed and were released. At gunpoint, the remaining prisoners, 1,186 of them, climbed into waiting boxcars of the El Paso and Southwestern Railroad, a subsidiary of Phelps Dodge. The train took the men to Columbus, New Mexico, 173 miles east of Bisbee, where many of the deportees remained for two months. Only a few ever returned to stay in Bisbee.[10]

It had all been announced on the night of July 11, following the instructions of Phelps Dodge Corporation's new president, Walter Douglas, when he arrived from Globe that day on his private railroad car, the "Cloudcroft."[11]

Before leaving Globe for Bisbee, Douglas made his feelings public and he made them clear:

> "There will be no compromise because you cannot compromise with a rattlesnake. That goes for both the International Union and the IWWs....I believe the government will be able to show that there is German influence behind this movement....It is up to the individual communities to drive these agitators out as has been done in other communities in the past."[12]

Sheriff Harry Wheeler earlier had been dubious about participating in any roundup. But a minor copper company official, George B. Willcox, together with Calumet & Arizona's general manager, John Greenway, succeeded in convincing Wheeler of the nefarious nature of the IWW and the purpose of the strike. The strike fund, they claimed, came from Germany. Wheeler, Willcox, and Greenway were all Spanish-American War veterans. Greenway and Willcox had both served as captains in Roosevelt's Rough Riders. Up until this time Wheeler's chief fear had been that the local Mexicans would start an uprising. Once they had dispelled such a rumor, the mine managers had but to redirect Sheriff Wheeler's sense of protective responsibility. When Wheeler inquired as to who would bear the expense of such an extravagant undertaking, Willcox assured the sheriff that the copper companies, not the county, would pay for everything.[13]

The Loyalty League learned of the roundup plan more than a week before the deportation. Several meetings of the league were held in the dispensary, strictly for Copper Queen employees, where Miles Merrill outlined the details for a roundup to be used "in the event of a riot." George F. Kellogg, manager of the local Bell Telephone office, attended the meetings, and he agreed to give the alarm when notified by Copper Queen officials, Miles Merrill or Sheriff Wheeler. Merrill gave Kellogg a list of Loyalty Leaguers containing 250 to 300 names. Kellogg was instructed to call each person on the list and say merely, "This is the Loyalty League call." League members already knew what to do: the call was their signal to act.[14]

But the deportation part of the plan remained a well-kept secret. The companies had taken great care to create the appearance that the decision to deport was spontaneous.

In late afternoon, July 11, Sheriff Wheeler called an 8:00 P.M. meeting for his followers at the Phelps Dodge dispensary. Even though he had arrived in Bisbee that day, Walter Douglas chose not to attend the meeting. Grant Dowell, manager of the Copper Queen operations, had ordered the meeting, and Sheriff Wheeler conducted it.[15]

John Greenway addressed about 100 "representative citizens" who had gathered in the dispensary, a building which was to remain Loyalty League headquarters for several months. Greenway implied to the men that the planned deportation had the knowledge and consent of the United States Government. Two weeks before the deportation, at the request of Sheriff Wheeler and Arizona Governor Thomas E. Campbell, the army had sent Lieutenant Colonel James J. Hornbrook to investigate conditions in Bisbee and ascertain if federal help was needed to maintain peace. Hornbrook observed that the situation was free of violence and decided against military assistance. Greenway implied in the meeting, however, that the officer had given his direct approval of the roundup and deportation.[16]

For almost three weeks, *The Bisbee Daily Review* had been describing the treasonous, despicable nature of the IWW. All the strikers in town fell into the category of "wobbly." Now the good citizens of Bisbee had a chance to show their patriotism and save their community. All the evidence clearly pointed to the contrary, but the men at the meeting accepted John Greenway's charges that Bisbee public places were alive with "terror" which included boisterous behavior, jostling, threats, and defiance.[17]

Moreover, the group heard that a dynamite charge with caps attached had been found under the Copper Queen Hospital only the day before. These conditions, claimed the speakers, constituted an "extreme situation." Grant Dowell told the group that a "cancerous growth" had developed in Bisbee, and he recommended an "operation." When asked for a vote of confidence, the audience responded unanimously. Dowell and Sheriff Wheeler warned the others not to discuss the matter with anyone, including Lieutenant Colonel Hornbrook. After the meeting was adjourned, many men were issued guns from the Phelps Dodge dispensary. At no time during this process or later were any official complaints filed with the sheriff's office or were any warrants drawn up or ever issued.[18]

The men then left, having been instructed to rendezvous at their various assigned posts at 4:00 A.M. The plan included directions for arresting "...on charges of vagrancy, of treason, and of being disturbers of the peace of Cochise County, all men who have congregated here from other parts and sections for the purposes of harassing and intimidating all men who desire to pursue their daily toil." Every "suspicious looking individual" was to be picked up and placed under arrest. Company officials ordered the arrest of a number of other Bisbee residents who had been listed as undesirable because of their outspokenness or admitted sympathy with the strikers. These sympathizers included many storekeepers, contractors, and professional people; some were prominent Bisbee citizens.[19]

Shortly after the July 11 meeting, Sheriff Wheeler got word that ex-Governor Hunt, a bitter foe of Walter Douglas, was on his way to Bisbee. Said Wheeler, "Should the old governor be in Bisbee after all of his friends had been taken out, he would be lonesome, and it will only be an act of kindness to send him along with his friends so that is what we will do." Thus it was decided that, if Hunt showed up the next morning, he would be placed in the ball park and shipped out to Columbus.[20]

At 2:00 A.M., George Kellogg, aided by several extra switchboard operators began making his calls. In addition to the Loyalty League members, Kellogg notified numerous members of the Bisbee businessmen's Citizen's Protective League. He made his last call by 4:30 A.M., but deputies continued to keep the switchboard busy with calls to friends and company sympathizers.[21]

Gathered in alleyways, behind fences, and in other dark places, the vigilantes waited in small knots, anxious and excited. To identify themselves, they tied white rags and kerchiefs around their arms. The instruction for secrecy was not followed; preparations attracted new recruits, while a telephone call brought two hundred reinforcements from Douglas. Within a short time, the number of vigilantes swelled to 2,000. At 6:30 A.M. they moved out.[22]

Also at 6:30 A.M., newsboys scurried through the streets of Bisbee delivering the *Review*. Within an hour or so, most of Bisbee's citizens had read Sheriff Wheeler's proclamation: "All women and children keep off the street today." Wheeler's statement told of the posse's objective and stated the charges of vagrancy, treason, and disturbance of the peace. He made clear his opposition to the strikers, and he also proclaimed that threats were "being daily made." He asked for aid and cooperation and requested that no shot be fired except in self-defense. He assumed full responsibility for the roundup. Wheeler's message concluded, "All arrested persons will be treated humanely and their cases examined with justice and care. I hope no resistance will be made, for I desire no bloodshed. However, I am determined if resistance is made, it shall be quickly and effectively overcome."[23]

In at least one instance, resistance was made. It was, to be sure, "quickly and effectively overcome." A former employee and an IWW cardholder, James Brew, awoke when vigilantes started to force their way into his rooming house. Brew had not participated in picket activity or other union demonstrations, but had been brooding alone for several days. When orderd out of his home, Brew answered with several shots. He killed Orson P. McRae, shift boss, Loyalty Leaguer and posse member. McRae, unarmed, had been assigned to a deputized detail of five men assigned to pick up IWWs from rooming houses. The deputies assisting McRae immediately killed Brew.[24]

Both men and women claimed that vigilantes beat them. One arrested man later stated that he saw Loyalty Leaguers knock down two women and drag them on the ground. Although not deported, Marco Benderack claimed that a gunman's beating permanently injured him. A consequent "paralytic attack" left him incapable of manual labor. William Gurovich said later that he and his family were robbed of a watch and chain and $172.50 by the same gunmen who took Gurovich away.[25]

Nancy Thomas later testified that gunmen Carl Fuller, Clarence Miller, and Billy Woods robbed her home. Charging into John Connor's home, Tom Madden struck Connor's wife a sharp blow with his elbow. In the street, one vigilante got on his knees and trained his gun on a man who had refused to be a deputy. Sixty-five-year-old Don Walsh, who had lived in Bisbee twenty years, was roughed up. George

Rice was eating breakfast when two men shoved their guns through the door and asked if he sympathized with the strikers. He said yes, and they took him away.[26]

When one man failed to be aroused by the deputies' knocks, three or four of the impatient gunmen broke down the front door, walked in, and pulled the man out of bed. When his wife interceded and begged the intruders to allow her husband to dress, she was pushed aside and the man was dragged out of the house in his night-wear. The wife threw his trousers to him through the window; stumbling and hobbling along, he dressed in the street.[27]

Eight-year-old Matt Hanhila saw his striker father spared similar ignominy. Sleeping in the living room, Matt was roused by a loud knock on the front door and looked up to see several men, armed with rifles, silhouetted against the sky. For a second, Matt's father, Felix, contemplated a .32 automatic above the door frame; but discretion prevailed, and Matt saw his father whisked away.[28]

The prosperity of Bisbee had attracted numerous independent merchants, contractors, professional people and other small businessmen who provided goods and services for the miners. To build goodwill, they naturally extended credit and, in many cases, shared the ambitions and uncertainties of the workers. During the strike they carried the men's accounts and give them encouragement. *The Bisbee Daily Review* described these sympathizers:

> Now there is a class of citizens here, fortunately in the small minority, but still a few, we are sorry to say, who are actually ready to encourage—yes, who have already encouraged—such a propaganda as we are now facing and slowly but surely stamping out.
>   Such citizens are little, if any, better than the 'wobblies' themselves....The citizen of your country who extends aid, comfort and abetment to his country's enemies is a traitor.

Two men who owned a grocery store were arrested and deported; they had given credit to miners. Vigilantes took over the store, sold many goods, and fought with each other over the sharing of the remaining inventory. A restaurant owner, Ilija Luka Gobowich, who had purchased $1,500 worth of liberty bonds with his savings and had given $25 to the Red Cross, found himself among those arrested. Though not an IWW, he was taken from his business at the point of a gun. He later stated, "I was forced to leave $150 in the cash register and 200 pounds of meat hanging in the meat house yet to be cooked. Meat in my ovens burned up, I guess, because the posse would not permit me to drag it from the stove."[29]

Father Brewster, vicar of the local Episcopal church, had helped the miners build a city park. The only church figure in town whom the miners could trust, he had gained the wrath of the corporations. Vigilantes sought him, and, had he not been out of town on business, the vicar, too, would have been deported.[30]

By 7:30 A.M., a huge group had been assembled, under guard, in the plaza in front of the Bisbee Post Office. Then, ten abreast, posse members and their prisoners began the two-mile march to the Warren Ball Park. Armed guards surrounded the procession, while spectators thronged at the rear. Miners loyal to their employers, observing the "big drive," instead of reporting for work hurried home to pick up a rifle and tie a white handerchief on their arms.[31]

One of the most colorful, dedicated, and zealous deporters was Dr. Nelson Bledsoe, a surgeon on the Calumet and Arizona Hospital staff. Armed with a Krag-Jorgensen rifle, a six-shooter in his belt, a cartridge belt full of revolver shells around his waist, and two *bandilleros* loaded with rifle bullets crisscrossed over his shoulders. Dr. Bledsoe appeared to one Mexican observer to look "just like Pancho Villa." Several people later testified that Bledsoe "looked like a wild man" and had a strong "light in his eyes." Others told how Bledsoe would not let deportees accept water offered them during the hot march from Bisbee. Three or four people claimed they saw Bledsoe in downtown Bisbee that morning walk up to a man who was holding a baby and talking to a lady. Without warning or apparent provocation, Bledsoe struck the man with his rifle so that the baby fell to the sidewalk. Bledsoe then forced the man to join the others already arrested. He continued to hit men in the line with his gun stock, even after other gunmen criticized him for being "too strenuous."[32]

While he supervised the roundup and drive, Sheriff Wheeler rode in an open Ford touring car owned and chauffered by Father Mandin, a local Catholic priest who had only recently acquired the impressive machine as a gift from his congregation. Mounted on the vehicle alongside Wheeler was a new 7.62 mm. Marlin machine gun with a loaded feed belt in position. As the car raced back and forth along the streets of Bisbee, Lowell, Bakersville, and Warren, Wheeler shouted instructions, exhortations, and praise.[33]

As the roundup proceeded to the Warren Ball Park, the number of those arrested rose. Once there, the crowd poured through the northwest gate and filled the grandstand, while the overflow occupied the baseball diamond. Vigilantes ringed the entire playing field, making way for the frequent additions to the collection of prisoners inside. Several of those arrested showed signs of being badly beaten; some had long, deep cuts. Throughout the morning, men were added to the collection. Many arrived from Bisbee, under guard, via streetcar. On the roof of the nearby Calumet and Arizona Office Building was another machine gun, trained on the ball park.[34]

During the hours in the ball park stockade, most of the prisoners were given a chance to recant the position and go back to work. No one tried to escape. Desperately, John Greenway pleaded with them to go back to work. So did some of the men's families, friends, and others. Women sympathizers outside the park, using strong, explicit language, urged the men not to weaken. They denounced the friends and family members who offered to intercede and get the men out. Some men showed contrition and were released; the rest answered the pleas of Greenway and others with catcalls, profane shouts, and songs. During this period, one of the arrested men, William Cleary, a well-known Bisbee attorney and long-time successful defender of the working man against the corporation, became their spokesman.[35]

Actually, almost anyone who either promised to go back to work or who could "get a respectable citizen to vouch for him" was released. At its peak, the number of arrested men reached around 2,000. This included 3 women, but they were among the first released. Lawyer Cleary supposedly promised them that he could make the copper companies, particularly Phelps Dodge, pay each one $10,000 in damages if they allowed themselves to be deported. Some gunmen admitted that their choice of sides was based more on expedience than on conviction. They knew, as one woman later testified, "Their jobs depended on what they did." When the train arrived, the group had been pared down to about 1,200 men. A number of men were not deported because there was simply not enough room for them on the train.[36]

Just before 11:00 A.M., twenty-three cattle and boxcars of the El Paso and Southwestern Railroad backed into the Warren station, and "immediately the wobblies gave the train a rousing cheer." Twenty-three cars for 1,186 men averaged more than 50 men per car. Some cars were reported to have had as much as three inches of manure on the floor.[37]

With the arrival of the train, the men seemed eager to start moving. John Greenway made one last desperate plea, begging them to go back to work. They responded with hoots and jeers. The armed guard, in two tight lines that faced each other, formed a winding gauntlet or corridor from the ball park gate to the train. Greenway, now mounted with a rifle across his saddle, helped guard the right-hand side of the exit gate. The prisoners were released from the park in groups of 40 and 50 and were led, as it were, through a cattle chute to the waiting cars. Within an hour, the train was loaded with men; among them, voluntarily, was the brother of Rosa McKay, a Cochise County labor representative to the state legislature. Vigilantes loaded some food, including bread and oranges, in the caboose for the 186 armed guards stationed on top of the cars.[38]

The executors of the roundup and deportation felt that the matter was their own affair and that no one in the outside world should interfere. Accordingly, Harry H. Stout, superintendent of the Copper Queen Smelter, used the fictitious title of captain, as he attempted to impose certain conditions of martial law on Bisbee. Calling it "military censorship," he ordered the Douglas manager of the Western Union Telegraph Company to cut off communications between Bisbee and the outside world. When she tried to telegraph President Wilson and United States Senator from Arizona Henry Fountain Ashurst, to inform them of the outrage, Rosa McKay, the labor legislatress elected the previous November on the Socialist Party ticket, was knocked down in the Western Union Office by gunmen. Later in the day, Mrs. McKay successfully sent her telegrams. When Stout attempted a similar censorship at the Bell Telephone Company, Manager George Kellogg refused to obey. But a few phone calls were made. To get the word to authorities outside Bisbee, alert Attorney Cleary, before he returned to Warren to be arrested along with the others, had slipped down to Naco, where he telegrammed federal labor investigator George W. P. Hunt in Globe: "Two thousand miners being deported this morning by corporation gunmen....Stop that train." The Western Union manager allowed Lieutenant Colonel Hornbrook to notify the adjutant general. And so, during the early stages of the affair, the news leaked out.[39]

Little time elapsed before the word reached the ears of elected authorities. Governor Thomas Campbell claims he heard about the deportation on July 12, when R. Allyn Lewis, a Phoenix stockbroker, called to give him the news. Governor Campbell discovered that he could not reach Bisbee by either telegraph or telephone. He then telegraphed Fort Sam Houston, Texas, asking for troops and saying he needed aid because he could not enforce martial law. Responding to William Cleary's message from Mexico, Federal Commissioner Hunt, together with Federal Mediator John McBride, immediately appealed to President Wilson to stop further deportations of strikers from Arizona towns "to prevent sympathetic strikes and industrial paralysis." Wilson notified United States Attorney General Whitney, who telegraphed Sheriff Wheeler demanding "by what authority of law are you acting. State fully what violations, if any, took place prior to decision to deport strikers." President Wilson contacted Governor Campbell immediately:

> May I not respectfully urge the great danger of citizens taking the law into their own hands....I look upon such actions with grave apprehensions. A very serious responsibility is assumed when such precedents are set.[40]

As the deportation train slowly pulled out of Warren at noon, it blew a warning whistle to several of the deportees' wives who, as they stumbled alongside, cursed Bisbee and its people. Overjoyed with the sight, John Greenway "took off his hat, hollered and clapped his hands." Ten miles east of Douglas, the train made its first stop, at Lee Station, where train crews were exchanged and water barrels were placed on the cars. During the stop at Lee, the train was guarded by 200 armed citizens "while machine guns on two knolls dominated the situation."[41]

The train then headed for Columbus, New Mexico, 173 miles east of Bisbee and close to the border of Mexico. While the guards allowed the railroad car doors to remain open, the men, forced to stand for many hours in crowded, airless cars, some in cow manure over their shoe tops, experienced extreme discomfort. The July heat (Columbus recorded one of the hottest days of the year) caused the men in those cars with water to exhaust the supply several hours before reaching Columbus that night. Some became nauseated. From inside the cars, they were unable to see where they were.[42]

When he learned that the deportees had arrived in New Mexico, Governor W. E. Lindsey ordered the arrest of those in charge. The train arrived in Columbus at 9:30 P.M. Local officials, after arresting F. B. King, district superintendent of the El Paso and Southwestern Railroad, who had been placed in charge of the deportation train, ordered that it turn back. King was released, but the train turned back westward. At 3:00 A.M. on Friday, July 13, it stopped in Hermanas, New Mexico, twenty miles west of Columbus. By this time the deportees had been without water for twelve hours. Hermanas would be their home for the next two days.[43]

Now more knowledgeable about the situation, New Mexico Governor Lindsey declared that the deportees at Hermanas should be treated humanely. He directed Luna County's Sheriff Simpson to "conduct the fugitives peaceably to Columbus...and feed them at state expense until the federal authorities take charge." He wired President Wilson, requesting that "the federal government take charge and dispose of the matter according to federal law and order." Quickly responding to the request, Wilson alerted his secretary of war. The War Department, on July 13, gave orders to General Bell—who relayed them to Colonel Sickel at Columbus—to bring the deported men from Hermanas to Columbus and "provide them with rations...if necessary to prevent great suffering." Colonel Sickel was instructed not to hold the men as prisoners.[44]

While at Hermanas, Cleary made a statement for the press, describing the purposes of the strike. At the same time, Cleary praised the attitude of the men and condemned the tyrannical way in which the deportation had taken place. A "machine gun was trained on the miners," he complained, even though at no time did any miner offer resistance. Cleary declared:

> While many of the men, it is true, are members of what is known as the IWW, nevertheless they are law-abiding and peaceful ....Many who have lived in Bisbee for years—some for as long as fifteen years and have their wives and families there now—are very anxious to return.[45]

There was little evidence that the men could return. On July 14, the *Bisbee Daily Review* stated:

> Any talk of their coming back is nonsense. They will not be allowed to come back. We have been slow to act but once started, it is a finish fight. The serious business of this district is the mining of copper ore, not the building of nightly schools of anarchism or idling on the streets or picketing public places and private works.[46]

Only about one hundred true IWW members were in Bisbee on July 12, 1917. (Three hundred more were "two-card" men.) Of these, only about twenty-five were considered to understand anything about IWW philosophy; not one Bisbee Wobbly who later testified against the deporters could demonstrate any knowledge of the IWW tenets. None of the older IUMMSW members who converted to the IWW participated as soapbox activists, and the most outspoken of these (such as James Chapman) were probably company-hired detectives. What is more, except for the organizers, the Bisbee IWW membership developed only after Charles Moyer's revocation of the Bisbee IUMMSW charter on July 3—only a week or two before the deportation.[47]

For the most part, Bisbee wobblyism represented the most dedicated—and frustrated—conventional unionists. Nothing, however, could have worked more to company advantage. By using the IWW radical charge as a blanket label for all the strikers, the copper companies had rid Bisbee and Arizona of the nucleus of political-labor leadership. AFofL leaders Frank Harmon, Charles Cavis, J. F. Jones, Fred Brown, and Frank Vaughan were among those deported. Thirty of thirty-nine members of the local Painters' Union were shipped out—not one was an IWW. Two-card men such as A. S. Embree and Charles Tannehill, also deported, certainly were pragmatic unionists and not doctrinaire wobblies.[48]

Immediately, the Bisbee Deportation became a national *cause celebre*. In Bisbee, the vigilantes set up a kangaroo court and deported several hundred more undesirables. However, some men at Columbus were asked, rather discreetly, to return to Bisbee; their mining skills were badly needed. A few accepted. The rest of the deportees began to drift out of Columbus to other places. Jobs were not scarce in wartime America. On September 17, 1917, the last of the deportees left the New Mexico camp, and it was closed. The next day, President Woodrow Wilson appointed a five-man commission to investigate the labor turmoil in Arizona. The commission, with Assistant Secretary of Labor Felix Frankfurter as secretary, left Washington on September 30. After visiting other Arizona mining towns, the investigators went to Bisbee, where they heard testimonies from November 1 to November 5.[49]

Acting on the commission's report, the United States Department of Justice started an investigation of the Bisbee Deportations. On May 15, 1918, twenty-one of Bisbee's leading mining company officials were arrested on charges of "conspiracy to injure, oppress, threaten, and intimidate United States citizens" under Section 19, United States Penal Code. Included were Phelps Dodge officials Walter Douglas, Gerald Sherman, and Grant H. Dowell. Sheriff Wheeler and John Greenway were in France by this time, serving with the American Expeditionary Forces. The defense filed for a demurrer, on grounds that no federal laws had been violated. The court upheld the defense counsel's request. The Justice Department then appealed the lower court decision to the United States Supreme Court. Late in 1920, the high court ruled in favor of the defendants, saying the case was a matter for the state courts.[50]

In the meantime, civil suits amounting to damages exceeding $6 million had been brought into Arizona courts. But the most dramatic trial—indeed the only criminal trial concerning the deportation that was ever conducted—took place from February to April, 1920, in Tombstone. Two hundred and ten Bisbee citizens were arraigned on charges of kidnapping, but one man, Harry E. Wootton, a Phelps Dodge employee, Loyalty Leaguer, and July 12, 1917, Bisbee vigilante, was picked as a representative. The defense argued that the IWW had presented a menace in Bisbee; it exhibited wobbly literature to prove that the IWW conspired to overthrow the government, to subvert the religious beliefs and patriotism of unsuspecting citizens, and to bring defeat to the United States in its war against Germany.[51]

Wootton was acquitted on the first ballot; all of the jurors agreed the deportation had been a good thing. The defense had claimed that its central justification for executing the Bisbee deportation was based on the "law of necessity," a legal argument based on a vague contention of self-defense, which presiding Judge Samuel J. Pattee explained did "not have to be a fear of really existent dangers but only of apparent danger, which is so compelling as to be real to him who views it." This strange argument was explained in an even stranger publication, "The Law of Necessity as Applied in State of Arizona vs. H. E. Wootton; the Bisbee Deportation Case." The booklet, ambiguous and onesided, was thought to be printed and circulated by the copper interests; the vigilantes and their chiefs had been exonerated conclusively. In fact, their innocence in this case forced almost all the civil suit plaintiffs to drop their suits. A few settlements for small amounts were reached out of court.[52]

NOTES

[1]"Personal," *Mining and Scientific Press,* Vol. 113, July 29, 1916, p. 183; *Arizona Republican,* September 24, 1915, p. 1; *Arizona Gazette,* September 30, 1915, p. 1; Walter Douglas, "The Strike in Arizona," *Mining and Scientific Press,* Vol. 3, November 20, 1915, pp. 771–772.

[2]"A Strike Without Disorder," *New Republic,* Vol. 5, No. 64 (January 22, 1916), pp. 304–306; Walter Douglas, "The Arizona Strike," *New Republic,* Vol. 6, No. 72 (March 18, 1916), pp. 185–186.

[3]George Soule, "Law and Necessity in Bisbee," *Nation,* Vol. 113, No. 2930 (August 31, 1921), p. 226; F. M. Murphy, "Thanks American Mining Congress for Arizona Work," letter published in *Mining Congress Journal,* Vol. 1, No. 9 (September, 1915), p. 443; "American Institute of Mining Engineers to Meet in Arizona," *Mining Congress Journal,* Vol. 2, No. 9 (September, 1916), p. 414; "Nineteenth Annual Convention of Mining Congress Was Great Success," *Mining Congress Journal,* Vol. 2 No. 12 (December, 1916), pp. 523–524; Cover, *Mining Congress Journal,* Vol. 2, No. 12 (December, 1916); *Mining Congress Journal,* Vol. 3, No. 1 (January, 1917), *passim;* "Arizona Chapter of Mining Congress Shows Long List of Achievements," *Mining Congress Journal,* Vol. 3, No. 5 (May, 1917), pp. 170–173.

[4]Industrial Workers of the World, *Proceedings of Tenth Convention* (Chicago, Illinois, November, 1916), pp. 61, 99; Fred Brown, "Transcript of Testimony Taken Before the President's Mediation Committee at Bisbee, Arizona, November 1–4, 1917." (Record Group 174, General Records of the Department of Labor); Vernon Jensen, *Heritage of Conflict* (Ithaca: Cornell University Press, 1950), p. 380; Fred Watson, interview, July 19, 1972; Harold Callender, "True Facts About Bisbee," *Dunbar's Weekly,* Vol. 14, No. 36 (September 15, 1917), p. 10; Grover H. Perry, letter to William D. Haywood, February 2, 1917 (*Simmons v. El Paso & Southwestern R.R.,* Exhibits, Special Collections, University of Arizona Library, Tucson); Metal Mine Workers Industrial Union #800 (IWW), *Bulletin Number One,* Phoenix, Arizona, February 24, 1917, and *Bulletin Number Two,* April 4, 1917 (Department of Justice files); Marlin Arms Corporation, "Bill of Sale to S. S. French, Gen. Manager, Phelps Dodge," April 10, 1917. (Copy in Department of Justice files.)

[5]Bulletin from Grover Perry, June 1, 1917 (*Simmons v. El Paso and SWRR*); "Demands of Metal Mine Workers Industrial Union No. 800" (in "Transcript...taken...at Bisbee,") pp. 351–352.

[6]Grover Perry, telegram to William Haywood, June 25, 1917 (*Simmons v. El Paso and SWRR*).

[7]Ibid; *New York Times,* June 29, 1917, p. 17, July 1, 1917; *Bisbee Daily Review,* July 6, 1917, p. 1; William Curnow, testimony, "Preliminary Hearings of Defendants in the Bisbee Deportation Trials," *Individual Transcripts,* Book 1, p. 18 (Arizona, Justice Court [Cochise Co. Precinct No. 41]); Jensen, pp. 401–403, Numerous Testimonies, "Transcript of Testimony..." and "Preliminary Hearings..."; Message of George W.

P. Hunt to the Special Session of the Third State Legislature" (Phoenix: privately printed pamphlet, n.d.), May 2, 1918, pp. 10–11.

[8]James Byrkit, "Life and Labor in Arizona, 1901–1921: with Particular Reference to the Deportations of 1917" unpublished Ph.D. dissertation (Claremont Graduate School), pp. 1–30, pp. 321–330.

[9]*Ibid.*, pp. 1–30.

[10]*Ibid.*

[11]*Arizona Republican,* July 11, 1917, p. 1; Arizona Record, July 11, 1917, p. 1.

[12]*Ibid.*

[13]William S. Beeman, "History of the Bisbee Deportations by an Officer in Charge of the Loyalty League," (Arizona Law Library and Archives, Phoenix, 1940.), pp. 3–4; George Soule, "Law and Necessity in Bisbee," *The Nation,* Vol. 113, No. 2930 (August 31, 1921), p. 226; Samuel Morse, "The Truth About Bisbee," (Arizona Pioneers' Historical Society, Tucson, n.d.), p. 7.

[14]Testimony of George F. Kellogg, "Transcript...taken...at Bisbee," pp. 3–8.

[15]Beeman, p. 7; Nelson Bledsoe, interview, August 15, 1968. Sheriff Wheeler later claimed responsibility for ordering the roundup and deportation. Witnesses stated, however, that Wheeler made no proposals of any action in the July 11 meeting (Kellogg, *loc. cit.*).

[16]Kellogg, *loc. cit.;* Beeman records that only about forty men attended (p.8); Robert Bruere, "Copper Camp Patriotism," *Nation,* Vol. 106, No. 2747 (February 21, 1918), p. 203; *Bisbee Daily Review,* July 1, 1917, p. 5; Bruere, *loc. cit.;* Thomas E. Campbell, "The IWW in Arizona; "Typescript Concerning Reconstruction of Labor Troubles in Arizona," San Fernando, California, 1962 (Arizona Pioneers' Historical Society, Tucson), no pagination. Later in the day of July 12, after the deportation train had left Bisbee, Lieutenant Colonel Hornbrook reportedly said, "It was the greatest piece of civilian work I have ever seen. I could have not done with my regiment what Sheriff Wheeler did with his deputies today." (Beeman, p. 10).

[17]"Deportations from Bisbee and a Resume of Other Troubles in Arizona," reprinted in "The Arizona Strike," *Arizona Mining Journal,* (August, 1917), p. 7; Beeman, p. 8; Kellogg, *loc. cit.*

[18]*Ibid.*

[19]*New York Times,* July 13, 1917, p. 1; *Bisbee Daily Review,* July 13, p. 1; Jensen, p. 405.

[20]Beeman, p. 10.

[21]Kellogg, *loc. cit.*

[22]*New York Times. loc. cit.*

[23]*Bisbee Daily Review,* July 12, 1917, p. 1.

[24]Robert Glass Cleland, *A History of Phelps Dodge* (New York: Alfred A. Knopf, 1952), p. 186; "Deportations from Bisbee...," p. 6. This source, an operators' journal, claims Brew fired before the deputies knew of his presence in the house. Deputy William Beeman said that McRae did not follow instructions by rushing ahead of his squad and attempting to break down the door. In a form true to the glamour of frontier legends, claimed Beeman, an armed McRae, with Brew's bullet in his heart, fired, as he fell, the shot which killed Brew. (Beeman, p. 9.) Another alleged "eyewitness" account says McRae, from the street, first ordered Brew to come outside. Brew, armed, stepped out and warned the deputy, "If you come through that gate, I will blast you." McRae entered the yard, Brew shot him, turned around, and went back in the house where he laid down his weapon. When he stepped back outside a few seconds later, he was unarmed and his hands were raised. Then, McRae's companions gunned him down. According to this same source, McRae and Brew had experienced an earlier conflict in Cripple Creek, Colorado. (Frederick Watson, affidavit, Bisbee, Arizona, August 31, 1970); *New York Times,* July 13, 1917, p. 1. For his sacrifice, Vigilante McRae was accorded the highest tribute the Bisbeeites could conceive. His funeral ceremony, scheduled to be held in the Post Office plaza, where the undesirables had been herded before the march to the Warren Ball Park, was preceded by a vigil. The *Review* announced: "The body will lie in state under a canopy on

the porch of the Phelps Dodge Mercantile Company's store building." (*Bisbee Daily Review,* July 15, 1917, p. l) On July 17, at Orson McRae's funeral, no mention was made of Brew or the fact that the vigilantes had no search warrants. Cleon T. Knapp gave the eulogy, contending that "O. P. McRae is as great a hero as any who has given his life upon the battlefields of Europe." He was buried, quite ceremoniously, in Bisbee's Evergreen Cemetary. However, a pension given to his widow by Phelps Dodge was subsequently revoked. She sued, but to no avail. (Watson affidavit, August 31, 1970.) "Jimmy" Brew was, by all who knew him, of excellent character and reputation." (Rosa McKay, "Mrs. McKay Writes of Bisbee," *Dunbar's Weekly,* Vol. 14, No. 32 [August 18, 1917], p. 9.) But he was allowed no chance to compete with McRae for martyrdom. Officials of the Copper Queen reportedly refused Brew's mother, who had come to Bisbee from Los Angeles upon hearing of her son's death, to view his body at the morgue. They forced Brew's fellow Workers to bury him in their plot by cover of night, quickly and quietly. (*Ibid.,* No. 29 [July 28, 1917], p. 8; McKay, *loc. cit.*)

[25]*The Messenger,* July 21, 1917, p. i.

[26]Callender, p. 12; Nancy Thomas, *Original Blanket Hearings,* Justice Court of Precinct No. 4,Douglas, Arizona, July–September, 1919, Book 1, pp. 161–171; Book 3, p. 322; William Eddy,*Ibid.,* Book 2, 322; Book 1, pp. 133–135, 81.

[27]R. McKay, *loc. cit.*

[28]Matt Hanhila, taped interview, Harwood Hinton Collection; Matt Hanhila, "The Bisbee Tea Party," Maricopa Open Door, Vol. 1, No. 1 (Fall–Winter, 1972), p. 13; Matt Hanhila, interview, March 13, 1972.

[29]Bruere, "Copper Camp...," (February 21), pp. 202–203; *Bisbee Daily Review,* July 12, 1917, p. 4; "Mark Larkin," unidentified clipping. George W. P. Hunt Scrapbooks (Special Collections, University of Arizona).

[30]Bishop William Scarlett, interview, March 13, 1972; Fred Watson and William Eddy, interviews, July 19, 1972.

[31]*Bisbee Daily Review,* July 15, 1917, p. 7; July 13, 1917, p. 1.

[32]Testimony of Anna Ballard, Tony Rodriguez, Richard Denning, Mike Pintek and others, Prelim. Ind. Trans., Book 1,*passim.*

[33]*Ibid.*

[34]John Pintek, Fred Watson, interview, July 19, 1972; Ind. Trans., Book 2, p. 109; Watson, affidavit.

[35]"Deportations from Bisbee...," p. 6; Watson, affidavit Leslie Marcy, "The Eleven Hundred Exiled Copper Miners," *The International Socialist Review,* Vol. 17, No. 3 (September, 1917), pp. 160–162; *Bisbee Daily Review, loc. cit.*

[36]"Deportations from Bisbee...," *loc. cit.,* Beeman, p. 10; John P. Chase, Original Blanket Hearings, Book 1, p. 33; Ballard, p. 166; *The Messenger,* July 21, 1917, p. 1.

[37]*Bisbee Daily Review,* July 13, 1917, p. 2; *Ind. Trans.,* Book 3, p. 222; *The Messenger, loc. cit.* The number of men deported varies in the numerous accounts. Both President Wilson's Mediation Commission's and the copper companies' statistics give 1,186 as the figure, (United States, Committee on Public Information, Official Bulletin, Vol. 1, No. 170 [November 27, 1917], "Report of President Wilson's Mediation Commission on the Bisbee, Arizona, Deportations, Including Its Recommendations as Made on Findings of Fact," p. 6; Fred Sutter, "Senator Sutter Makes Reply," *Arizona Mining Journal,* Vol. 2, No. 1 [June, 1918], p. 48; Phelps Dodge Corporation, Copper Queen Branch, "Employees to Columbus," "Transcript...Taken...at Bisbee," p. 287.).

[38]*New York Times,* July 13, 1917, p. 1; Testimony of Richard Denning, *Original...,* p. 1003; *Bisbee Daily Review,* July 13, 1917, p. 2; *Ind. Trans.,* Book 3, pp. 32, 82.

[39]Bruere, "Copper Camp...," (February 21), pp. 202–203; Kellogg, p. 15; R. McKay, *loc. cit.;* Rosa McKay, telegram to President Woodrow Wilson, July 12, 1917, (copy in Department of Justice Files, 186813-4.); Bruere, *loc. cit.;* Kellogg, *loc. cit.;* New York Times, July 13 1917, p. 3. Cleary obviously chose to be deported. After returning to Warren, he joined the men at the ball park and then elected to board car number five with sixty-four other deportees. This selfless conduct failed to evoke a scintilla of admiration from the *Review (Bisbee, Daily Review, loc. cit.);* Lt. Col. James J.

Hornbrook, telegram to adjutant general, July 12, 1917, Adjutant General Files 370.61 (Bisbee, Ariz.). (Copy in Department of Justice Files.)

[40]Campbell, "The IWW in Arizona," no pagination; *New York Times*, July 13, 1917, p. 3.

[41]Dominic Catero, *Orig. Blanket Hearings*, Book 1, p. 54. *Bisbee Daily Review*, July 13, 1917, p. 1.

[42]Brown, *loc. cit.*

[43]*New York Times*, July 14, 1917, p. 1; *Bisbee Daily Review*, July 13, 1917, p. 1.

[44]*New York Times, loc. cit.*, p. 4; Brigadier General James Parker, Commanding Officer, United States Army, Southern Department, San Antonio, Texas, telegram to adjutant general, July 13, 1917, Adjutant General Files 370.61, Southern Department. (Copy in Department of Justice Files.)

[45]*New York Times, loc. cit.*

[46]*Bisbee Daily Review*, July 14, 1917, p. 4

[47]Brown, "Transcript...taken...at Bisbee," pp. 24–30; Kellogg, *Ibid.*, p. 19; Frank J. Vaughan, *Ibid.*, p. 46; Massey, *Ibid.*, p. 50.

[48]*Ibid.*

[49]Byrkit, pp. 36–49, 356–375, 395–400, 407–416.

[50]Byrkit, pp. 440–445.

[51]Byrkit, pp. 445–450.

[52]*Ibid.*

III

The Rise of Unionized Farm Workers

The United Farm Workers of America

DEATH, TAXES, AND POVERTY have always been with us and, if the West has been a model of the nation, so have the farm workers. Unlike mining, there is nothing romantic about stoop labor in the hot sun. There is nothing exciting about hoeing cotton or picking oranges. Money is all that keeps the wageworker in the fields and, in the West, the money is rarely good. However, the farm worker is an authentic western character, a part of the western scene ever since that day when the transcontinental railroad turned California into the nation's premier agricultural state. As the last hammer blows echoed into the desert at Promontory Point, the search was already on for a cheap and docile farm-labor force.

Until 1900, the answer to California's boom agriculture labor question was the Chinese. Thousands of Chinese had come to the golden state to build the Central Pacific Railroad and thousands were left stranded when the golden spike was pounded home. The mines, already brimming with the disillusioned gold seekers of '49, refused to accept the human flotsam discarded by the Central Pacific, and there was no industrial base to exploit the surplus of cheap labor. No work in the mines, no work on the railroads, and no work in the factories left only a single alternative—the farms. Fortunately for the California economy, there was more than enough field work to absorb the surplus labor pool.

What was the status of California agriculture in 1870? Carey McWilliams is his *Factories in the Field* notes that 516 men owned more than 8 million acres of California's best lands in 1871. A complicated series of Mexican land grants, American railroad grants, and speculative land ventures had left the control of most of the good farmland in the hands of a very few; the yeoman farmer never had a chance. From the very beginning, California agriculture was boom agriculture and, as Henry George put it in 1871, "California [was] not a country of farms, but a country of plantations and estates."[1] On labor's end of the equation, this meant that those first Chinese pickers encountered not a host of hardy homesteaders, but rather an organized agricultural establishment which well merited the McWilliams title of factories in the field. However, even that title did not do justice to a system which discarded its labor at the close of harvest, which paid the lowest wages in America, and which would ultimately be taxpayer-subsidized through the extension system, the Reclamation Service, and the land-grant colleges. For years, California agriculture was able to masquerade as merely a collection of family farms, a simile which would bring to mind General Motors posing as the corner garage.

By the turn of the century, Chinese labor had helped harvest the oranges of Southern California which had created the Sunkist cooperative, the wheat of Northern California which inspired Frank Norris's *Octopus,* and the cotton which pushed California ahead of many a southern state as a supplier of raw material to the textile industry. Loyal service had not brought honor. California laborers feared Chinese competition with unbridled passion and that passion would soon turn to a particularly bitter streak of nativism. The Chinese Exclusion Act barred Chinese immigration after May 6, 1882, and similar acts, strongly supported by California, would prevent all new Chinese from entering the country until the 1920s. Riots against Chinese began in California in the 1870s and continued for half a century. All of this left agriculture in a terrible pinch; there were no longer enough Chinese to keep the wheat, oranges, and cotton harvested. Thus entered the bindlestiff.

Tramping was an old and honorable pastime long before America came of industrial age. E. J. Hobsbaum once called the tramp "the artisan's equivalent of the Grand Tour."[2] Tramping was a way in which a young man could work his way around the world or around the states. Inevitably, many of the young tramps who started in Maine or Massachusetts ended up picking cotton in California. It was a way to keep the tramp going. By 1900, the tramps of the nation began to supplant the Chinese in those factories in the fields. Perhaps it was not a coincidence that the IWW began its climb to prominence at about the same time.

We have already seen that the free speech fights were designed as publicity campaigns for agricultural organization. What we have not seen was the rather disappointing response to IWW organization after the various free speech battles were won. The IWW did have marked success in bringing the migrant lumberjacks into the fold, but the agricultural bindlestiffs were a different lot entirely.

Who were the tramps? Take for a moment the case of Axel Olson, a turn-of-the-century Swedish immigrant who was brought into the United States as an agricultural laborer in Kansas. Olson recalled vividly the long train ride from New York through Chicago to the great plains of Kansas, a lonely ride for a young man who spoke not a word of English. In St. Louis, he had tried in vain to buy a sandwich, but his money could not make up for a total lack of communication. He would eventually settle for a glass of water out of a vending machine. "It cost a penny," he remembered. The job itself, when he arrived, was hardly worth the trip from Sweden. A couple of Swedish farmers took turns exploiting Axel and his brother; they never received more than $15 a month for a job that lasted eighteen hours a day and six days a week. The year Axel and his brother spent in the midst of Kansas wheat was 1912, the very year that the IWW was organizing thousands of Axel Olsons in California and the West. Olson would escape farm labor by tramping west; thousands just like him would tramp their way right into the IWW's Agricultural Workers Organization.[3] For many, the need for such an organization was demonstrated in 1913, in what would later be called the Wheatland Hop Riot.

Wheatland, California, was hot in the summer of 1913. The agricultural valleys of California often boast of more 100-degree days than the deserts of nearby Arizona. What made Wheatland even hotter during the summer of 1913 was some 2,800 angry workers—tramps, immigrants, migrant families, and even college boys. All had been lured into the area by Durst Ranch broadsides which promised good wages, plentiful work, and decent living conditions. E. C. Durst had never intended to honor the spirit of those broadsides. When 2,800 pickers showed up, he cut the going wage for hop picking by 10 percent (from $1.00 per hundredweight to 90 cents), refused to allow water in the fields (even though temperatures were hovering in the 105-degree range), and rented tents on a barren hillside for $2.75 a night. His only concession to the workers' demands for drinking water was a lemonade wagon, which made its way through the fields selling a citric acid and water mixture for 10 cents a glass (the wagon was conveniently operated by a cousin). Thus, it was not surprising that the IWW found the Durst Ranch an organizer's dream in early August; IWW workers "Blackie" Ford and Herman Suhr were welcomed whenever they talked union. Yet, that union was not to be.

Jack London would later comment upon the affair at Wheatland as not a strike, but rather a "spontaneous, unpremeditated explosion."[4] The IWW drew up a list of demands, including a uniform pay scale, free drinking water, and decent camp conditions, but those demands were never given a chance. Panicked by the thought of 2,000 angry pickers, Durst attempted to break up a protest meeting on August 3, 1913. His deputies fired their shotguns into the air and, in an instant, the meeting became a mob scene. Four men died that day, including the Yuba County District Attorny E. T. Manwell. Ultimately, the two wobbly organizers would receive life sentences for their part in a riot, which labor economist Carleton H. Parker blamed almost entirely on Durst.[5] Wheatland would be the last gasp of IWW farm unionism in the Southwest. True labor organization would wait for other developments.

Other developments which would lead to the day of Cesar Chávez and the United Farmworkers of America can be traced to two separate events in the 1920s. First, the Mexican Revolution of 1910 and the completion of railroads in northern Mexico brought thousands of refugees north, refugees willing to do anything to escape the violence and uncertainty which was revolution. These refugees would become the new farm-labor force of the Southwest, the national group which would ultimately displace the Chinese. By 1930, Mexican workers were the largest single ethnic group in the fields of the Imperial Valley, and their numbers increased yearly. At almost the same time, many independent small farmers in the Midwest and South were discovering that the agricultural depression could easily convert landowners to tenant farmers. Tenancy was on the rise and seemed to be the wave of the future, until the New Deal stepped in with aid for agriculture. However, the tenants' hopes were soon dashed when the AAA and other New Deal programs proved to be less than an advantage to tenant farmers. The results of that discovery would lead to the Southern Tenant Farmers Union.[6]

H. L. Mitchell was the organizer of the STFU and he watched his creation become a farm-labor union, as farm tenants took another drop in status from tenants to pickers. Mitchell's approach to those years is the subject of the first essay in this section. As his essay explains, the war years turned a number of midwestern tenant farmers into migrant workers, who found their hopes of upward mobility dashed on the rocks of the government's new Bracero Program. By the end of the war, the STFU had become a labor union rather than a tenant's organization. The 1946 name change to National Farm Labor Union merely stamped an AFL label on an already active farm union. Mitchell's narrative are the words of a labor veteran, a man who made labor history.

As history shows, the National Farm Labor Union was no more successful in organizing the Southwest than the wobblies had been. Yet, the thirties and forties were not without their successes. Perhaps the most interesting of those successes took place in California and Hawaii, where the International Longshoremen's and Warehousemen's Union, led by Harry Bridges, turned from unloading ships to unionizing pickers. This often neglected aspect of western labor history is explored by Edward Beechert in the second essay of the section, an essay devoted to the unionization of farm workers in Hawaii. Not only is the Hawaiian tale interesting as a union story, it also details the problems of race and organization. The effects of racial divisions on early attempts of agricultural workers in Hawaii to organize is one of the principal themes of this paper and therefore requires little elaboration. The so-called "racial strikes" conducted by Japanese and Filipino plantation workers during the early decades of this century reveal, in a particularly stark fashion, how racial differences retarded the development of unionism among Hawaii's agricultural workers. Despite efforts, mainly by outsiders, to promote greater unity within the agricultural work force, ethnic, rather than class-conscious, plantation workers too often acted in ways which guaranteed that the racist strategy, which their employers had so carefully devised and assiduously followed, would have its desired results. That the agricultural workers of Hawaii were successfully organized in the 1940s seems to have resulted less from a conscious decision by the workers to put aside race as a primary determinant of behavior than from the fact that the ILWU, the militant union that finally brought organization to the plantations, would not countenance anything less than complete unity. However, that unity was not the ultimate answer for Southwest farm labor.

No history of the farm workers would be complete without a discussion of Cesar Chávez, the United Farmworkers, and California's struggles to find a legal framework for farm labor. Art Carstens was very much a part of the legal side of that fight. As a professor of Industrial Relations at the University of California at Los Angeles, he was one of the drafters of the famed Agricultural Labor Relations Act of 1975. His is the third essay in this section.

Carsten does three things in his paper. First, he reviews the early history of agricultural labor relations in the golden state. Second, he reviews key events which led to the elevation of Chávez and his organization in the recent history of the farm-workers movement. Finally, he analyzes and assesses the future of the California Agricultural Labor Relations Act. In all of his paper, he proceeds with none of the emotionalism found in many accounts of the origins of the UFW.

Without doubt, the California Agricultural Labor Relations Act of 1975 is the most important single piece of current labor legislation. It provides a legal framework for an occupational category which has existed outside the mainstream of labor law for the last forty years. As intriguing as the law itself, however, is the manner in which Governor

Jerry Brown took a personal hand in guiding it around the pitfalls provided by the state legislature. Carstens gives us an insider's view of the entire legislative process.

While California was working on a strong agricultural labor law which promised many benefits to farm labor unions, other western states considered the model presented by California's conservative southeastern neighbor. The Arizona legislature had enacted a labor law in 1972 of quite a different stripe. Coming at the end of Chávez's first successful organizing efforts in California, the Arizona farm-labor law bore much of the language of the Taft-Hartley Act and few of its protections for unions. Perhaps the most important section of the act allowed landowners to sue unions for damages suffered during a strike or other labor action. This proved a fine *de facto* method of outlawing strikes without exposing legislators to the political embarassment that an outright strike ban might cause. The law also put severe limitations on the use of picketing and strikes for recognition. All in all, it was a conservative answer to the success of the United Farm Workers Organizing Committee, led by Chávez. Arizona growers still speak of it as an alternative to the California ALRA.

Does the California law hold out the ultimate hope for farm labor? The California experience since 1975 has not been totally positive. As Professor Carstens' paper relates, the financial state of the ALRB seemed incapable of withstanding the burdens of over 400 representational elections in a year. The drive for Proposition 14, which promised to ameliorate the financial problems of the ALRB as well as modify some of the antiunion aspects of the original legislation, succumbed to a well-financed campaign of the Farm Bureau and owner organizations. The willingness of the state legislature to fund the ALRB during the Proposition 14 fight could merely have been temporary political expediency. Nothing at all has been done to solve the bitter split-vote feuds and numerous procedural problems which Proposition 14 was also intended to solve. In fact, only the withdrawal of the teamsters from the fields has simplified the complexity of California agricultural labor relations. Only time will tell the effect of that action.

Even if the Agricultural Labor Relations Act is not the last word in farm labor legislation, the explanation Professor Carstens gives of it is an important contribution to contemporary history. No history of farm labor could be complete without some mention of the historic act and its immediate consequences.

Taken together, the three papers in this section paint a limited but accurate picture of the farm-labor movement. While much of the bitter Chicano element of the story is abbreviated, the important facts are there. Farm-labor unions, as we know them today, began with the struggles of the ILWU and other radicals in the thirties. The union movement blossomed with the incorporation of the STFU and the AFL into the larger effort in the 1940s. It came of age with the rise of Chávez and the United Farm Workers in the early sixties. Finally, in 1975, the California Agricultural Labor Relations Act promised to give the same kind of protection to farm unionists that the Wagner Act provided for their thirties industrial brethren.

While agricultural labor unionism may lack the scope, magnitude, and capacity to influence national affairs in the way that its more mature industrial counterpart has done, farm workers seeking to build collective economic power through organization have, nonetheless, produced a rich and instructive history that is worthy of careful inquiry. The three following papers represent an intriguing sample of an exciting new field.

NOTES

[1]Carey McWilliams, *Factories in the Field* (Boston: Little, Brown, and Company, 1939), pp. 20–25.

[2]E. J. Hobsbaum, "The Traping Artison," *Economic History Review,* Series II, III (1951), p. 313.

[3]Interview with Axel Olson, Victor, Colorado, August 14, 1979.

[4]Melvyn Dubofsky, *We Shall Be All* (Chicago: Quadrangle Books, 1969), pp. 294–299.

[5]Carleton H. Parker, *The Casual Laborer and Other Essays* (New York: Harcourt, Brace, and Rowe, 1920), pp. 61–89.

[6]The best story of the STFU can be found in David Conrad, *The Forgotten Farmers* (Urbana: University of Illinois Press, 1966).

Little Known Farm Labor History
1942–1960

H. L. Mitchell

MOST HISTORIANS INTERESTED IN FARM LABOR seem to overlook the period from 1942 to 1960. Only a few books have been written about this era. The LaFollette Civil Liberties investigations came to an end in the early days of World War II, and there were no more reports on farm labor. The CIO efforts to organize in the farm field ended even earlier. The only organization to survive was the Southern Tenant Farmers Union and its successors, the National Farm Labor Union A.F. of L. and the National Agricultural Workers Union AFL–CIO. About 1960, the Agricultural Workers Oganizing Committee of the AFL–CIO became active in California, and from it came the United Farm Workers of America, led by Cesar Chávez.

FARM LABOR IN WORLD WAR II

The growers of food and fiber in the Southwest saw the war as an excuse for importing a cheap supply of labor from Mexico, to exploit in their "factories in the fields." Their representatives in Washington had already persuaded the federal government to enter into an international agreement with the Republic of Mexico for the importation of thousands of workers for the anticipated farm-labor shortages.

In Arizona, a special type of silk-like cotton ("pima" cotton) was grown. The cotton growers of this state, and others from California, New Mexico, and West Texas enlisted the aid of the United States Army in bringing workers from Mexico into this country. They claimed that the pima cotton grown in 1942 was going to rot in the fields because of the lack of experienced cotton pickers. The growers demanded the immediate importation of 5,000 workers from Mexico. Spokesmen from the United States Army claimed that the pima cotton was needed as a substitute for Chinese silk, used in making barrage balloons for directing field artillery.

A War Manpower Commission had been established to provide workers for all industries. On the commission were representatives of industry and agencies such as the United States Departments of Labor and Agriculture, the AF of L and the CIO, the Farm Bureau, the Grange, and the Farmers Union, but there were no direct representatives of farm labor. The United States Employment Service had the responsibility for recruiting all workers, and the Farm Security Administration was assigned the job of transporting workers required in agriculture.

As soon as it became known that jobs were available in other areas of the country when there was no work in the mid-south (Alabama, Arkansas, Mississippi, and Missouri), the Southern Tenant Farmers Union demanded that American citizens be given the first opportunity for such temporary employment. The first move made by the union was to circulate petitions requesting authorizations to represent the workers individually and collectively. Over 8,000 such authorizations were secured in sixty days. A wage conference was called in Memphis, Tennessee, on September 7, 1942. There were over 300 workers representing the petition signers in attendance at this meeting. The conference accepted the minimum wage fixed in the international agreement with Mexico—thirty cents per hour—which was about twice as much as was currently being paid farm workers in the mid-southern states. The conference fixed a union rate of $2.00 per 100 pounds for picking cotton as the equivalent of the rates fixed for Mexican nationals. Ten thousand circulars were printed and they were distributed before sunrise on the morning of September 9th. The circulars advised everyone to remain at home until the rate of pay was established. The plantation owners were stunned. There were no arrests. There was not even a threat of calling out the National Guard to break the strike, as had been the pattern before. Circulars demanding the government fixed rate were not even torn down when they were posted on fences and barn doors around the plantations.

2000 COTTON PICKERS GO WEST

The union had thoughtfully invited representatives from all agencies of government concerned with farm labor to attend the wage conference held in Memphis. The United States Employment Service, the Farm Security Administration, and the War Manpower Commission each sent men to attend the meeting. Within two weeks, the cotton-picking wage rate of $2.00 per 100 pounds was established in the mid-south states. The union offered to supply 2,000 experienced

cotton pickers to harvest the pima cotton in Arizona and other southwestern states in November. At the insistence of AF of L representative Frank P. Fenton, then director of organization, and CIO representative Clinton S. Golden, United Steel Workers of America, (these two
men were alternates for President William Green of the AF of L and
President Philip Murray of the CIO), the Southern Tenant Farmers
Union was invited to meet with the War Manpower Commission in
Washington. Among those also present at this meeting in early October was General Lucius Clay, who wanted assurance that the union
could mobilize its members and transport them to Arizona as quickly
as he could move troops. The union offered to assist the United States
Employment Service in recruiting and transporting its members to
Memphis if the Farm Security Administration would provide trains
for the trip to the West. When all the cotton had been harvested in the
South, the union sent 2,000 workers to pick cotton in the West. A
capable union leader was aboard each train, but when the train arrived at a railway siding near Eloy, Arizona, there was no housing, no
food, and no employers. The men and women refused to let the train
move until agents of the Farm Security Administration arrived, and
when they did arrive, they quickly provided food, housing, and jobs at
the promised rate of pay. There were similar foul-ups elsewhere. At
McNary, Texas, the workers were unloaded from the train and transported by truck to a huge ranch. There was no housing, and
the employer refused to pay the rate promised. There was a strike
that was settled by a young man from Austin, Texas, Clay Cochran,
who later became the director of the Rural Housing Alliance in
Washington. Cochran sent a telegram to C. B. Baldwin, the FSA
administrator in Washington, saying, "Job issues settled, strike over,
all quiet west of the Pecos."

500 WORKERS GO TO FLORIDA

Early in 1943, 500 more workers were sent to harvest fruits and
vegetables in Florida. John Beecher, then a Farm Security Administration farm-placement officer, recalls how a trainload of workers
arrived in Palm Beach. The men and women were all wearing a green
union button, its emblem a cotton boll with a plow, hoe, and the letters
STFU on it. Beecher was afraid that the Florida growers would refuse
to accept the men and women. However, the field bosses didn't learn
for some days that they had union workers on the job.

CONGRESS PASSES A LAW

The nation's large farm operators, mobilized by the American
Farm Bureau, were determined that farm workers should not become

unionized as a result of the war emergency. A temporary law was passed by Congress that permitted the importation of foreign workers for employment in agriculture. Government agencies were prohibited from fixing wages and from providing transportation for domestic agricultural workers, unless each worker had the written consent of his county agricultural extension agent to accept employment outside the county in which he resided. This effectively ended the union's program of cooperation with government agencies in providing its members with temporary work out of the South.

SOLDIERS WORKING ON FARMS

Several large-scale farm operators in New Jersey, claiming labor shortages, persuaded the United States Army to furlough men to work on farms. Among these huge farm operations was the Seabrook Farms of Bridgeton. But in this instance there was a closed-shop union contract that covered even farm employees hired for temporary work. In return for union representation, each worker was required to pay twenty-five cents per week for union dues. There is no record that any of the soldiers furloughed for farm work objected to the dues collection, but the Farm Bureau of New Jersy did take offense and alerted the newspapers. The union leader was held up as a traitor to the country, hampering the war effort by insisting that his union contract be enforced. The problem was solved temporarily when the employer and union agreed that no more soldiers would be hired on Seabrook Farms.

NAZI WAR PRISONERS ON THE FARMS

By 1943, thousands of prisoners of war had been captured in Africa and brought to the United States, where they were put to work on farms all over the country. Theoretically, the employer had to pay the United States Treasury the current rate of pay for the use of prisoners of war. Seeing an opportunity to get cheap labor, food processing plants also applied for German war prisoners. Local communities became alarmed at the idea of Americans working in the same plant with Nazi war prisoners, and young Jewish refugees from Hitler's concentration camps, who had been pilloried in the press for insisting that furloughed soldiers pay union dues of twenty-five cents a week, took action. Leon B. Schachter, business manager of Local No. 56 of the Amalgamated Meat Cutters and Butcher Workmen of North America, AF of L, contacted the Southern Tenant Farmers Union. An organized migration plan was worked out, under which more than 12,000 workers from the midsouth were sent to work on temporary jobs in New Jersey and other mid-Atlantic States. The men and women were employed both in food-processing plants and on farms.

THE UNDERGROUND RAILWAY

Workers were recruited by the Southern Tenant Farmers Union, and transportation was provided by the employers. Wages and working conditions, including housing, were the responsibility of Local No. 56, which held contracts in most of the plants and on some of the larger farms. Local and state employment services were bypassed by the unions, and local agents of the Employment Service in Arkansas had union representatives jailed on charges of "interfering with labor." Trucks and cars loaded with workers going to Memphis to board trains were turned back in Arkansas, Mississippi, and Alabama. The STFU in turn protested to the War Manpower Commission and the Department of Justice that local farm workers were being held in a new form of peonage. One of the officers of the union, Vice President F. R. Betton (a black man), termed the STFU project an "underground railroad."

Meanwhile, workers in the fields had found a new bargaining weapon. If plantation owners refused to pay union wages, they told the boss they were going to the union to get shipped out to jobs in New Jersey. Consequently wage rates and working conditions continued to improve until the end of the war. The union began collecting membership dues at the rate of $3.00 annually, and an economic basis for the organization was established for the first time. Negotiations for affiliation with both the CIO and the AF of L were started.

AF OF L ENTERS THE FARM FIELD

In August of 1946, the AF of L Executive Council granted a charter to the newly renamed National Farm Labor Union (formerly the STFU). The organization was invited by the California Federation of Labor to come and organize the "factories in the fields" in that state. Financial and other support was given by the state federation and many of the central labor union councils. The National Farm Labor Union campaign in California was directed by Hank Hasiwar. He was the most adaptable as well as the only professional trade-union organizer ever involved in organizing farm workers. One of the first things Hasiwar did was to marry a lovely Mexican-American girl who had a radio program on a station in Bakersfield. Delfina De Anda played and sang Mexican songs, while her brother broadcasted the news of the union during noncommercial breaks in the program. With the encouragement of a former IWW organizer, Fred West, then secretary of the Kern County Central Labor Union, Hasiwar organized the huge DiGiorgio Fruit Corporation Ranch. When the owner, Joseph DiGiorgio, refused to meet with representatives of the workers, 1,100 men and women, including whites, blacks, and Mexican Americans, walked out. The huge corporation farm was given guards by the Kern County sheriff, and there was an attempt to wipe out the leadership of the strike by gunfire one night, when a meeting was being held in the home of the local secretary, Hattie Shadowen. The president of the NFLU Local No. 218, Jimmy Price, was shot in the face and almost bled to death before he could be transported to a Bakersfield hospital, eighteen miles away. (When the company doctor of the DiGiorgio Ranch was called, he refused to give first aid to Price.) The gunmen were never apprehended, although Governor Earl Warren offered a huge reward and also sent in state investigators. So much attention was attracted to the DiGiorgio strike that the Hollywood Film Council made a movie called *Poverty in the Valley of Plenty;* the head of the Screen Actors Guild, Ronald Reagan, was very active in making this movie. The movie was shown to the House Labor and Education Committee in Washington, and an investigation was requested by the union. A subcommittee was subsequently sent to Bakersfield, among whose members was a young congressman from Southern California who assumed the role of defender of the DiGiorgio Fruit Corporation. He questioned union witnesses as if they were criminals on trial for their lives. At the end of the first day's hearing the congressman went to Hank Hasiwar and H. L. Mitchell and promised to straighten out the growers if the organizers were again accused of being communists. Hasiwar was infuriated and threatened to beat the hell out of the congressman, but Mitchell persuaded Hasiwar not to attack Richard M. Nixon.

During the strike, the corporation brought in exconvicts from San Quentin Prison, to assist the sheriff in guarding the ranch property. Early one morning, five picketers were beaten almost to death by the excons. They were taken to the hospital, and word spread rapidly through the farm-labor camps and communities. A crowd estimated at 1,000 "okies," armed with rifles, shotguns, and pistols, assembled at the main gate of the DiGiorgio Ranch. They were prepared to go in and clean out strikebreakers, company thugs, and officials from the entire ranch, but were persuaded to await the arrival of Hank Hasiwar at 7:00 A.M. One young okie said to Kern County sheriff, John Lousalot, "We are going to shoot you first." But Hasiwar and the older men persuaded the mob to go home; the strike had been lost and there was no point in hundreds of people being killed. Perhaps historians would have had more to write about if the "okies" had attacked that day.

NIXON AND FARM LABOR

Richard Nixon filed an unofficial report condemning the union, and had it inserted in the Congressional Record. The DiGiorgio Fruit Corporation lawyers filed suit for $2 million alleging libel against each organization and individual who had any part in the making of *Poverty in the Valley of Plenty.* Lawyers for the Hollywood unions and the A.F. of L. agreed to withdraw the film from circulation and settled the suit for $1.00. Alexander H. Schullman, attorney for the National Farm Labor Union, wanted to contest the lawsuits all the way to the United States Supreme Court, but only the National Farm Labor Union would agree; other unions did not want to be involved further. In 1961, when the AFL–CIO launched the Agricultural Workers Organizing Committee, someone found a copy of the movie and showed it at union meetings. Lawyers for the DiGiorgio Corporation promptly filed suit and reportedly collected, $50,000 from the AFL–CIO.

In his report, Congressman Richard Nixon advanced the theory that, since Congress excluded farm workers from the National Labor Relations Act, such workers had no right to organize and bargain collectively.

In 1949, there was a strike of over 20,000 cotton pickers in the San Joaquin Valley. Rates for picking had been reduced by a dollar per day, and DiGiorgio strikers engaged in mass picketing in caravans of "jalopies," as their old cars were called. A long string of cars rolled from field to field, calling out the workers, and the strikers won their demands. Among those in the caravans was Cesar Chávez, a young migratory worker who got his first union card from the National Farm Labor Union.

A NEW PRESIDENTIAL COMMISSION
ON MIGRATORY LABOR

Conditions among migratory farm workers were so appalling during the winter of 1949 that the union called upon President Harry S. Truman to name a presidential commission to investigate. The Commisssion on Migratory Labor in American Agriculture was appointed, and issued a report a year later. This report became the basis for all farm-labor legislation, and eventually the twenty-year-old law, permitting the temporary importation of Mexican nationals under contract, was brought to an end.

STRANGERS IN OUR FIELDS

The union conducted a three-point program, exposing the evils of farm labor, from 1947 to 1960. First, it called public attention to the plight of American farm workers, especially those of Mexican descent who soon became the largest group engaged in farm work. The second phase was to lobby in Washington, and, as a result, legislation was proposed and introduced in Congress. The union's representative of the Federal Advisory Council of the Bureau of Employment Security—that was included in the United States Department of Labor—often found not only organized labor but public members and industrial employers sympathetic. The third part of the program was in the nature of guerrilla warfare, and consisted of hit-and-run strikes in every California valley, involving almost every crop. Wages were usually increased as a result but no lasting union was organized. Then, a final effort to secure recognition and a union contract was made in the Imperial Valley in 1951. About 4,000 men and women, nearly all of Mexican descent, struck the fields during the melon harvest. Illegal aliens were arrested by union members under California's Citizens Arrest Act and turned over to the Border Patrol for deportation. Mexican trade unions assisted the American workers by picketing border-crossing points with baseball bats. Twenty-eight larger employers offered to negotiate contracts with the union, but then the United States Department of Labor ordered 7,500 Mexican nationals under contract into the Imperial Valley. The strikebreakers were not the Mexican workers but a former mayor of Boston, an Irish politician, and Maurice Tobin, the secretary of labor of the United States.

THE LOUISIANA STORY

In the early 1950s, the National Farm Labor Union turned its attention to the South again. Strong local unions of dairy farmers and fruit and vegetable producers were organized. A local of 3,600 strawberry farmers was organized on the basis of a cooperative marketing agency. After successful operation for three years, its officers were convicted of violating the Sherman Anti-Trust Act, fined, and given suspended prison sentences by the United States District Court in New Orleans. Judge Christenberry refused to accept a settlement, worked out by attorneys for the Department of Justice and the union, and imposed maximum sentences. Within the same time period, sugar-cane-plantation workers were organized by the union, with both moral and financial support from the Roman Catholic Archdiocese of New Orleans. A strike for union recognition was broken by injunctions issued by local courts, based on the theory advanced by Richard M. Nixon that Congress had excluded farm workers from the National Labor Relations Act, and they, therefore, had no right to organize or "act in concert." The injunction was upheld by the Louisiana Supreme Court, but upon appeal by the union on a "pauper's oath," the injunctions were ordered set aside by the United States Supreme Court.

Meanwhile, the National Agricultural Workers Union, as it was called after 1954, was seriously handicapped by the loss of its best organizer, Hank Hasiwar, who had been among those convicted by the Eisenhower administration of violating the antitrust law in the case of the strawberry farmers. Hasiwar was given a two-year prison sentence and placed on probation. He was forbidden to work for a union during that time. Remnants of the union remained in Louisiana and were put together again in 1960, when the National Agricultural Workers Union merged with the Amalgamated Meat Cutters and Butcher Workmen of North America.

HOW THE AFL–CIO BECAME INVOLVED
IN ORGANIZING FARM WORKERS

As soon as the two labor federations of the AF of L and CIO merged in 1955, a campaign was started to persuade the organized labor movement to launch an organizing drive. This was supported by Walter P. Reuther, A. Philip Randolph, and other leaders of the AFL–CIO. A National Advisory Committee on Farm Labor was formed, with members that included Mrs. Franklin D. Roosevelt, Norman Thomas, Frank P. Graham, and Helen Gahagan Douglas. This committee held a public hearing in Washington, during which the AFL–CIO made a firm commitment to launch an organizing campaign among the nation's farm workers. Out of this AFL–CIO action came first the Agricultural Workers Organizing Committee and then the United Farm Workers of America.

The most authoritative work in this period has been done by Dr. Ernesto Galarza, who served as an organizer and research and education director for several unions. His books include *Strangers in our Fields, Spiders in the House—Workers in the Fields, Merchants of Labor, Barrio Boy,* and *Farm Workers and Agri-Business in California, 1947–1960.* Another recommended book is *A Long Time Coming: The Struggle to Unionize Farm Workers,* by Dick Meister and Anne Loftis.

Racial Divisions and Agricultural Labor Organizing in Hawaii

Edward D. Beechert

THE MULTIETHNIC COMPOSITION of the Hawaiian labor force and the peculiar context into which Hawaii's ethnic immigrants were placed has combined to give the island commonwealth a unique labor history. It all began with sugar.

As the Cubans and Jamaicans before them, the sugar barons of the islands soon discovered that native workers were inadequate to meet the manpower demands of the plantation system. Successive waves of Chinese, Japanese, Filipinos, and others swept into the cane fields to supplant native Hawaiians, as the islands moved toward closer ties with the American mainland. By 1909, the most important of the new ethnic groups was the Japanese. In that year, a group of nonplantation intellectuals organized the Higher Wage Association, whose goals were an increased wage of $22.50 per month (over the existing scale of $18.00) and a wage scale that would guarantee Japanese workers equal pay to workers of other nationalities.[1] It was hardly a radical demand, but the planters reacted both immediately and negatively. Over $2 million was spent importing strikebreakers of other ethnic identifications—Chinese, Portuguese, and Koreans—who would have little sympathy for the striking Japanese. The strikers themselves were arrested on conspiracy charges, tried, and thrown in jail; planter control of the courts was never in doubt.[2] Only afterward were the worst abuses of the system corrected. Slight changes in wage scales gave the Japanese the equality they had demanded, and improvements in cane-cutting bonuses and housing helped allay the latent hostilities of all sugar workers.[3] However, the pattern was set.

Between 1909 and 1937, the islands would suffer a number of strikes which were basically racial in nature. None of the actions brought victory to the workers, but they did involve Filipinos and other ethnic groups in the fray. The strike of 1920, for instance, found Japanese, Filipinos, and Koreans working together so effectively that planters and the Hawaiian government begged Congress to relax the ban on the importation of Chinese labor; they viewed Chinese labor as absolutely necessary to break the "Japanese menace."[4] But if it was the Japanese who took the lead in early island strikes, it was the Filipinos who led workers out of the fields in 1937.

The strike of 1937 was organized and led by an intensely Filipino union called Vitora Luviminda. Taking its name from the Filipino patriot, General Artemio y Vitora, and a combination of the names of the three major islands of the Philippines, Vitora Luviminda got much of its direction from Antonio Fagel, a Filipino nationalist who came to the islands in 1934.[5] From the start, every action of the organization was carefully monitored by the Hawaii Industrial Association, a rather ham-handed industrial espionage operation founded by Hawaiian businessmen to keep radical unions in check.[6] Despite the efforts of both spies and union, the troubles of 1937 developed out of a spontaneous conflict over a change in cane-cutting rates rather than industrial espionage or union activity. Before either side could intervene, the dispute was taken up by some 1,500 Filipinos and a like number of sympathizers. On May 1, 1937, a parade of 2,500 people marched four miles, from Maui's port town to the county seat, in support of the strike.[7] Indeed, before things finally quieted down, the NLRB, the CIO, and the WPA all took a hand in the strike. The labor board investigated a company-inspired beating of Antonio Fagel (the first time that the federal government had intervened in an island strike), the CIO gave aid and support to Vitora, and island planters used their control of the WPA to find strikebreakers.[8] Yet, it was the courts which finally brought an end to the strike.

In mid-May, 1937, the planters offered strikers the first concession in the history of Hawaiian agricultural labor relations. If, noted the planters' "statement of policy," the workers returned to the fields, management would guarantee a wage increase and meetings with strikers' representatives on any future dispute.[9] Union refusal of this offer resulted in the arrest of Fagel and nine other strike leaders for unlawful imprisonment of a strikebreaker. With events becoming ever more ominous, Fagel appealed to Ed Berman, the CIO representative in Honolulu and editor of *The Voice of Labor.* It had been Berman who first brought an NLRB investigator into the fray and, indirectly, Berman who had forced the planters to issue their conciliatory "statement of policy."[10] Berman went to work.

It proved impossible to get legal council for the union in Honolulu, so Berman turned to the International Law Defense in San Francisco. Grover Johnson, an experienced labor lawyer, was retained by Berman and, as the strike continued to drag on, Johnson set sail for the islands. Disembarking only days later, Johnson discovered that the trial was already underway—a not uncommon practice in territorial labor cases.[11] The subsequent trial vividly illustrated the power of the planter community and the extent of change in labor's status in Hawaii.

The trial was moved to Honolulu. Circuit Court archives and materials in the ILWU library indicate that the reason for the move was to avoid the certain spectacle of Filipino workers being defended by an experienced attorney.[12] Both the presiding judge and prosecuting attorney were chosen because of their planter ties. The judge, a former staff attorney for the Hawaiian Sugar Planters Association, was unlikely to forget his former loyalties. To aid him, the HSPA paid a staff counsel $100 a day to serve as prosecuting attorney, a position which would allow him to wax eloquent on the sins of sugar workers.

The Honolulu trial was the last in a long series of clumsily rigged antilabor trials. Subsequently the HSPA had to learn to cope with skilled attorneys for the defense and a strong CIO. In the meantime, eighty-five different groups of jurists had to be called in order to empanel a jury for the proceedings, which strangely contained no Filipinos.[13] It took only a short time for the jury to find all defendants guilty and to sentence each one to between four and thirteen months probation. The leader, Fagel, alone chose to serve out the sentence, speculating that probation would likely result in a return to court and, in any case, would prevent him from organizing.[14]

Before this strike was brought to an end, the modern labor movement had arrived. While Fagel was struggling with the spontaneous ethnic strike, other workers in Hawaii were forging ties with the power and skill of mainland labor organizations. Linked by ship to the mainland, Hawaii responded quickly to the events of 1934–35. Seamen from Hawaii observed the maritime strike of 1934 and were fired with enthusiasm, returning to Hawaii in 1935 to begin the long process of organizing. Longshoremen in Hilo and Honolulu joined in between 1935 and 1937.

Enthusiasm ran high and into stone-wall opposition. Harry Kamoku, the organizer of the Hilo longshoremen, returned to Hawaii from job positions in San Francisco and Seattle. He was the proverbial seaman mentioned by historians.[15] A considerable legend has been generated about these "radical seamen" who came ashore. One recent account describes the situation:

> (Hall) arrived in Honolulu in 1935 with a reputation as a skilled labor organizer....He was suspended from the Seamen's Union when his efforts to bring Hawaiian waterfront labor into the CIO-affiliated ILWU were disclosed, and he began immediately to organize longshoremen, truck drivers, hotel employees, and sugar and pineapple workers.[16]

It would be difficult to assess from the above the role of the Hawaiian seamen in the organization of labor. Hall arrived in Hawaii at about the same time as Harry Kamoku and Harry Kealoha. Kamoku returned to his home in Hilo and began organizing, and Kealoha worked on the waterfront in Honolulu. The report of the NLRB trial examiner put it very simply in one hearing, on the complaint of Harry Kealoha against Castle and Cooke.

> In the latter part of August or the first of September, 1935, Harry Kealoha came to Honolulu and began the organization of the longshoremen.... Kealoha is a native of the Territory and a Hawaiian, but prior to his return...he had been away working in various places as a sailor, longshoreman and other activities for 14 years.[17]

Efforts to organize in Hilo met with little resistance, and Kamoku was able to form a unit and apply for a charter in the ILA on November 10, 1935. Employer resistance was at a higher level in Honolulu.[18] Activity there was accompanied by a steady drumbeat in the Hawaiian press, which alternated between charges of "communistic leadership" and "outside agitators."[19]

The Hawaii charter applications became entangled in the conflict between Harry Bridges, west coast director of the ILA, and the president, Joe Ryan. The conflict originated in the rejection of the settlement of the 1934 longshore strike, negotiated by Ryan and Dave Beck,[20] and continued throughout 1935 and 1936, eventually disrupting the Maritime Federation of the Pacific. Under Bridges' leadership, the longshoremen turned from the craft-union struggles of the AFL to the newly organized CIO, which was operating under the banner of the International Longshoremen and Warehousemen's Union (ILWU).[21]

An appeal to Bridges from the executive committee of the Honolulu local describes the situation:

> "Brother William Craft (ILA organizer) has tried every means in the effort of installing a charter for both ports, but somehow Ryan has held out on us.... The majority of the men have elapsed in the past due to the lack of a Charter.... The Honolulu and Hilo locals have tried every means by which we could receive that charter."[22]

At the same time, a strong petition was sent to Ryan. "You have repeatedly failed to comply with Bro. Craft's demands, which reasons given by you [sic], for withholding the installation of our charter are very vague in detail."[23] A series of telegrams between New York, San Francisco, and Honolulu resulted only in Ryan's demands for pledges of loyalty and accusations of disruption against Bridges.[24] The struggle culminated in the removal of Bridges as president of the West Coast ILA. Ryan offered the post to Craft, who indignantly refused.[25] The conflict between Ryan and Bridges was also reflected in the conflict between Dave Beck and the Teamsters Union. The longshore drive to organize allied workers, announced as the "march inland," inflamed AFL craft sensibilities and those under the jurisdiction of Dave Beck.

The resulting conflict moved the longshoremen into the CIO, and Hawaii was swept up in the complex quarrel—one that would end up in the United States Supreme Court before the right of the ILWU to exist was confirmed.[26] To the longshoremen in Hawaii, it seemed that once again Hawaii was a victim of mainland race prejudice. The view was widely shared among both labor and business people in Hawaii.[27]

The island unions watched with interest the breaking away from the AFL and the pending affiliation with the CIO. Earlier in the year, the Hawaiian Islands Federation of Labor had begun to fall apart because of the conflict between craft unionism and the drive to industrial unionism, and the poor quality of leadership. In Hilo, the problem emerged when Harry Kamoku announced a "march inland," with the formation of a council of unions, both AFL and CIO. The CIO representative, Edward Berman, reported that "in Hilo the longshoremen have been for the past two months on a steady and uninterrupted march inland...."[28] Hawaiian longshoremen were invited to the West Coast of the mainland, to work as permit men in order to strengthen their attachment to the movement. The close and effective attention given to Hawaii by Bridges and the officers of the ILWU played an important role in strengthening and encouraging the fledgling locals.

The Hawaiian workers were anxious for a charter. For example, the Port Allen Waterfront Workers Association inquired of the secretary-treasurer, Matt Meehan, what the procedures and obligations were to affiliate with the CIO.

> The Port Allen Waterfront Workers Association wishes to become an independent local of the CIO. But before being affiliated to the CIO, we want to obtain the following information: 1) Will we be part of the Pacific Coast organization with both moral and financial support? 2) What procedure should be used by this union to be affiliated? 3) After being affiliated, how much and in what way will the Union be obligated to the CIO?[29]

Bridges informed the local that new CIO charters would be issued in the International Longshoremen and Warehousemen's Union. As to help, he offered to explore the issue. "I am taking up the matter of getting an organizer to your area. This, however, may take a little time and will move [*sic*] on as soon as possible."[30] When the charters were issued, Edward Berman, editor of the labor newspaper, *Voice of Labor*, was appointed Hawaii director of the CIO—an unpaid position.

The level of enthusiasm was high. The Port Allen group wrote Bridges that they had been "organizing the waterfront and plantation workers with a promise of affiliating with the CIO. So far we have organized over 3,000 workers on the island of Kauai....We need help badly. Will you send one or two organizers from the mainland to help us in our hard struggle?"[31] The letter reflects the belief of the island workers that mainland connections would provide the margin necessary to win out over the island oligarchy.

Ed Berman, after conferring with Henry Schmidt of Local No. 10 in San Francisco, wrote to Meehan urging an organizing campaign beyond the waterfront. Pointing to the approximately 65,000 workers in agriculture, canneries, and allied industries, he urged swift action to bring them into the union. He estimated that he would need at least $3,000 and about six months for the effort.

> "Returning with me to Hawaii will be Brothers Aukau and Bert Nakano of Hilo who worked as permit men in Seattle and San Francisco for the past six months and Brothers Amoka and Kawano, who worked in San Francisco for three months. These men have been trained in West Coast traditions and can bring a real message."[32]

The enthusiasm and high spirits were soon put to the test by the seasoned opposition of the employers. In Hilo, the waterfront employer decided on the strategy of informal recognition without the formality of an NLRB election—in other words, a gentlemen's agreement.[33] It is indicative of the informal atmosphere and self-confidence prevalent in Hawaii that the group in Hilo accepted this proposal, but it did not bring labor peace. Spontaneous walkouts continued just as in the past. The Interisland Steamship strike of 1938 would bring savage violence to the Hilo waterfront.

This strike was notable for its eighty-day duration and the efforts made in interunion cooperation. There were no significant racial issues, and the unions made a serious effort to submerge craft-industrial union differences. Despite the violence and the length of the strike none of the leaders were arrested on the usual conspiracy charges used in all other previous major strikes in Hawaii.[34]

In Honolulu, where the strike originated, the unions involved were the Inland Boatmen's Union, ILWU Local No.1–37, and the

Dry Dock Workers of the Metal Trades Council, AFL, of Honolulu. After halting operations for several weeks, the steamship company began operations at the smaller outports of the territory. This was followed by resuming service with one of the regular vessels, manned by scab seamen. Picketing and threats of violence immediately began.

The Hilo unions planned to meet the scab ship with a large-scale community type demonstration, reflecting the labor unity of the Hilo Industrial Council. Despite the plans for passive resistance, a police riot ensued. The police opened fire with buckshot on the demonstrators, who were conducting a sit-in on the dock apron. Fifty-one people were wounded, many severely.[35] The eventual settlement of the strike proved to be a very small victory, when measured against the demands and the extent of the struggle. The unions failed to win a union shop, in the form of maritime hiring halls or wage parity with the West Coast. "The men return to work with their ranks intact. They return better and veteran unionists as a result of this struggle." The CIO organizer was obviously taking a long view—one which proved to be correct.[36]

Once again, the agreements which ended the strike were informal, gentlemen's agreements. However, the companies did move to correct the worst abuses and to ameliorate conditions which had produced the strike.[37] The Interisland Company informed the NLRB director that:

> It is our opinion that there exists no necessity for such [a representation election] at the present time. We are informed and believe that the majority of our stevedore employees are members of the Longshoremen's Association.[38]

The company recognized "the principle of collective bargaining" and proposed a "guaranteed wage" to stabilize working conditions, and promised to provide "stevedores with a means of living, during such times as we are unable to provide enough work to enable a man to support himself by his earnings." Company authorities also pointed out, however, that the agreement was entirely voluntary and subject to amendment—"at any time, subject to notice." For Hawaii, this was a long step on the way to successful collective bargaining.

Union activity on the plantations began when Berman was appointed CIO organizer, and a charter was issued by the United Cannery and Agricultural and Packinghouse Workers (UCAPAWA) on September 30, 1937. The first unit was formed at McBryde Sugar Company.[39] A committee to begin organizing was selected, consisting of James Cooley, Jack Hall, Calixto Piano, and George Goto, to assist Ed Berman.

The task was easier to plan than to execute. By following the progress of the campaign through the pages of the intensely anti-union Kauai newspaper, it is easy to detect difficulties and some progress amid the rhetoric and ritualistic pronouncements of total failure. The resident labor commissioner from the Philippines, a consistent union foe, began an antiunion campaign. He proposed to organize "committees" on each plantation that would bring complaints and misunderstandings to the attention of management. This effort was supported by the management of the three Kauai plantations.[40]

That the CIO effort was meeting resistance was evident when meetings were confined to the relatively few public buildings on the island, creating travel problems for workers on the more remote plantations.[41] Events at an NLRB hearing suggest the atmosphere that prevailed on Kauai in 1937–38. A plantation manager named McBryde had been charged with unfair labor practices. When Ben Shear went to Port Allen to heal a split in the longshore local, the plantation manager had issued warnings to his workers not to attend the meetings on threat of being "fired out." Mauro Andaya, curious, went to the Port Allen meeting, which was also attended by several plantation officials. After Richard Mamdamba, the interpreter, spoke, the manager was heard to say, "Don't worry, I'll fix that guy." The next day, Mamdamba had little to say, and he did not show up at any more meetings.[42] Andaya then became the interpreter for the meetings, which had to be translated into Japanese and Ilocano. Andaya was immediately offered a position in the social welfare department of the plantation, which he refused. Subsequently, the plantation hired two touring Filipino missionaries, to urge resistance to the labor talks. At the end of the 1937 season (September), Andaya was fired and his family was evicted. According to the manager, Andaya was not fired "due to union activities" but had "created discord among the entire workers in this plantation, including every other nationality." However, after one day, the manager offered Andaya his job back—after the NLRB office in Honolulu had been called. Andaya said, "I am still working, although I have lost the confidence they used to have in me."[43]

Before the workers won recognition, another union activist was fired by McBryde. In July, 1940, the case of Frank Silva earned new prominence for the organizing campaign. A popular athlete, supervisor, and union activist, Frank Silva was fired for the alleged reason that he had played soccer for a rival plantation club—against company orders. This mingling of union concerns with popular and heated athletic rivalries resulted in the appointment of an Emergency Board of Labor by the territorial governor. After an investigation, the board concluded that Silva had been fired for union activity rather than a breach of plantation athletic club rules.[44] On October 24, 1940, the industrial employees under McBryde voted 200 to 40 for UCAPAWA. A modest but significant beginning.

Meanwhile, the ILWU was moving steadily to improve its Hawaiian organization. The 1939 convention voted to form an Hawaiian Islands Organizing Committee.[45] This committee was to be funded, in part, by a return of the island per-capita payments.[46] Armed with a mandate and financing, the Hawaii local moved to set up an organizing committee. Invited to the meeting as fraternal delegates were representatives from the two UCAPAWA locals on Kauai, the Transport Workers, the Quarry Workers, and also Jack Hall, a CIO organizer. A combined total of some 520 per-capita payments was estimated to be the base available for organizing. Three organizers, Jack Kawano and Fred Kamahoahoa of Honolulu and Bert Nakano of Hilo, were to be hired at $60 per month each.[47] There was optimism that the thirty-five cents per capita could be raised by vote to fifty cents. On a budget of $182 per month, with hopes of increasing the amount to $260, the two longshore locals set out to secure contracts at all Hawaiian ports.

Reports from the two UCAPAWA units were then heard and discussed. Arashiro, from McBryde's plantation, urged "solidification of the waterfronts of the territory so that agricultural workers would have the protection for their organization, which in turn would make recognition of the agricultural workers possible."[48] The delegates observed that the seasonal peak of the pineapple industry made that industry "one of the major points of concentration."

Arashiro indicated optimism in securing changes in the basic law to permit organization of field workers. Labor on Kauai had actually supported the election of J. B. Fernandes over a plantation official in November, 1938. At the next session of the legislature, Senator Fernandes introduced a bill to permit organization of agricultural workers.[49] Although this effort failed, the effort was indicative of a new level of sophistication in seeking labor's goals. In 1948, a Kauai Progressive League was organized and actively supported labor candidates. Their nominee for the territorial senate narrowly defeated the head of the oldest planter family in the islands, Elsie Wilcox of the Lihue Plantation.[50] This victory was followed shortly by the October 24, 1940, election, in which McBryde employees supported UCAPAWA.

The fortunes of labor were further advanced by a series of hearings held by the Agricultural Adjustment Administration on sugar industry wage rates and job classifications. Jack Hall appeared for the

UCAPAWA units, having filed a complaint on the value of perquisites.[51] A related investigation by the Bureau of Internal Revenue into the question of nonpayment of social security taxes on perquisites furnished to industrial workers by the plantations was also under way. An estimated $1 million was due for the years since 1937.[52]

Perhaps the best clue to the rapidly maturing status of organized labor in Hawaii was the appointment of an international representative of the ILWU, who would report directly to the international executive board.[53] Clifford O'Brien's first report indicated alarm at the casual Hawaiian style. He found the longshoremen's strike at Port Allen, Kauai, for example, tied to the effort to organize agricultural workers. Also, workers were being "borrowed" from the plantations for military contractors. These workers were paid their regular plantation rates and perquisites, while the plantations, as labor contractors, received approximately sixty-two cents per hour per worker. Plantation wages at that time were only forty-two cents, plus nine cents for perquisites. The arrangement was defended by the plantations as "a legitimate reimbursement for their expenditures, overhead, and lost sugar production."[54]

O'Brien reviewed the results of Pearl Harbor in a vivid letter on December 23, 1941. Longshoremen of Japanese ancestry were excluded from the waterfront. All labor legislation, including the National Labor Relations Act, all wages and hours legislation, and all contracts were suspended. The *Herald,* Hall's newspaper, was closed down. O'Brien asked to be removed from the payroll as he would probably be working at a defense job shortly, although he agreed to continue to act as international representative "until the situation over here has sufficiently crystallized to enable us to make a sensible decision as to whether there's going to be enough opportunity to work to justify the salary."[55] The displaced Japanese longshoremen actually improved their earnings by moving into construction work and an effort to force the Japanese back to the plantations was defeated. However, the gross inequity in the use of plantation labor on military jobs would become an important factor in strengthening union sentiment when organizing resumed in 1943–1944.

O'Brien, continuing his report, wrote:

> As the picture stands there will not be much chance to continue our organizational programs, with the exception of the dock clerks in Honolulu and the strengthening of our Kauai organizations and the now remote possibility of plantation and pineapple cannery workers.[56]

> Their disposition is to go too far to protect agricultural workers —if we get beat, they'll get discouraged, etc....Jack Hall, politi-

cally somewhat successful on Kauai and depending largely on agricultural workers has gone much too far in encouraging this.[57]

O'Brien was also beginning to encounter the techniques of Hawaii employers in negotiating the Honolulu longshore contract.

> Sorry to be taking so damn long on this job, but it is difficult to get people to move at all over here, and these employers have privately stated to Geurts (mediator) and to me that they expect by minor concessions to kill the Union with Kindness toward them so that there'll be a loss of interest in the Union and hence no Union next time. They also state openly that they'll bargain and bargain but they won't give anything important. This technique, just enough to meet the Wagner Act, is devastating and has been used to smash two (Kress) unions here.[58]

Despite this gloomy outlook, O'Brien wrapped up a new longshore contract by January 9. The contract, while good, failed to secure either a union security clause or a central hiring hall—a cherished goal.

By July, the locals were asking that O'Brien be returned to the islands because of the number of grievances to be arbitrated and the problems of organizing.[59] O'Brien agreed to return for one year. He immediately plunged into the task of building the longshore locals and exploring the problems of organizing warehousemen and teamsters.[60]

The pattern which would be used in later organizing began to emerge at this time: full reporting to the international; a constant lookout for sources of trouble (whether from within or without); and a steady pressure to streamline and consolidate patchwork local organizations. O'Brien urged a consolidation of ILWU activities and the CIO office in Hawaii, doubting that Jack Hall could do the work of editing a labor paper and carry on as CIO organizer. "Frankly, with all his abilities, I do not believe Hall can do both effective organizational work and newspaper editorship," he said.[61]

The rising tide of military preparation was beginning to intrude on labor organizing. The military had threatened to use personnel as longshoremen several times in 1941. The Territorial Disaster Committee recommended to the governor that plantation workers who had left the plantation for higher-paying defense jobs be shipped back to their old jobs and old pay, and that "their places in defense work and stevedoring be taken by military personnel."[62]

A future problem loomed suddenly in the form of the Territorial Board of Harbor Commissioners appropriating money for the development of bulk-sugar-loading facilities on several territorial wharves and an experimental facility on Maui. The value of mainland affiliation was evident in the request: "Please rush all available information on bulk processes."[63] Sugar organizing, meanwhile, moved from Kauai to the island of Hawaii, when UCAPAWA asked for recognition at the Olokele Sugar Company, outlining a unit of 600 in the industrial branch.[64] Recognition was expected to give impetus to later organizing on Oahu, and evidence of organizational activity can be seen in the three sets of unfair practice charges that were filed between May and October, 1941.

However, the bright picture of organizational gains vanished in the smoke and fire of Pearl Harbor. On December 20, 1941, most labor and wages were frozen. Labor agreements became null and void according to the military governor's General Order No. 38.[65] This was the first of several confused moves which were made in an attempt to cope with the frantic situation. Later, in March, 1942, a second order produced a conflict in jurisdiction between the Office of Military Government and the War Labor Board, a conflict which persisted until the return of civilian control in 1943.[66]

The war years produced few permanent gains. Disputes with the military, organizational and jurisdictional fights with the AFL, and the arrest of organizers by the provost marshall of Maui sabotaged several organizing efforts. However, organizers had gotten a toehold on Maui, and Jack Hall had begun informal negotiations with five major Maui plantations by late 1944.

Meanwhile, the international executive board had dispatched an experienced agricultural organizer to Hawaii. Frank Thompson of Sacramento, head of ILWU Local No. 17, had been involved in organizing agricultural workers in the San Joaquin Valley of California. Veteran of many battles with formidable California agricultural corporations and of attacks by government, he was well prepared to take on the task in Hawaii.[67] Work was divided between Hall and Frank Thompson, and Hall was to handle details with the War Labor Board, the NLRB, and the Department of Labor, as well as public relations and political action. Thompson was assigned to functional matters, such as the consolidation and organization of locals, the making of financial arrangements, and the training of local leadership. Both would participate in negotiations whenever possible.[68] In this division of tasks lay the key to the success of the union, both in Hawaii and on the mainland. Particularly important were the consolidation of units, the training of leadership, the skillful handling of government agencies, and use of political action. Meticulous attention to detail had long been a feature of ILWU administration. Hall and Thompson reported at length every week, or at least every two weeks, to the mainland, and responses were prompt and detailed.

Despite the efforts at informal negotiations, no agreement was reached, and an NLRB recognition hearing was held. The subsequent ruling, handed down January 12, 1945, consolidated eleven representation petitions.[69] The ruling was a sweeping victory for the union, granting representation to all employees except field workers engaged in cultivating and harvesting. The unit was defined as beginning with the transportation of the cane from the field.

A subsequent election demonstrated the pent-up enthusiasm for union organization: a total of 2,628 votes were cast with the union winning 2,496. Only 132 votes were cast against the union. Consequently the industry abandoned the hearing route, agreeing to consent elections. A total of nineteen consent elections were held in 1945 throughout the territory. The results were equally overwhelming: 5,568 votes for the union, 222 against. In all, the union won thirty-three of the thirty-five plantations that were operating in 1945.

The efforts in 1945 to establish the union can only be outlined. One issue came up frequently—the demand for field workers to be included in the union. Given the plantation housing system, it was difficult to refuse these workers, and the issue was particularly troublesome. Hall had long been disposed to organize all plantation workers. He had tried in 1939 to secure a "Little Wagner Act" but had failed. Organizers in 1945 were concerned about the divisiveness of excluding field workers; given the composition of the work force on many plantations, such divisiveness could have exacerbated racial tensions. Also a sophisticated employers' group could use excluded workers to impede organizational efforts. The executive board position was:

> The basic policy outlined in earlier correspondence is still sound not only for sugar workers but for agricultural workers as well. Security and long-range collective bargaining by the agricultural workers lies in successful organization and collective bargaining by the sugar mill workers. We are still a long way from seeing daylight in the sugar industry and any efforts to organize agricultural workers would weaken rather than strengthen our organization concentrations.[70]

The correspondence between Hall, Thompson, and Goldblatt reveals an organizational strength that was new to the islands. From an office in Washington, D. C., the officials were prepared to bring assistance and pressure whenever appropriate. Whether they were talking to the president of Castle and Cooke about employer-labor cooperation, a continuation of the ILWU pledge of "no strikes" for the duration of the war, or seeking the help of the national CIO staff on pending NLRB cases, a report was made. Discussions with staff counsel of the War Labor Board, with Secretary Ickes to counteract "this campaign of sabotage by the Island interests against workers' basic rights," or with John J. McCoy, assistant secretary of war about hiring a hall for longshore were all reported with the above actions in one communication. The letter includes another problem also:

> The International has been opposed up until now to sending any of the leading (ILWU) officials or principal Research people to the Islands.... If possible, get the OK of the WLB in the Islands to put on a staff assistant (for research).[71]

The efficiency of internal organization, thorough preparation, and analytical research of the highest order, combined with a firm militancy and belief in the ability of the working man to organize, were important elements in the ultimate success of the ILWU. Never before had island workers been an integral part of such a comprehensive organization. Mistakes and defeats occurred, of course, but the organization leading up to a strike in 1946 proved strong enough to survive the startling blows which were used against the union, before the planters and island oligarchy finally conceded that the union was in Hawaii to stay, something not totally conceded until the long strike of 1958. Despite the difficulties of hopping among four islands, organizing the sugar industry, pineapple canneries, can plants, three railroads, a soda works on Maui, and longshoremen, Hall found time to stimulate political action. He conducted a registration drive on Oahu, hoping to sweep six territorial house seats in addition to victories in other districts. To this end, he forged an alliance with "several influential AFL unions." The result in the next legislation session (1945) was to get the "Little Wagner Act" passed, which effectively removed the problem of how to divide plantation communities without giving the employer an opportunity to drive a wedge into the union. Because housing was set up according to racial groups, omitting field workers often divided families as to union participation.

By November, 1945, the union had won 132 separate elections in sugar, pineapple, railroad, stevedoring, and miscellaneous industries, involving 10,984 workers. The union lost six elections covering 177 workers, but nevertheless, over 15,000 of the jurisdiction had become dues-paying members.[72] The entire sugar industry, made up of thirty-three plantation companies and including the agricultural field workers, was covered by the agreement reached in 1945. The union was able to secure an irrevocable, voluntary, dues checkoff, providing for substantial union security. The Hawaii Employers' Council even accepted the technique of permitting the dues checkoff upon certification.

The process of consolidating the multiple units began immediately. As a result, the union officers were confronted with a bewildering variety of imperative assignments. Not only did they have to consolidate the sugar units to prevent employer splitting tactics, but they had to find and train local leaders, develop grievance procedures, and carry on further organizing. The goal was to merge the multiple sugar units into one consolidated local, with strong unit leadership in each company. By December, 1945, the units had been consolidated down to three locals.[73]

Field workers were incorporated under the Hawaii Employment Relations Act by means of a cross check, which meant considerable work for unit leaders. Reports of the process indicate difficulty with communication between nationalities and even between members of the same group. As might be expected, some units were more diligent than others; nevertheless, the work was consistently pushed ahead, with the target being to complete the signing up of field workers before the 1946 contract negotiations. There were many problems, some of them having their locus in racial differences and antagonisms. One type of problem was that encountered at Olaa. Young Japanese workers who didn't speak the language well had considerable difficulty in explaining the process to older workers who didn't speak English. Unfortunately, untrained unit members had to be used to complete the process.[74]

In anticipation of these problems, the executive board of the parent union arranged to send selected island workers to San Francisco for union training and education. A comprehensive program of union leadership training was set up, and twelve unit leaders were sent for three months of intensive training. These men returned in time to participate and lead in the sugar strike of 1946.[75]

The union came to the 1946 contract negotiations with its organization complete. Field worker registrations had been completed by mid-year, and the contract expired in August. By June of 1946, over 20,000 of the 24,000 workers in the sugar industry had been signed into union membership.

The 1946 union contract demands stand in sharp contrast to the efforts of previous years. The sugar workers were now able to deal with employers on an equal basis. A significant demand was for a ten-month contract, which would move the expiration date up into the harvesting season. Workers also asked for a union shop, a minimum wage of sixty-five cents, a wage increase of eighteen and one half cents, a classification system (under discussion since March, 1946, with no progress), a forty-hour week, a nine cents per hour value for perquisites, and a ban on discrimination by race, creed, or color, political belief, or union activity.

Some of the demands were very complex. The union asked for improvement in housing and a voice in any housing fund.[76] On the issue of perquisites, the union had long been agitating on the determination of the value. A suit on back pay under FLSA standards had been settled out of court by the plantations on January 10, 1946, in which the plantations had agreed to pay $1.5 million or settle overtime claims. Since the value of the perquisites entered into the calculation of compliance payments to the industry, the employers were probably anxious to be rid of the system. In 1944, the union had filed complaints against no less than fourteen types of violation of FSLA rules. The union had also asked for a determination of the reasonable costs of perquisites furnished employees in the sugar industry.[77] The basis of the union request was that the employer-assigned cost of perquisites, set at six cents per hour, was without regard to quality, type, or quantity of services furnished. Thus, it was likely that the sugar industry was not meeting minimum wage standards of forty cents per hour in many cases.[78]

These charges struck directly at the basic structure of paternalism, which had long been one of the keys to control of the work force in Hawaii. Eviction from housing was usually the first employer response to any serious demands by a worker, and the question was how to convert or abandon such a system. Both employer and union wanted the system changed, however diametrically opposed their reasoning.

During the negotiations to settle the suit for back pay, the union exposed the soft spot in the employers' position. If the planters were considered as landlords, then the union would demand that overtime after forty hours be paid to all maintenance people. If the planters claimed the houses were essential to production, they would then become liable to pay back-claims of six cents per hour, since housing had been furnished for the convenience of the employer and could not be counted to meet the minimum wage.[79]

Negotiations quickly stalled on these issues of perquisites, wages, and union security. Meanwhile, the union had begun elaborate strike preparations. With a new membership, newly selected local leaders, and an infusion of 6,000 new immigrant workers, the union faced a task of enormous proportions. An elaborate structure of strike committees was organized—from the international down to the unit level. Local strategy committees received daily reports from the unit strike committees. The island committees then made a daily report to the territorial committee. In effect, a two-way communication was thereby established. Each unit was responsible for appointing nine subcommittees: picket, organizing, police, relief, finance, transportation, publicity, morale, and women's corp. The police committee was organized to prevent sabotage, provocation, or other mischief. The organizing committee was to gather up any remaining unsigned field workers. Throughout the seventy-nine-day strike, this plan functioned effectively. Food committees were organized both to meet nutritional needs and to provide an opportunity for the development of community spirit. Teams were assigned to hunt and to fish, and gardeners were solicited to plant vegetables.

The employers agreed to maintain essential camp services, and the union assigned maintenance personnel to do the necessary tasks, asking them to contribute their earnings to the strike fund. On August 30, one small unit reported that its preparations were complete and that it had collected a strike fund of $1,550. The chairman of Local No. 142, unit 12, concluded his report:

> All in all, our unit members are ready for the strike, but sincerely hopes that it could be avoided.[80]

For the first time in the labor history of the sugar industry, management agreed not to evict the strikers. The prospect of over 20,000 homeless workers and their families, spread over the entire territory, was no doubt a factor in this decision. Instructions to supervisors, issued prior to the strike, contained the following provision:

> If inquiries are made to you with respect to whether strikers will be permitted to remain in their houses, tell them that the policy of the company will be to permit them to remain so long as they remain in the legal status of employees on strike.[81]

Compare this with the 1937 strike, when selective instant evictions were a major weapon of the employer; or with 1920, when some 12,000 strikers were evicted in the middle of a flu epidemic. Approximately sixty-five people died of influenza among the 1920 strikers.

Some plantations went so far as to arrange credit for the strikers at the company store. In one such situation, credit equal to the previous month's pay was allowed.[82]

Any effort by employers to continue operations was doomed by the coincidence of a nationwide maritime strike, which began on September 5, 1946. The union was thus not confronted with the job of preventing the flow of sugar. Hawaii longshoremen's contracts expired on September 30, 1946. It is unlikely that the longshoremen's union would have reached a contract agreement very rapidly if the sugar units had still been out. The value of one big union was self-evident, even if they did not have to take this course.

The settlement met most of the sugar workers' expectations. They did not win the union shop, but did improve the irrevocable dues checkoff. The so-called employer security clauses—no strike, no lockout, no discrimination, and a discharge clause—were major employer issues.[83] The union demanded that the nondiscrimination clause be expanded to include race, political activity, and religious beliefs. The employers had argued against these, saying their inclusion would exacerbate the very conditions prohibited. The discharge clause was to be amended to include subjecting dismissals to grievance procedures and, more importantly, consultation with the union prior to the formulation of house rules.[84] Perquisites were converted to a basic wage rate along with a classification system. The method of conversion frequently resulted in a premium, or "red circle," rate for the worker.

The settlement was impressive. Even more impressive was the solidarity of the union during a seventy-nine-day strike. It was a convincing demonstration to the rank and file of the effectiveness of the unified, closely knit organization. The active involvement in meeting the innumerable problems was a powerful lesson in labor education. The units, backed up by effective and sensitive organization, were able to meet the problems of personal difficulty that a long strike always creates. Food supplies were not always timely, utility workers did not all contribute their earnings in the manner prescribed, personal financial problems developed—but the gamut of problems was met openly and most were resolved. A final demonstration of success was seen in the November election, when the Political Action Committee carried on its territory-wide campaign. No less than thirty-five PAC-endorsed candidates were elected to the legislature, ensuring a strong prolabor body.[85]

The union emerged from the 1946 strike with an impressive organization, widespread public support, and a strong political position. This unusual strength would be tested in the fire of a massive counterattack by management, which would not cease until the union demonstrated again, in 1958, the validity of its aims and the durability of its organization.

NOTES

[1]Ernest Wakukawa, *History of the Japanese People in Hawaii*, p. 127; also U.S., Bureau of Labor, *Report of Commissioner of Labor on Hawaii*, 1911, Bulletin 94, p. 734.

[2]Interview with T. Kawahara, Pacific Oral History Program, University of Hawaii. Mr. Kawahara was the bodyguard of strike leader Fred Makino.

[3]Bureau of Labor, *Report on Hawaii*, 1911, p. 8.

[4]U.S., Congress, House Committee on Immigration and Naturalization, 67th Congress, 1st Session, Joint Resolutions 158, 171, June 20–30, July 7, 1921; Part 1; and Part 2, July 22, 27, 29, and August 1–4, 10, 12, 1921, "Labor Problems in Hawaii."

[5]David Sturtevant, *Popular Uprisings in the Philippines, 1840–1850* (Ithaca: Cornell University Press, 1976) for examples of this type of organization; also *Voice of Labor,* June 17, 1937.

[6]Report of E. J. Eagen, NLRB investigator of Several 1937 labor complaints in Hawaii. His shocked and scathing report on the crudities of management posture in Hawaii was made public in the 1940 hearings of the NLRB. U.S., Congress, House Special Committee to Investigate the National Labor Relations Board. 76th Congress, 2nd and 3rd Sessions, December 11–23, 1940. Eagen Report, V. 22, pp. 4524–4539 and 4598–4624.

On the HIA, see ILWU Library in Honolulu, "Affidavit of R. F. Hykland," HIA agent assigned to William Bailey, editor, *Voice of Labor,* 1937 Puunene Strike File.

[7]Interview with Carl Damaso, President, Local 142, ILWU, Pacific Oral History Program. Also, *Honolulu Star Bulletin,* April 1, 1937. Eagen Report, p. 4616.

[8]*Honolulu Star Bulletin,* May 7 and 8, 1937.

[9]*Voice of Labor,* May 13, 1937.

[10]*Ibid.*

[11]*Honolulu Star Bulletin,* June 17, 1937.

[12]First Circuit Court Archives, Case No. 1996, Gr. 14288, 1937; copies of correspondence between William Lymer, special prosecutor, and county attorney T. A. Bevins indicated that they feared the effect of the trial on "locals." ILWU, 1937 Puunene Strike File.

[13]Eagen Report, p. 4600. Also, *Hawaii Hochi,* September 13, 1937.

[14]*Honolulu Star Bulletin,* September 10, 1937.

[15]Gavin Daws. *The Shoals of Time,* p. 359; and Lawrence H. Fuchs, *Hawaii Pono,* pp. 237–238; and interviews with Fred Low and Dan Haleamau. November 21, 1965. The latter two were charter members of the Hilo longshoremen's local (Pacific Oral History Program, University of Hawaii).

[16]Theon Wright, *The Disenchanged Isles* (1972), p. 85.

[17]NLRB, Case XX–C–55, George Pratt, Trial Examiner, August 14, 1937; also printed, in part, in *Honolulu Star Bulletin,* September 9, 10, 11, 13, 14, and 15, 1937. This report was edited, to remove material unfavorable to the companies.

[18]Interview with Fred Low, longshoreman, Pacific Oral History Program; *Honolulu Star Bulletin,* November 22, 1935.

[19]See *Honolulu Star Bulletin,* February 8, 1935, June 11, 1935 and August 19, 1935. "The experience of the Pacific coast ports is plain warning not to allow these professional agitators and alien seditionists from getting (sic) a foothold here," September 24, 1935; on September 26, 1935, an editorial discussed "Moscow influence" on the waterfront; October 12, 1935, "It was an evil day for the islands when they (seamen and longshoremen) descended on this port." A consistent effort to portray all union efforts as the work of outsiders carefully ignored local Hawaiian or Japanese.

[20]Charles Larrowe, *Harry Bridges* (1972), p. 53.

[21]ILWU, *The ILWU Story* (1962), p. 30; Larrowe, *op. cit.,* pp. 126–127.

[22]Executive Committee to Harry Bridges, 1/21/37, ILWU Archives, San Francisco.

[23]Local 137 Files, Petition and letter to Ryan, signed by fifty members, January 21, 1937.

[24]Local 137 Files; Telegrams, February 21, 24, 25, 26, 1937.

[25]ILWU, San Francisco, History Archives, Ryan to Executive Board, Pacific Coast District, February 20, 1937.

[26]Larrowe, *Harry Bridges,* pp. 119–131.

[27]*Honolulu Star Bulletin,* October 10, 1937.

[28]ILWU, San Francisco, Archives; Berman to Bridges, June 8, 1937.

[29]ILWU, San Francisco, Organizing, Hawaii: Kando Shibao to Meehan, July 10, 1937.

[30]ILWU, San Francisco, Bridges to Harry Kealoha, July 28, 1937.

[31]ILWU, Organizing Correspondence, 1937–43; Territorial Organizing Chairman to Bridges, September 23, 1937.

[32]*Ibid.*, Berman to Bridges, October 26, 1937.

[33]ILWU Local 136; Bulletin, C. Brewer and Co., Hilo Terminal and Transportation.

[34]Hawaii Education Association, Social Education Plans Committee, *The Interisland Strike*, May 26–September 17, 1938, p. 100; Territory of Hawaii, Attorney General, *Report on the Hilo Massacre of August 1, 1938*. Units of six unions in Hilo were directly involved in the demonstration: three units of ILWU, two Ladies Auxiliaries, United Auto Workers Local 586, United Laundry Workers, Hilo Transport Workers, and Hilo Quarry Workers international.

[35]Territory of Hawaii, Attorney General *Report*, pp. 34–40.

[36]*Honolulu Star Bulletin,* August 18, 1938.

[37]Hawaii Education Association, *The Interisland Strike*, pp. 149–50.

[38]Local 136 Files; C. Brewer and Co. to E. S. Eagen, May 5, 1937.

[39]*Hawaii Hochi,* September 30, 1937.

[40]*Kauai Garden Isle News,* October 12, 1937, December 7, 1937, and January 4, 1938.

[41]*Ibid.,* December 7, 1937, October 26, 1937.

[42]NLRB, McBryde Sugar Company, 1938, Unfair Labor Practice Charge, statement of Mauro Andaya, A. C. Wills, field examiners, ILWU Local No. 142 Files.

[43]*Ibid.*

[44]Emergency Board of Labor, Report to the governor of Frank Silva v. McBryde Sugar Company, August 10, 1940. The board concluded that constitutional rights were "but nothingness if an employer is permitted to visit punishment on employees for making his own choice on recreational matters...even serfs in medieval times had time which was their own choosing."

[45]ILWU, 3rd Biennial Convention, *Officers' Report.*

[46]Conference of Hawaiian Locals, ILWU, May 16–17, 1940, Local 142 Files, p. 1.

[47]Transcript, ILWU Conference, May 15, 1940, p. 4.

[48]Transcript, ILWU Conference, May 17, 1940, p. 7.

[49]*Honolulu Star Bulletin,* February 15, 1939.

[50]*Honolulu Star Bulletin,* October 7, 1940.

[51]*Star Bulletin,* November 8, 1940.

[52]*Star Bulletin,* January 13, 1941. Amendments by Congress extended the exemption of agricultural workers on January 1, 1940. However, this did not change the Territorial Unemployment Act as to the definition of industrial and agricultural workers.

[53]Jack Kawana to Matt Meehan, January 1, 1941, ILWU, Hawaii Local 137, 1937–1945.

[54]Clifford O'Brien to Harry Bridges, April 15, 1941, ILWU Correspondence.

[55]O'Brien to Bridges, December 23, 1941.

[56]*Ibid.*

[57]O'Brien to Bridges, May 20, 1941.

[58]O'Brien to Bridges and Meehan, June 9, 1940.

[59]Ichiro Izuka to Harry Bridges, July 28, 1941; Harry Kamoku to Harry Bridges, August 4, 1941.

[60]O'Brien to Bridges, August 5, 1941; O'Brien to Robertson, September 12, 1941.

[61]O'Brien to Bridges, September 20, 1941.

[62]O'Brien to Bridges, October 8, 1941.

[63]O'Brien to Bridges, November 4, 1941.

[64]*The Herald* (formerly the *Kauai Herald),* December 1, 1941.

[65]Gwenfread Allen, *Hawaii's War Years* (1950), pp. 310–311.

[66]*Ibid.*

[67]Interview with Frank Thompson, Pacific Oral History Program: also, Goldblatt to Hall, July 26, 1944.

[68]Hall to Goldblatt, July 26, 1944.

[69]NLRB, In the Matter of Pepeekeo Sugar Co., et al., *Reports*, Vol. 59 pp. 1532 ff.

[70]Goldblatt to Hall, December 29, 1944.

[71]Goldblatt to Thompson, November 14, 1944.

[72]Frank Thompson, Report to Executive Board, November 1, 1945.

[73]Thompson to Goldblatt, December 28, 1945.

[74]Interview with K. O. and Y. A., Pacific Oral History Program.

[75]Goldblatt to Hall, December 7, 1945.

[76]Territorial Wage Conference, July 10, 1946.

[77]Hall to Goldblatt, July 26, 1944.

[78]Petition to L. M. Walling, Administrator, Wage and Hour and Public Contract Division, Department of Labor, ILWU Local 142 Files, July 24, 1944.

[79]Report to Executive Board on FLSA negotiations with the HSPA, Goldblatt, January, 1945.

[80]Strike Strategy Committee Reports, August–November 1946.

[81]Hilo Sugar Company, Instructions to Supervisors, July 1946, ILWU Local 142 Files.

[82]Local 142, Unit 12, August 30, 1946.

[83]See Paul Brissenden, "The Three Clauses in Hawaiian Labor Agreements," *Political Science Quarterly,* March 1953, pp. 89–108.

[84]These clauses have never had the crippling effect they were intended to have. All discharges were pursued by the union with full vigor and effectiveness. For example, when a driver was dismissed in 1948 for alleged drunken driving of a company vehicle, the union representative was able to get the charges dismissed by showing a lack of evidence and prejudiced testimony. As a further example of the somewhat meaningless nature of the clauses, management conducted a sixty-nine day lockout at Olaa Plantation, terming it a union strike. Interviews with Jack Hall and Chester Meske, Pacific Oral History Program.

[85]*Honolulu Star Bulletin,* November 4, 1946.

Farm Labor:
New Forks in Old Trails

Arthur Carstens

WHO WILL GROW THE FOOD AND FIBERS needed to feed and clothe the millions of Americans and persons in other lands? Who will control the land on which these products are grown? What must be done to enable those persons who work in the fields to share more equitably in the benefits of our social and economic system? Must field workers who plant and harvest our crops remain at the bottom rung of our social and economic ladder? This is what our present farm labor problem is all about.

These questions have been asked since the first settlers arrived in America 400 years ago. New England settlers agreed that the welfare of their communities depended upon ownership of individual plots of land, to be tilled by the owners and their families. Celebrating the bicentennial of the landing of the Pilgrims, Daniel Webster drew these conclusions:

> Our New England ancestors were nearly on a general level with respect to property. Their situation demanded the parcelling out and division of land and it may be said fairly that this necessary act fixed the future frame of our government. The consequence has been a great subdivision of the soil and a great equality of condition; the true basis most certainly of popular government.

A century later the head of the Wisconsin State Historical Society defined the prevailing rural character in these terms:

> Study reveals Agriculture as one of the main supports of American Democracy because it is an occupation embracing millions of free men who own property and cultivate land on a somewhat equal basis.

> A farm represents a 'living' but neither an actual or potential modern fortune. The family-size farm is the American ideal that means in effect that the owner and his son or sons can perform the actual work. Hired men are the exception rather than the rule.

[142]

This view of how agricultural enterprise should be operated contrasted sharply with the view held in the South. Large plantations rather than family farms came to dominate the southern states. Plantations produced commodities such as tobacco and cotton for export rather than food and fiber for the farm family or for local markets. Plantations were worked by slave laborers, often belonging to absentee masters.

South Carolina's Senator Hammond gave Congress the southern view of the role of the plantation system in the early 1880s:

> In all social systems there must be a class to do the mean duties, to perform the drudgery of life. It is a class requiring but a low level of intellect and but little skill. Its requisites are vigor, docility, fidelity. Such a class you must have, or you would not have that other class which leads progress, refinement, civilization.

In California, even before the Civil War, a third form of man's relation to land was being laid down. At the conclusion of the war with Mexico, a variant of the south's plantation appeared in California. Slave labor was rejected, but a pattern of concentrated land ownership and dependence upon landless laborers was established.

In 1854, the "California Farmer" expressed the prospect in these words:

> California is destined to become a large grower of cotton, rice, tobacco, sugar, tea, and coffee, and where will the laborers be found? Americans will not become the workingmen of our rice and cotton plantations. In the South this is the work of the slave, but California is a free state. Then where shall the laborers be found? The Chinese ... that population educated and schooled and drilled in the cultivation of these products are to be to California what the African has been to the South. This is the decree of the Almighty and man cannot stop it.

Although all three forms of land control and ownership continued to exist, support for the family farm gained increasing support. In response to popular pressure, Congress passed the Homestead Act in 1862:

> an Act that would enable settlers to acquire 160 acres free from all charges except a minor filing fee. To insure permanency of settlement the Act specified that before title to the land was gained, the individual must live on the homestead for five years.

The Homestead Act was a legislative first of its kind, and not all the difficulties that would confront homesteaders could be foreseen. Flaws in the act and its administration, for example, allowed individual speculators and companies to acquire vast tracts. But as a result of the act, farm tenancy grew from 26 percent in 1880 to 43 percent in 1935.

Congress became concerned over the substantial number of homesteaders who lost or gave up their homesteads and, after extended hearings, it concluded that a National Reclamation Act, to provide water to family farms, would enable many homesteaders to hold on to their land. Consequently, the Reclamation Act of 1902 was passed. The act specifies simply:

> No right to the use of water for land in private ownership shall be sold to a tract exceeding 160 acres to any one landowner, and no such sale shall be made to any one landowner unless he be a bona fide resident on such land, or occupant thereof residing in the neighborhood of said land.

Congressman Newlands, a supporter of the act, remarked:

> Lord Macauley said that we would never experience the test of our institutions until the public domain was exhausted and an increased population engaged in a contest for ownership. The very purpose of this bill is to guard against land monopoly and to hold this land in small tracts for the people of the entire country.

> Convey this land to private corporations and doubtless this work will be done, but we would have fastened on this country all the evils of land monopoly which produced the great French revolution and which caused the revolt against the church monopoly in South America and in recent times the outbreak of Filipinos against Spanish authority.

In the three-quarters of a century since the Reclamation Act was passed, the drift toward concentration of land ownership continues. A million family-sized farms were consolidated out of existence during the 1950s and another million met the same fate during the 1960s. In addition, it is estimated that one smalltown businessman goes under for every six family farmers who quit their farms. Credit regulations, marketing orders, and subsidy legislation have combined to frustrate the goals of the Homestead and Reclamation acts.

As farms increased in size, there was a need for workers to plant and harvest crops. Growers first turned to Chinese immigrants, who became available in large numbers once the railroads were completed. In 1870, Chinese workers made up one-tenth of the farm labor supply, and, by 1884, Chinese people constituted more than one-half of California's field workers. Mass unemployment during the 1880s, plus the exploitation of Chinese workers, led to the growth of the anti-Chinese movement, and Congress passed a Chinese Exclusion Act.

The depression of the 1880s and 1890s drove more and more "white" workers to the farms as laborers. When these white workers launched an organizational attack that promised some favorable results, thousands of Japanese workers joined also. Japanese immigration was halted in 1908, but shortly thereafter, 9,000 Hindus were allowed into the country to work on farms.

The discontent of farm workers increased and reached its climax with the Wheatland Riot of 1913, a landmark in California labor history. About 3,000 workers had been recruited by the owners of the Ralph Durst hop farm, but conditions were so bad that the workers drew up a few demands, including fresh drinking water twice a day, one toilet for every hundred workers, and separate toilets for men and women. They also asked for higher piece rates. When these demands were presented to the owner, he struck the spokesman for the grievance committee across the face. A riot followed; two workers were killed along with a deputy and the district attorney. Many persons were injured by club-swinging deputies. The riot initiated a period of violent repression of workers and set back by a decade the organizational efforts of farm workers.

Between 1920 and 1930, the number of Mexicans in California increased by 400 percent, and, at the close of the decade, more than 75,000 Mexicans were working on California farms. Fearful that the Mexican migration might be stopped, growers began to import large numbers of Filipinos also, 30,000 of whom arrived in California by 1930. Auto immigrants from the East—predecessors of the *Grapes of Wrath* legions—also began arriving. These were the small farmers who had lost their midwestern farms. Organizational efforts were now halted completely, because the farm labor market was glutted.

In the early 1930s, the nation again was made aware of the plight of the farm worker. In 1933–34, ninety-nine strikes involving 87,000 farm workers occurred in the United States. Forty-nine of these strikes involving 68,000 workers took place in California. Citizens became aware that the hired man was not just another member of the family, and learned that the family farm was in decay and was rapidly being displaced by industrial agriculture. By 1929, there were 7,900 of these industrial farms, 2,900 of them in California. Farming in California had become a business, not a way of life.

The New Deal triggered a farm revolt. Deeply rooted economic, social, and racial resentments were compounded by the discriminatory nature of the new legislation. The National Recovery Act and the Agricultural Adjustment Act encouraged the organization of businessmen, urban labor, and farmers to improve their lots.

But farm workers were excluded from both programs and were provided only such help as they could find in government-supported transient camps.

Pickers in the cranberry bogs of Cape Cod walked out in 1933, and onion workers in Ohio struck. In New Jersey, Agricultural and Cannery workers struck Seabrook Farms—a huge integrated farm factory. Citrus workers struck in Florida. But farm-labor unrest reached a high point in California. Under the leadership of the Cannery and Agricultural Workers Union, 1,000 pear pickers struck in Santa Clara County, and later, this union led a cotton strike in the Fresno area in which 10,000 workers took part.

The farm strikers received very little help from New Deal sources. Instead, the president focused his attention on the plight of the small farmer, organizing the Rural Resettlement Agency for the purpose of grubstaking impoverished farm families until they achieved self sufficiency. Although this program appeared to be entirely consistent with the traditional view of the virtues of the American family farm, it proved to be the New Deal's most controversial program as it threatened the corporate farm. Even though thousands of families benefitted, the program was terminated, and support programs designed to help small farmers were redesigned to provide subsidies for corporate farm enterprises.

In the late thirties, the attention of the country was again turned to war, and labor gluts turned into labor shortages. Thousands of additional Mexican workers were recruited to fill places in the fields, left vacant by workers who moved to the cities or by the forceful evacuation of the Japanese interned in wartime camps. When the war ended, growers continued to recruit Mexican workers, and, when the Mexican government expressed concern over wages paid and working conditions provided, the United States simply opened the borders and allowed large number of workers to enter, in violation of Public Law 68 which defined the rights of the braceros.

In the years that followed, the administration of worker immigration was transferred from department to department. Although regulations gave Mexican workers the right to organize, the Department of Labor advised them to take their grievances to their employers. Growers posted signs telling workers it was illegal to strike.

Beginning in the late 1950s, the regulations and practices involved in the importation and use of Mexican workers came under closer scrutiny. "We must," said Congressman Teague, "make our program more respectable." Congress refused to extend Public Law 68, which formed the basis of the importation regulations, and a new era of work relations began.

With the termination of the law, the threat of large numbers of newly imported workers was greatly reduced. As the work force became stabilized, farm workers began to turn their attention to means of improving their economic and social status. The freedom rides of 1961, the march on Washington when Dr. Martin Luther King delivered his history-making speech "I Have a Dream," the arrival of large numbers of concerned young people in Mississippi—all served to remind farm workers and community leaders of the growing flood of discontent that was developing among many groups.

Established unions once more began to send organizers into the fields. Paul Schrade and Roy Reuther from the Auto Workers met with Cesar Chávez, whose leadership capacities were beginning to receive national recognition. William Kircher, National Director of Organization for the AFL–CIO was assigned to help. Representatives of the longshoremen's union also appeared (the teamsters had already established themselves), as did Communist organizers.

In September, 1962, in Fresno, California, Cesar Chávez founded the National Farm Workers Association. His hope was to organize workers one by one without a contract, until the union became strong. Chávez was more concerned about building a movement than an organization, but his approach worried many traditionally minded organizers who had grown accustomed to formal structures.

The union began to grow. The first strike was held in 1965 on a rose farm but was lost. Then came the well-known grape strikes, during which Mexican and Filipino workers joined hands. In October, 1965, the union initiated a boycott of grapes, and, with the help of student activists and other volunteers, began to picket stores and piers. Gradually, the union began winning contracts, and, in the late 1960s, won its strike against the DeGiorgio Company and also won a representation fight with the teamsters.

The effort to build an effective union continued. As growers began to recognize that they could no longer thwart union organization, they turned to the teamsters with whom they preferred to negotiate. An intensive jurisdiction fight began, but the boycott, the series of cross-country marches, and the active support of clergymen and civil rights activists all helped the union to survive and grow.

In 1974, Jerry Brown became governor of California. Chávez had already determined that some form of legislation was needed, and he requested his attorney, Jerry Cohen, to draw up a list of issues to be considered in a proposed farm-worker law. At a Sacramento rally, with 20,000 farm workers persent, Chávez stressed the need for a strong law. Brown agreed and ordered his staff to draft the necessary legislation. But when the first draft was made public, Chávez was shocked and rejected it as totally inadequate. In an interview with Jacques Levy, Chávez is quoted as follows:

> The Governor began to ask, 'What's wrong with this, Chávez?' and we began to negotiate. Jerry Cohen talked with Leroy Chatfield who talked directly to the Governor. Jerry has a brilliant mind. He's got a really good way of getting the most complicated legal stuff and either complicating it beyond any hope, if it needs to be done, or just going to the core and explaining it very simply. And he was at his best because it was negotiating over legal language.
>
> There were some very hectic all night meetings. We compromised as much as we could. Finally we said, 'This is the minimum we will accept.'
>
> The compromise would set up a five-man board to run secret elections. It would permit the largest number of people to vote, requiring elections to be held at the peak of the season so that migrants could vote. It was geared so that elections would be held quickly, so that we wouldn't get caught waiting for an election for two or three months, until everyone was gone. It would permit workers to vote on preexisting teamster contracts and set up voting on the basis of all the workers on a ranch instead of by crafts. It also dealt with unfair labor practices, guaranteeing that a worker could not be fired because he openly declared himself for one union rather than another. And it prevented an employer from telling a worker that if he didn't vote for the teamsters he was going to get fired. It also permitted strikers to vote.
>
> We gave up some of our rights to the boycott, but we insisted on the right to the primary boycott, and—if we won an election—the right to ask people not to shop at a store selling a product from a grower where we had won an election. That meant that if we won an election and the grower would not sign a contract, we would have the right to bring economic pressure to him.
>
> About 7 P.M. a call came from Jerry who told me the governor is getting together all the agribusiness here in Sacramento. They've agreed to the proposal. But they have some preconditions. I found out that the growers would agree to accept the compromise provided we did two things—that we agreed that nothing should be changed, not even a period, and that they would hear me personally that we were supporting it.
>
> So when they got the phone hooked up to the loudspeaker in the governor's office, Governor Brown got the growers one by one to identify themselves and state publicly that they were for the bill.
>
> Jerry tells me that the growers were sitting at the table when the governor asked me if I would support the bill, they all moved out to the edge of their seats, looking at the loudspeaker. And when I said, 'Very definitely,' they all broke into smiles and applauded.

Allan Grant, the president of the California Farm Bureau and an active participant in drafting the act, also described his experience to Levy.

We were trying for twelve years to get farm labor legislation. I started working on this before Governor Reagan was elected. Therefore, we were pleased that Governor Brown saw fit to work so hard on it. He could do some things that the former governor couldn't because he is a Democrat and he had a Democratic legislature.

All the farm organizations supported the governor's bill with the exception of one or two. The boycott was the only minor reason. It did affect us. It put a lot of grape growers out of business and it had some effect on lettuce. But more important was the violence that took place, the property destruction and the very strong antipathy felt between the two unions.

The growers had gotten along with unions for several years and they are just the same as any other employer. They could adjust to whatever situation came along, and the cost would be passed on to the consumer.

Governor Brown added these comments:

When the amended bill was heard in committee, there was opposition from the teamsters, the building trades and the packinghouse workers. So it was just a matter of resolving all three in such a way as to keep the growers and Chávez also supporting the bill. On the day of the next senate committee hearing, May 19th, Jack Henning, head of the state AFL–CIO, called. I invited him in and he brought Jimmy Lee of the building trades. I saw his amendments. I already had Rose Bird draft some alternate ones.

By this time it was 1 P.M. and we were still trying to get the votes. Three senators wouldn't commit themselves one way or the other; so it was unclear how the vote would go unless we could get the support of the building trades and the teamsters. The bill was scheduled to be heard at 1:30 P.M. We invited the teamsters down, then the growers, then everyone involved. I had Henning and Lee in my office with Rose and my staff. Jerry Cohen was down at the other end of the room. The teamsters were in another office, the Farm Bureau and the Agricultural Council in a second and the Western Growers in a third. The negotiations kept going and we postponed the committee.

We solved the teamster problem and the packinghouse workers problem, but it was about 6:30 P.M. before we finally got an amendment satisfactory to both the building trades and Cesar Chávez.

We had just gotten notice that the senate hearing was about to adjourn the hearing for another week. So Rose Bird, under some very trying circumstances, wrote some language that was taken from section 8(e) of the National Labor Relations Act. That did it. The bill was endorsed by all parties and passed the committee unanimously that night.

We got what appears to be a solution. I think the bill is a reasonable bill. I think it has the economic tools that the unions need and are reasonable in light of American history. In my judgment the bill sets a model for the entire country.

Precisely what benefits and obligations were included in the Agricultural Labor Relations Act of 1975? Prior to the acceptance of the act, California allowed employees to freely designate a representative for purposes of collective bargaining. But the California Supreme Court had also reasserted the long-recognized rule that determination by management to bargain should be left free to the interaction of free economic forces. From time to time, economic forces were assisted by local sheriffs and district attorneys. The primary goal of the ALRA (Agricultural Labor Relations Act) was to insure peace in agricultural fields and to bring stability to labor relations. The act specified that the ALRB was created to:

    a. conduct elections to determine what union should represent a given group of farm workers.
    b. investigate unfair labor practices.
    c. determine appropriate bargaining units.
    d. perform other duties delegated to its appointed members.

The ALRA is a pioneering piece of legislation and therefore it is important to understand the problems that have been confronted in the efforts to implement it.

Determining the Majority Representative

The first step in the collective bargaining process is to determine who will represent employees. The act specifies that the organization to be designated as the majority's choice pursuant to a secret election shall be the certified representative for purposes of bargaining.
Because of the highly seasonal nature of farm employment, it is necessary to conduct elections quickly. The act specifies that this must be done within seven days of the filing of a petition. The use of authorization cards (permitted by NLRB) to show majority status is forbidden by ALRA.

Timing of the Election

Under ALRA, the union requesting an election must allege that the number of persons currently employed is not less than fifty percent of the employer's peak agricultural employment. To insure that the election is in fact held during this critical period, the board is required to hold the election within a maximum of seven days. Once a union is certified, another election may not be directed for twelve months.

Contracts Currently Existing—No Bar to an Election

The ALRA provides that no collective bargaining agreement executed prior to the effective date of the act shall bar a petition for an election. Agreements arrived at prior to the act are not automatically cancelled but become void upon ALRA's certification of an election. The effect of this provision is that some 400 teamster contracts existing at the effective date of the act are subject to voidability.

Elimination of the "Sweetheart" contracts

ALRA also specifies that it is an unfair labor practice for an employer to enter into a collective bargaining agreement with a labor organization not certified pursuant to a secret bargaining election.

The Secondary Boycott

The secondary boycott is one of the concerted forms of action utilized by labor to enforce an objective. It is a tool used to induce one employer to stop doing business with an employer with whom the union has a dispute. Through utilization of the secondary boycott a labor organization may prevent delivery of goods to a secondary employer, may discourage consumer buying of the primary employer's goods, or may discourage all consumer trading with a secondary employer.

The ALRA prohibits the harshest form of boycott, stopping delivery of goods from a primary to a secondary employer, but it permits a consumer boycott that includes the boycotting of a particular product handled in the store and it also permits efforts by the union to discourage the public from all trading with a store. This type of boycott can only be carried on by the union when it has already won an election and uses the boycott to secure demanded terms of a bargaining agreement.

The Appropriate Bargaining Unit

The ALRA provides that the bargaining unit shall be comprised of all farm employees and that the board may determine the appropriate unit where an employer operates two or more noncontiguous farms. Construction workers are specifically excluded from the bargaining unit but the act requires the board to include machine operators and truck drivers.

Union Security

There are various union-management arrangements relating to employee membership in a given union. Although California law recognizes a closed shop arrangement which requires an employer to hire only members of a given union, the ALRA prohibits the closed shop. Instead it approves a new form of union shop which allows a collective bargaining agreement that may require, as a condition of employment, membership in the certified union within five days of hiring. During harvest seasons, migrant farm workers may work for many farmers within short spans of time. For the protection of migrant workers, the ALRA also provides that no workers shall be required to pay dues more than once a month.

The Access Rule

The United States Supreme Court has stated: Organization rights are not viable in a vacuum. Their effectiveness depends in some measure on the ability of employees to learn the advantages and disadvantages of organization from others. When alternative channels of effective communication are not available to a union, organizational rights must include a limited right to approach employees on the property of the employer. Under such circumstances, both statutory and constitutional principles require that a reasonable and just accommodation be made between the right of unions to access and the legitimate property and business interest of the employer.

With these Supreme Court guidelines in mind, the board of the ALRA issued the following guidelines:

A. Access onto an agricultural employer's property shall be available to any one labor organization for no more than four thirty-day periods in any calendar year.

B. Each thirty-day period shall commence when the labor organization files in an appropriate regional office two copies of a written notice of intention to take access onto the described property of an agricultural employer, together with proof of service of a copy of the written notice upon the employer.
   If a petition for election is filed, the right of access shall continue until after the election. If a runoff or rerun is required, the right of access shall continue until after the said election.

C. Access shall be limited to two organizers for each work crew provided that if there are more than thirty workers there may be one additional organizer for every fifteen workers.

D. Upon request, the organizers shall identify themselves by name and labor organization.

E. The right of access shall not include conduct disruptive to the employer's property or operations.

In the six months following the enactment of the Agricultural Labor Relations Act, over 400 union representation elections were held. Because of the large number of elections and the challenges and counter-challenges that followed each vote, the ALRA ran out of funds before the close of the fiscal year. The legislature demanded some basic changes in the act before it would provide more funds. The governor refused to comply, and the ALRA closed its doors from March, 1976, when all its money was spent, to July, 1976, when the new fiscal year began.

In an attempt at self-protection, the farm workers submitted to Proposition 14, and when it became evident that this proposition had received enough public support to be placed on the November ballot, the legislature included funding for the board in its budget.

Proposition 14 proposed these changes:

a. required that a new board be appointed.

b. made provisions for access to the field by union organizers for short periods of time before and after work and during lunch breaks.

c. required employers to furnish lists of employees on the payroll to ALRA so that determination could be made of voter eligibility.

d. allowed the board to order payment of treble damages as a penalty for unfair labor practices.

e. increased the number of signatures needed for decertification from thirty to fifty percent.

f. directed the legislature to appropriate funds to permit the board to carry out its functions.

Proposition 14 was defeated in the November election, although, as a result of the election, the board possibly had more legislative support than it did during the previous term. Opposition to Proposition 14 was generated in part by huge corporate contributions, as well as an unfavorable reaction of many citizen to a series of strikes in San Francisco and Los Angeles. Ironically, many citizens who still viewed agriculture in terms of small farms were swayed by the television commercials paid for by corporations, which presented an elderly couple peering anxiously and nervously through their picture window at the approach of a "union type goon" trampling through their rose garden.

A union is only a tool that can serve many purposes, which includes meeting the important bread and butter demands of its members. The farm workers' union, as of 1980, had not yet defined the boundaries of its concerns. Whether it will remain a union that can be joined by anyone or, like many unions, will require workers to be hired before considering them eligible for membership, remains an open question. It is possible that a court decision will result in the division of vast western landholdings into 160 acre tracts. How will the union relate to such efforts to encourage the growth of family farms? Should the union place limits on land ownership? Should it provide better credit? And must farm workers remain migrants? With the availability of air transport and speedy communication, cannot the union meet sudden seasonal needs in the same way that it provides forest-fire fighters? Can the farm-workers' unions follow the example of the longshore industry and provide a degree of income, health, and safety security for its members? How?

IV

Mexican Labor, North and South of the Border

Mexican Labor and the
American Southwest

There is a verse about midway in Ralph Chaplin's *Solidarity Forever* which goes:

> It is we who plowed the prairies; built the cities where they trade:
> Dug the mines and built the workshops: endless miles of railroad
> laid. Now we stand outcast and starving midst the wonders we
> have made: But the union makes us strong...

In a few lines, it seems to sum up the tale of Mexican labor during the last half century. Unrestricted immigration filled the Southwest with hardworking Mexicans, fleeing the economic crises which accompanied the Mexican Revolution, hardworking immigrants who soon became the major labor force in the mines, the fields, and many factories. Yet, Mexican labor was an unorganized entity. For fifty years, Mexican workers had to put up with a Mexican scale, or simply low wages, until the United Farm Workers, the International Union of Mine, Mill, and Smelter Workers, and the Amalgamated Clothing and Textile Workers came along. The last decade has seen Mexican unions become the cutting edge of the southwest labor movement. However, the story of the last decade has roots which predate even the Mexican Revolution.

While the first recorded Mexican farm-workers' strike did not occur until 1930, Mexican unionists had organized south of the border well before the turn of the century. Various mutual aid societies had arisen in several trades during the 1860s, and these proto-unions kept alive the spirit of labor throughout the regime of Porfirio Díaz. Yet, while workers north of the border flocked to the Knights of Labor or the American Federation of Labor, there was no comparable labor federation in Mexico itself. The event which did most to focus attention on Mexican workers on both sides of the border was the great mining confrontation at Cananea, Sonora, in 1906.

Much has been written about the Cananea strike, a strike which had profound effects on labor, the mining Southwest, and Mexican politics. In simplest terms, Cananea was a strike against Colonel William C. Green's tiny mining empire which had been set up with the aid of Porfirio Díaz. As a strong booster of outside investment, Díaz had won Greene's Sonoran enterprise with a host of incentives, which were paid despite the fact that Greene openly discriminated against Mexican miners. American miners working side by side with the Mexicans received up to three times their pay for identical work. This neatly played into the hands of the Flores Magón brothers, the three syndicalists who had been publishing the anti-Díaz *Regeneración* since 1900. The Flores Magóns had been trying desperately to harness Mexico's anticlerical forces into a broad anti-Díaz coalition, such as their Partido Liberal, without much success. Then came Cananea with proven ties between anti-Mexican discrimination (working class discrimination) and the Díaz regime; as the strike continued in early June, 1906, these ties became even more evident.[1]

The strike itself began on June 1, when Mexican miners demanded an end to the iniquitous "Mexican scale." Greene's immediate reaction was to view the strike as a riot, with widespread threat to life, limb, and property. He was convinced that the Mexican army was incapable of handling the situation, and he was equally convinced that the Western Federation of Miners was behind the whole affair. He proved to be wrong in both assumptions, although the WFM did try to support the Cananea strikers with limited funds and the presence of Mother Jones. However, he was not proven wrong until he and his supporters created an international incident in Sonora.

The incident would later prove to be almost as famous as the strike. On June 2, Greene asked for the aid of the Arizona Rangers, an armed force which was particularly adept at breaking strikes. Walter Douglas of Phelps Dodge had, in turn, agreed to arm the rangers—free of charge—from the stores of the Phelps Dodge Mercantile Company in Bisbee. Colonel Thomas Rynning of the rangers did his part by dredging up an old agreement which allowed the Arizona force to cross the border in cases of "hot pursuit." Admittedly, breaking a strike more than fifty miles from the border could hardly be considered "hot pursuit" of a criminal, but Americans had become quite accustomed to treating the border in a cavalier manner during the Díaz regime. Only the patent embarrassment of Sonoran governor, Rafael Yzable, gave the affair some legitimacy. Rather than let the rangers cross into Sonora unimpeded, Yzabel had agreed to swear the entire contingent into the Mexican Army as volunteers. Thus, the amenities were observed and the rangers proceeded on to Cananea. Their stay there would be short-lived.

No sooner had Rynning and his Americans arrived on the scene than out of the blue came Colonel Emilio Kosterlitsky and a force of tough Mexican *rurales*. Kosterlitsky demanded the immediate with-drawal of Rynning's group. Rynning, who had often spoken of his deep admiration for Kosterlitsky, complied. The strike died within a few weeks.[2] Yet, an incident had occurred which gave major impetus to the Flores Magóns, the Partido Liberal, and *Regeneración*. In July, 1906, the Partido Liberal set forth an official program at a meeting in St. Louis, which would be closely followed eleven years later in the constitution of 1917.[3] Mexico's labor movement had begun to come of age.

Mexican labor would continue to mature over the next few years. While the liberals tried to ally themselves with Emiliano Zapata, other strikes and forces pushed Mexican labor in a different direction. The Flores Magóns continued to move their labor allies in an anarcho-syndicalist direction, which naturally led north of the border to an alliance with the WFM and the IWW. It also lead eventually to an abortive revolution in Baja during 1911, when Joe Hill, Jack Mosby, and other famous wobblies joined the liberal ranks. Jack London even hosted a Los Angeles rally for the Baja warriors, but it was all in vain. The Flores Magón and their *magonistas* were doomed to lose, and Ricardo Flores Magón would die in the perpetual dark of blindness eleven years later in America's Fort Leavenworth. Writing from his cell, he noted bitterly, "My comrades are generals, governors, even presidents...rich, famous...while I am poor, unknown sick... branded as a felon....But my old comrades were practical men while I am a dreamer, which I prefer to be."[4] As the revolution died in Baja, its northern support died as well. Eugene Debs, carefully cultivated by the Flores Magóns, found the *magonista* constitution too impractical and too anarchistic. The *Appeal to Reason,* which had kept the faith during much of the revolution, turned away from the Mexican dreamers. Victor Berger, the American socialist, issued a statement which condemned the rebels as antisocialist.[5] Mosby would die mys-teriously, Hill would be shot in Utah, and Ricardo died in prison. They were all noble losers.

The first two papers in this section debate just this point: were the Flores Magóns indeed nothing but noble losers? John Hart, an expert on the syndicalist movement in Mexico, writes a rather forceful de-fense of the *magonistas* and other members of the Partido Liberal Mexicano, placing them in a historical line of labor development which can be traced back to the 1860s. Rodney Anderson, on the other hand, dismisses the entire *magonista* period as nothing but the glorious posturings of intriguing romantics. The two authors are par-ticularly at odds over the issue of the Río Blanco strike of 1907. Yet, regardless of the debate, the significance of Mexican labor does not end south of the border but continues to be an issue in the American Southwest.

What transformed Mexican labor from a national issue into an international question? First, the seven years of revolution, 1910–1917, did little to protect an already endangered Mexican economy. One of the issues at Cananea had been the eroding worth of the Mexican miners' pay in pesos. Inflation became an ever increasing problem in the period after 1907, a problem which Díaz was never able to solve. The political and military turmoil which came after Díaz made the situation ever worse. Thousands of Mexican workers looked north to the United States for a haven against a broken economy and constant danger. By 1920, California and the Southwest had absorbed some 300,000 Mexican immigrants, and more continued to come. If the problems of revolution were the prime reasons for northern movement, the economic maturation of the American Southwest was a close second. The opening of new mines, new agricultural areas, and new factories meant that the Southwest could take in the new immigrants without serious consequences. Many employers looked upon the lower wage scale of Mexican labor as the silver lining of the immigrant cloud.

By the 1920s, Mexican immigrants had become the major ethnic group in Arizona and New Mexico mines, California fields, and even in Chicago sweatshops. The southwestern implications of the demographic trend were not lost on organized labor. Unfortunately, the nationwide impotence of unions in the decade of the "American Plan" rendered them unable to take advantage of the situation. That impotency would end with the coming of the New Deal, the National Industrial Recovery Act, and the 1935 National Labor Relations Act. By 1937–1938, the unions were well into a major Mexican organizing drive.

In the Southwest, the Mexican drive would be most marked in the efforts of the International Union of Mine, Mill, and Smelter Workers (partially explained in section one) and the various CIO unions that tried to organize California's pickers. The latter effort was not successful, but the Mine-Mill became the champion of Mexican rights in many a miner's heart. As Ernesto Verdugo, a veteran of the Mine-Mill organizing drive at Ray, Arizona, recalled, "They may have called our little union Communist, but it sure fought for us."[6] Mine-Mill's fight brought new locals into the fold in Ray, Globe, and Morenci, Arizona (all old WFM camps), as well as in previously unorganized mines in New Mexico. Part of the Communist Party line at the time was an attack upon racism (as in the Scottsboro boys case), and the IUMMSW concentration upon Mexican miners fit right into such a political push. However, the real success of the Mine-Mill among Mexican workers would not come until the later 1940s and early 1950s, a period which corresponded to the rise of Reid Robinson in the IUMMSW organization. Robinson, originally a strong anti-Communist from Butte, began to moderate his stand against left-wing elements in the IUMMSW when he was elevated to the vice presidency in 1940. It may have been coincidence, but as the Mine-Mill turned left, it also turned to Mexican miners.[7]

There were a great number of issues which helped the IUMMSW in its Mexican drive. Kennecott, for instance, still used a modified Mexican scale in its Ray operation, and the IUMMSW fought long and hard against it. A number of New Mexico operations simply paid miners working in Mexican-dominated mines less than those working in similar Anglo-dominated places. Such a policy was used to keep the wages of all miners low, with the implied threat that Mexican wages would come to Anglo operations if union demands seemed excessive. The Mine-Mill finally faced this situation in the famed Silver City, New Mexico, strike of the fifties, which became the basis for the film, *Salt of the Earth*. The Silver City victory which broke the Mexican scale once and for all gave the IUMMSW its last breath of life in the Southwest. Unfortunately, as the first essay in this section explains, it was a case of too little too late. Mine-Mill and its Mexican miners would be swallowed by the United Steelworkers in 1967.

While the IUMMSW met with some success in organizing Mexican miners, few of the farm workers' organizations had any success until the mid-1960s. The *bracero* master contract forbade the use of Mexican aliens as strikebreakers, evidence showing that *braceros* broke the NFLU Di Giorgio strike of the 1940s and proved an insurmountable obstacle to the United Packinghouse Workers when they tried to organize farm workers in the 1950s. The farm-labor drive slowed to a walk in the 1950s as the UPWA and others (particularly Ernesto Galarza of the old NFLU) campaigned against the Bracero Program. Even the AFL–CIO's massive attempt to organize pickers under the banner of the Agricultural Workers Organizing Committee came to naught during the *bracero* era. Obviously, labor had not learned the lesson that the key to Mexican labor in the states was to be found south of the border. That lesson was made manifest in 1964, when Public Law 78 (the *bracero* law) was repealed.[8]

The final essay in this section deals with the problems of the Bracero Program and Mexican migrants, from a Mexican and Marxist perspective. Professor Maciel questions American policy over the past half century as merely a capitalist exploitation of workers. The paper points out an important fact: that the solution to the problem lies with organized labor. Only when organized labor becomes aware of both the northern and southern facets of the problem will a solution be found.

Current evidence points to labor's slow realization that the Mexican problem cannot be solved by repealing Public Law 78 and marching to Sacramento. While Cesar Chávez and the United Farm Workers did quite well during the late 1960s and early 1970s, progress slowed with the upsurge in illegal immigration in the late 1970s. The AFL–CIO's answer to the problem of immigration had always been the enactment of a law forcing harsh penalties on the employers of illegals. Such a law had little chance of passage in the late 1970s and probably has less chance in the 1980s. However, some farm-worker organizers saw salvation in a different light. Why not, they asked, organize the illegals before they cross the border? The plan was bold, but, in one case, it worked.

In the end, the problem of Mexican labor in the 1980s is quite similar to the problem confronted by IWW organizers during the teens. Mexican workers labor for wages on boths sides of the border, and only the union that recognizes that fact will make headway against the illegal tide of the future. As long as the Southwest has the jobs and the Mexican north has substantial unemployment, illegal immigration will be a fact of life.

NOTES

[1]Victor Alba, *Politics and the Labor Movement in Latin America* (Palo Alto: Stanford University Press, 1968), pp. 52–55.

[2]Charles Douglas Hill, "The Arizona Rangers: Frontier Law and Order in the Twentieth Century," Unpublished M.A. Thesis, Arizona State University, 1977, pp. 71–95.

[3]Alba, *Politics,* pp. 52–55.

[4]William W. Johnson, *Heroic Mexico* (New York: Doubleday and Company, 1968), p. 365.

[5]Lowell L. Blaisdell, *The Desert Revolution* (Madison: University of Wisconsin Press, 1962), pp. 188–204.

[6]Interview with Ernesto Verdugo, Superior, Arizona, March 22, 1980.

[7]Vernon Jensen, *Nonferrous Metals Industry Unionism* (Ithaca: Cornell University Press, 1954), pp.30–48.

[8]Joan London and Henry Anderson, *So Shall Ye Reap* (New York: Thomas Crowell, 1970), pp. 10, 115–140.

The Struggle for Independent Unions in Mexico, 1854–1931

John M. Hart

SINCE THE BEGINNING of modern Mexican unionism in the 1860s, the leaders of organized labor have been courted, praised, threatened, supported, and suppressed by an interventionist government in search of social and political stability. One of the fundamental divisions between radical and moderate labor leaders since 1865 has been the relationship of the workers' movement to the state. Both sides have traditionally stressed the importance of an independent union movement, but the moderates have consistently invited government intervention, actively supported political candidates, and openly praised the government as the workers' ultimate hope in their conflict with employers. The radical unionists have usually, but not always, rejected government involvement, refused to participate in elections, viewed the state as an "agent of the bourgeoisie," and called for "class struggle" and "social revolution" in order to create a society controlled by the workers.[1]

The interactions of organized labor with the state began in 1867, shortly after the defeat of Maximilian and the return to power in Mexico City of the liberal government led by Benito Juárez. The returned liberals included artisan labor leaders Epifanio Romero and Juan Cano. This pair supported the idea of a small artisan-based workers' movement, created out of the older artisan guilds and stressing life and disability insurance offered through "mutualist societies." However, they found that the artisans and factory workers had already been organized by radicals led by Santiago Villanueva, who espoused the revolutionary and anticapitalist doctrines of Pierre Joseph Proudhon and Charles Fourier. The radicals belonged to a secret society known as La Social and used an older established artisan group, La Sociedad Artística Industrial, as a central workers' council for their publicly observable organizing activities.[2] The liberal gov-

[164]

ernment and its moderate artisan allies were forced to compete with the radicals for control of the nascent labor movement.

Romero and Cano joined the Sociedad Artistica and failed in a quick electoral attempt to unseat Villanueva and place the organization under the aegis of the government. They then formed a rival group, which received an annual subsidy of 1,200 pesos from the government and a large former church and its grounds to use as a meeting place. The successful and affluent moderates challenged Villanueva again, and a vote merged the new group into the Sociedad Artistica, with Romero and Cano in charge. Mexico's first central workers' council therefore became a group whose expenses and facilities were provided by the government. The state had successfully initiated a workers' management policy which still continues.[3]

The radicals refused to accept the open alliance with the government, and in 1869, they created a rival workers' central called the Círculo Proletario. The new and radical *círculo* soon recruited almost all of the important labor leaders of the 1870s and 1880s, including some who later became moderates. The new activists carried on labor organizing in the textile mills and among the artisans, including the typographic workers, tailors, hat makers, cobblers, and stone workers.[4]

By 1870, the organized workers were ready to form the first official central workers' council in Mexico. The Gran Círculo de Obreros de Mexico convened on September 16. The radicals won the first election for the leadership of the Gran Círculo, when Villanueva defeated Cano despite the latter's endorsement by President Juárez. During 1871 and 1872, the *círculo* conducted a successful campaign and organized several thousand workers in the Mexico City area and outlying towns. The red and black flag of the Mexican labor movement, which symbolized socialism and anarchist independence from government, was adopted at that time.[5]

In late 1872, Villanueva died, and by 1873 the moderates won control of the *círculo*. It soon received a monthly allotment of 200 pesos and a regular meeting place from the government. By 1874, the *círculo* numbered 8,000 members, and, in conjunction with workers' groups from other cities, a national labor congress, the Congreso General Obrero de la República Mexicana, was created.[6] At that point, the labor leadership was about equally divided. The radicals were more prone to strike and to organize lower echelon workers than the moderates, and they continued to oppose any relationship with the government. As a result, the national congreso was totally free of state intervention, and the Mexico City *círculo* continued its close ties with the government. The *círculo,* which supported the reelection of President Lerdo de Tejada, suffered a severe setback when Lerdo was overthrown by Porfirio Díaz.

During the next three years, Díaz alienated the national labor movement leadership to the extreme. In 1880, the 50,236-member *congreso* and its 100 unions affiliated with the European-based anarchist International Workingmen's Association. La Social, the anarchist secret society and control group of the *congreso,* had sixty-two affiliated sections nationwide. La Social called for the workers' control of factories, *campesino* control of landed estates, and the abolition of the government. The labor radicals overreached themselves, and the national *congreso* and La Social were destroyed by the armed forces during the years 1881–1883, in the midst of widespread labor strikes and agrarian rebellions that swept central Mexico.[7]

During the 1880s many former radicals and La Social members, such as Pedro Ordónez and Carmen Huerta, accepted government positions and continued in the leadership of unions, which were now authorized by the Díaz regime. The government's labor management policies were a combination of the financial and social prestige incentives of the Juárez and Lerdo administrations and the decision to use force, when necessary for control. The latter expedient was utilized with decreasing frequency during the economic growth and optimism of the mid-1880s and 1890s. Labor moderates throughout this era pointed to sizeable growth in the GNP, stable real wages, and high hopes for a better future, and they urged cooperation with government and capital.[8] Radical labor activities continued, however, as was revealed in the countless wildcat strikes during the last fifteen years of the nineteenth century. On these occasions, an assortment of government arbitrators, including former labor radicals employed by the government, strikebreakers, and sometimes armed forces were used to restore order.[9]

It was only in the troubled economy after 1900 that radicals were again able to make gains against the moderates and the Díaz government's labor control policies. In 1905, the revolutionary newspaper, *Regeneración,* published by the Partido Liberal Mexicano (PLM), reached 20,000 copies per edition. It carried violent attacks against the government and capitalism. The deeply troubled Mexican government worked hard to suppress it, but, during 1906, in the midst of increasing labor unrest and sponsored by small donations collected throughout Mexico, it reached 30,000 copies per edition. By 1906, the PLM had forty-four clandestine guerilla units and clubs operating within the five zones into which they had divided Mexico.[10] Grass-roots labor radicals, led by nine identified Mexicans and several Americans, were responsible for the famous strike at Cananea in 1906. Several PLM representatives were also on the scene, and the government interpreted the events at Cananea, both at the time and later, as a workers' uprising.[11]

The 1907 textile lockout and strike and workers' rebellion at Río Blanco in Orizaba was the most spectacular instance in which labor radicals overturned moderate government-supported labor leaders. Workers attacked the factory, town, and residences of the "sell out" labor officials. The Orizaba area had been a site of labor unrest as early as the 1870s. In the 1890s, the Río Blanco workers formed a "resistance society," to protect themselves from the "capitalists, foreigners and government." In 1901, they created another "resistance group in order to regain their lost rights. In 1906, a PLM organizer, José Neira, was among a group of twenty-seven workers who formed the Gran Círculo de Obreros Libres (GCOL) in Río Blanco, that affiliated with the PLM. The government declared the GCLO subversive, however, and it was dispersed by the authorities. Shortly thereafter, government officials, including the local judge, an Orizaba political boss, and the governor of Veracruz, approved the creation of a new GCOL under the leadership of a low-level shop timekeeper, José Morales. Labor historian Luís Araiza has described the new leader of the GCOL as "more concerned with interests of the industrialists than those of the workers." The GCOL soon organized throughout the Orizaba, Puebla, and Tlaxcala regions nevertheless, and radicals were denied admission to the Río Blanco meetings.[12]

After intense labor strife and a lockout that lasted more than two weeks, the Río Blanco workers were scheduled to return to work on January 7, 1907. The contract rejected all worker demands and provided for new and hated identity books, containing worker employment and discipline records. In Puebla, the GCOL leader, in his address to the assembled workers, cited the endorsement of the archbishop, God, church, and country before gaining a majority acceptance. In Río Blanco, Morales' approval vote was spoiled by shouts of "revolution," "death to Porfirio Díaz," and "down with the dictatorship."[13]

The next day, the workers rebelled, the company store was burned, the local *rurales* refused to intervene, and angry workers calling for the overthrow of the government attacked the company stores of neighboring factories. Scores of workers were killed during one incident. The bitter workers attacked the cluster of houses that

were used by Morales and the GCOL leadership, but, in anticipation
of such wrath, they had already escaped. The contagion of the rebellion was not easily controlled. Eighty workers from the Cerritos factory
burned a pawnshop. By January 8, hundreds of workers were in jail,
and, on the following day, ten were summarily executed. The most
knowledgeable source estimates that 200 workers were killed and 400
made prisoners. Soldier losses amounted to some twenty-five killed
and thirty to forty wounded. The end result was that over 1,500
workers were suspended from their jobs in five factories.[14]

After the Río Blanco rebellion, working-class unrest continued to
smolder, and heavy troop concentrations were needed in both
Orizaba and Mexico City to maintain control. In Puebla, a new
government-sponsored union, the Gran Confederación de Obreros,
was created out of the remnants of the GCOL. The confederation's
bylaws prohibited strikes and stressed cooperation with employers
and government. Later in January, the La Magdalena Textile Factory,
a radical stronghold since 1876, was closed by strikers. The nearby La
Hormiga Plant was also struck, but reopened following occupation by
the *rurales*. Refugees from Río Blanco were found to be involved in
both episodes. In April, wildcat strikes in Orizaba were broken by
troops and the threat to use 1,500 strikebreakers from Oaxaca.

In 1908–1909, strikes again involving Río Blanco participants
closed down La Hormiga and San Antonio de Abad in Mexico City,
which was closed twice in 1909. Troops were used to clear 1,500
workers from their housing area near La Hormiga, and an army
cleanup of radical infiltrators, subversive literature, and weapons was
conducted. Strikes in the Mexico City, Puebla, and Orizaba zones
continued throughout 1907–1910.[15]

The first stage in organized labor's participation in the revolution
of 1910 began in 1909 and extended to the fall of 1914. During that
time, groups of radicals, organized by Spaniard Amadéo Ferres and
Colombian Juan Francisco Moncaleano, coalesced into the Casa del
Obrero Mundial, which became the national workers' central. The
casa called for the overthrow of capitalism and the state. It was hostile
to both the Madero and Huerta governments and successfully com-
batted efforts of pro-Madero moderates to establish a union, the Gran
Liga de la República Mexicana, supported by the new Department of
Labor. Direction of the *casa* was given through a secret control group,
known as Luz in 1912 and Lucha in 1913 and 1914. The members of
Luz and Lucha advocated anarcho-syndicalism. By the end of 1914,
the *casa* was too large and too spread out nationally for one group to
direct, and leadership passed to twenty-three unpaid committees run
by equally impoverished secretaries who were members of the na-

tional directorate. The number of enlisted syndicates soared past seventy-five.[16]

The second stage of organized labor's involvment in the revolution began in the fall of 1914 and was confirmed in February, 1915, when the *casa* allied with the bourgeois-led constitutionalist faction of the revolutionary forces. The *casa* made such an arrangement in return for full authority to organize workers' councils and syndicates throughout Mexico. The *casa* leaders had no illusions about an inevitable conflict with the bourgeois constitutionalists, but they already counted 50,000 members in their syndicates and anticipated an easy victory. They formed a Comite de Propaganda and divided it up into fourteen commissions, which were then set out into the provinces to organize the nation's workers. In return for the constitutionalists' agreement to allow working class organizing in the areas under their control, the *casa* contributed 12,000 men nationwide to the constitutionalist military effort. Thus, during this stage of the revolution, an urban alliance of workers and bourgeoisie emerged in opposition to the armed peasantry of Villa and Zapata, which the urban elements regarded as "reactionary." The urban alliance fell apart as soon as Villa was defeated in the spring of 1915. When Zapata proved unable to mount an effective attack, President Carranza ordered the 7,000 workers from the Mexico City area, and their frightening "red batallions" demobilized.[17]

The third stage in the revolutionary process, pitting the bourgeoisie against the urban workers, began in the spring of 1915 and continued until August, 1916. The new constitutionalist government allied with the Mexico City, Puebla, and Veracruz industrialists and businessmen, in a fight with the *casa* which followed class lines and included violent street battles between workers and troops, and demonstrations and strikes involving the returned red batallion veterans. The end came on August 2, 1916, when some "revolutionary" generals, including the principal commander of the constitutionalist forces, General Alvaro Obregón, who were previously sympathetic to the *casa* and even encouraged its opposition to President Carranza, betrayed the workers. Troops occupied Mexico City, seized the *casa's* offices, and arrested its leaders, and the anarcho-syndicalist group, the largest independent labor organization in the nation's history, was declared subversive and was outlawed.[18]

The urban workers and their radical leaders were defeated. Later, many joined the CROM, the government-supported forerunner of the present-day Confederación de Trabajadores Mexicanos. In 1921, others entered the anarcho-syndicalist Confederación General de Trabajadores (CGT). The CGT's strength lay in the traditionally militant unions of central Mexico, but never exceeded 80,000 members. The CROM was at least twice as large. During the 1920s, violent street battles between the CGT on one side and the CROM, police, and army on the other were frequent occurrences. But, during the post-revolutionary years, the government's position steadily improved. By 1931, the aging CGT leadership, which was losing potential younger members to Marxism, was confronted by a new labor code (Ley del Trabajo), which required government licensing of all unions, approval of all strikes, and compulsory arbitration. The new code was hardly compatible with independent unionism, but the industrialists of Mexico City cooperated with the government in the effort by providing funds for the new arbitration *juntas*.[19] By 1931, a stabilized and once again powerful Mexican government was able to reassert its authority over the independent and radical tendencies in Mexican labor, as it had done for so much of the time since 1867.

NOTES

[1]The most useful studies for the aspect of Mexican labor history discussed here are Manuel Díaz Ramírez, *Apuntes Históricos del Movimiento Obrero Y Campesino de México 1844–1880*, (México: 1938), John M. Hart, *Anarchism and the Mexican Working Class, 1860–1931*, (Austin: 1978), James D. Cockcroft, *Intellectual Precursors of the Mexican Revolution 1900–1913*, (Austin: 1968); also Rodney D. Anderson, *Outcasts in Their Own Land, Mexican Industrial Workers 1906–1911*, (DeKalb, 1976); Ramón Eduardo Ruíz, *Labor and the Ambivalent Revolutionaries Mexico, 1911–1923*, (Baltimore, 1976); Moises González Navarro, "La Huelga de Río Blanco," *Historia Mexicana*, (April–June, 1957):510–533; Jacinto Huitrón, *Origenes E Historia del Movimiento Obrero en México*, (Mexico, 1975); and Hart, "Urban Working Class and the Mexican Revolution: The Case of the Casa del Obrero Mundial," *The Hispanic American Historical Review*, February, 1978, pp. 1–20.

[2]Hart, *Anarchism*, pp. 43–45.

[3]Ibid., p. 45; and *El Hijo del Trabajo* (Mexico), No. 82, February 17, 1878.

[4]*El Hijo del Trabajo*, Nos. 4, May 9, 1876, and 12, July 9, 1876; Díaz Ramírez, *Apuntes*, pp. 33–34; and Hart, *Anarchism*, 45–46.

[5]Díaz Ramírez, *Apuntes*, pp. 37–38; Hart, *Anarchism*, pp. 46–48; and *El Socialista* (México), Nos. 4, May 9, 1876, 1, July 9, 1871, 61, March 1, 1874, and 15, September 29, 1872.

[6]*El Obrero Internacional* (Mexico), No. 9, October 27, 1874; *El Socialista*, Nos. 165, February 27,1876, and 166, March 5, 1876; and Hart, *Anarchism*, p.49.

[7]*El Socialista*, No. 34, September 26, 1882: *La Internacional* (México), Nos. 8, August 25, 1878, and 14, October 6, 1878.

[8]For a full discussion of the moderate position in the late Porfiriato see Anderson, *Mexican Industrial Workers*.

[9]Hart, *Anarchism*, pp. 74–82; and González Navarro, *Las Huelgas Textiles en el Porfiriato*, Puebla, 1971.

[10]Armando Bartra, "Ricardo Flores Magon en el cincuentenario de su Muerte," *Supplemento de Siempre*, No. 1015, December 6, 1972; and Cockcroft, *Intellectual Precursors*, p. 124.

[11]Manuel González Ramírez, *Fuentes para la Historia de la Revolución Mexicana*, Vol. III, Mexico, 1956, p. 45: Esteban B. Calderón, *Genesis de la Huelga de Cananea*, México, 1956, pp. 19–33; and Cockcroft, *Intellectual Precursors*, pp. 136–137.

[12]Luís Araiza, *Historia del Movimiento Obrero Mexicana,* Vol. 2, México, 1966, pp. 99–102; *La Revolución Social* (México), November 18, 1922; González Navarro, *Las Huelgas Textiles,* p. 226, and *La Historia Moderna de México, El Porfiriato, La Vida Social,* México, 1957, p. 326.

[13]González Navarro, *El Porfiriato,* pp. 324–331. Araiza, *Historia,* Vol. 2, pp. 105–111.

[14]González Navarro, *Las Huelgas Textiles,* pp. 79–80 and 409; Araiza, *Historia,* Vol. 2, pp. 115–121. For a version which estimates smaller casualties at Río Blanco, see Anderson, *Mexican Industrial Workers,* pp. 166–169.

[15]For reference to unrest in the wake of Río Blanco, see *El Imparcial* (Mexico), January 8, 1908, May 28, 1908, May 29, 1908, April 23, 1909, April 25, 1909, May 13, 1909, May 14, 1909, July 25, 1910, and July 26, 1910; and *El País* (México), July 24, 1910, and July 27, 1910; all cited in González Navarro, *Las Huelgas Textiles,* p. 409, and Anderson, *Mexican Industrial Workers,* p. 194.

[16]"Manifiesto Anarquista del Grupo Luz," *Luz* (México), July 15, 1912; José Ortiz Petricioli. *Cincuentenario de la Casa del Obrero 1912–1962,* México, 1962, p. 7; and Huitrón, *Orígenes.* For a detailed analysis see Hart, "The Urban Working Class and the Mexican Revolution: The Case of the Casa del Obrero Mundial," *The Hispanic American Historical Review,* January, 1978, pp. 1–20.

[17]José Colado, "El Proletariado nacional unificado a Carranza," *La Vanguardia* (Orizaba, June 5, 1915; Araiza, *Historia,* Vol. III, pp. 78–91; and Rosendo Salazar and Jose G. Escobedo, *Las Pugnas de la Gleba,* Vol. 1, México, 1923, pp. 116–119.

[18]"Ecos de 13 de Octubre," and "Justicia Social," *Ariete* (Mexico), October 24, 1915; "Destruyamos los viejos moldes," *Ariete,* December 12, 1915; "La Huelga General de Obreros del Distrito Federal," "Los Obereos y la Revolución; La Huelga Actual," and "La Huelga, su origen, su desarrollo, sus consecuencias," *Acción Mundial,* May 22, 1916; Salazar and Escobedo, *Las Pugnas,* Vol. I. pp. 165–184; Araiza, *Historia,* Vol. 3. pp. 106–178; Huitrón, "La Casa del Obrero y la Revolución Social," Regeneración (México), August 12, 1943; and Hart, "The Urban Working Class and the Mexican Revolution," *The Hispanic American Historical Review,* January, 1978, pp. 15–20.

[19]"Comienza el terror blanco en México," *Bandera Roja* (México), June 5, 1921; Miguel T. Ochoa, "Asesinos," *Nueva.*

The Historiography of a Myth

Rodney Anderson

A MYTH IS FAR EASIER TO CREATE than to destroy, for, in the process of its development, it attracts its own vested interests for which the myth itself plays some vital function. In the academic world, a myth often serves the purpose of an intellectual "safe house," a means by which a weak argument can be disguised as something already proven and hence which does not have to be subjected to the usual methods of criticism. Often a myth serves as its own evidence of authenticity. Slavery was correct because blacks were inferior as seen by the fact that they were slaves. And then, all too often, a myth simply makes a good story, and no one likes to give up a good story.

One such tale concerns the role that Mexican anarchists presumably played in the important series of labor conflicts which took place in the half-decade prior to the Mexican Revolution of 1910. Almost all traditional, as well as most recent scholarship, alludes to this role, and more than a few scholars have asserted quite strongly that Mexican anarchists, under the leadership of Ricardo Flores Magón, were instrumental in those conflicts, winning workers in large numbers to their cause.[1]

The story begins on February 5, 1901. On that day, the forty-fourth anniversary of the signing of the 1857 Constitution, fifty delegates from liberal political clubs around the nation met in San Luís Potosí at the First Liberal Congress. The movement ostensibly favored only political reform and "good government," but it was clearly at odds with Don Porfirio Díaz, ruler of the country. The leaders of the congress were a group of young intellectuals, among them Antonio Díaz Soto y Gama, Camilo Arriage, and Ricardo Flores Magón, the latter being the person who would dominate radical opposition to Díaz and his successors for years to come.[2]

By the fall of 1902, all leaders of the first (and last) liberal Congress were in jail, because of their opposition to Díaz and his regime. Most were released soon afterwards, but, for greater security and freedom of operation, many took up residence, first in Texas, and

[172]

then, when harrassed by Díaz agents, in St. Louis, Missouri, in February, 1905. It was from St. Louis that the Mexican Liberal Party (PLM), as they now called their group, took up the fight to overthrow the Díaz regime. Increasingly disillusioned with liberalism as a means to bring political and social change to Mexico, a majority of the exiled leadership of the PLM had become committed to the anarchist cause by the summer of 1908. What is significant however, is the fact that this was a secret conversion. They continued to call themselves the Mexican Liberal Party and to espouse programs that were progressive, but hardly radical. Ricardo Flores Magón explained this tactic when he wrote to his brother, Enrique, on June 13, 1908: "All is reduced to a mere question of tactics. If we had called ourselves anarchists from the start, no one, or at best a few, would have listened to us. Without calling ourselves anarchists, we have been firing the people's minds with hatred against the owner class and governmental caste."[3]

For five years before the rest of Mexico decided to rid itself of the dictatorship of Porfirio Díaz, the PLM and its supporters throughout Mexico struggled alone against the regime. Continually harrassed by agents in the hire of the Mexican government and by hostile North American authorities, the PLM nonetheless managed to lead two revolts against Díaz—in 1906 and 1908. The latter was planned and carried out with the majority of PLM leadership in United States federal prisons, on charges rising out of the 1906 uprising. Both revolts failed, but the PLM continued its fight, increasingly trying to enlist the support of Mexico's emerging industrial proletariat. "Destroy the factory, cave in the mine, burn the estates," exhorted one PLM newspaper of its working-class readers.[4] It was around the PLM's appeal for working-class support, and its involvement in labor conflicts, that the myth began to grow.

Mexican industrial workers had every reason to listen to the PLM because, during the first decade of this century, inflation, unemployment, low wages, and deplorable living and working conditions, were common characteristics of their lives. Yet, economic hardship has never automatically driven people to revolution, nor were most Mexicans strangers to such misery. The PLM believed, however, that the traditional apathy and resignation that was commonly thought to inhibit rebellion among Mexican working people was no longer a problem. The Mexican industrial proletariat, they believed, were ready for revolution.

Mexican industrial workers were a product of the unprecedented economic growth of the previous quarter century. Encouraged by the iron peace imposed by Porfirio Díaz, an industrial economy had emerged during the decades following the dictator's triumph over his adversaries. Industrial production doubled between 1876 and 1900, and primary product exports, encouraged by a vastly expanded railway system, grew at an even faster rate.[5] At the same time that the wealth of their nation was increasing, the living conditions for most Mexicans were declining. Population increases had deteriorated living conditions in the burgeoning cities and had depressed wage rates in all but the most skilled working-class occupations. After 1900, inflation and recession added to the lot of Mexico's working people.[6] Health and safety conditions were poor, even by the standards of the day.[7]

Throughout most of the regime of Porfirio Díaz, labor policy echoed the laissez-faire principles of classical economics. Francisco Bulnes, well known to contemporaries as the period's most arrogant, cantankerous intellectual, succinctly summarized government policy. Speaking in Congress, he rejected a plea for "just remuneration" for Mexican workers, scornfully pointing out the "absurdity" of such an idea. "The words 'just remuneration' have no meaning in economics," he declared. "In economics, nothing is just or unjust. Labor is a product like corn, wheat, or flour and is subject to the same law of supply and demand."[8]

With little official support for their grievances, Mexican industrial workers and artisans began organizing on their own. However, a promising labor movement begun in 1870 was repressed by the government in the early 1880s,[9] and despite intermittent strikes during the 1880s and 1890s, the first decade of the twentieth century began with few workers, except those on the railroads, organized. But, by 1906, organized labor had made inroads in cotton textiles, tobacco, and mining, and had vastly expanded on the railroad lines. Beginning early that year, the industrial peace enforced by the Díaz regime began to crumble under a series of unprecedented strikes. In 1906 alone, there were twenty-seven strikes—more strikes involving more workers than in the previous five years combined—and this unrest continued unabated through the following year. In response to a worsening economy, the strikes declined by mid-1908, but the number of labor organizations continued to increase. Mexican labor was coming of age.[10]

In 1911, the Díaz regime was overthrown by a widespread popular movement, and, in the decades that followed, a clear picture of pre-revolutionary workers was obscured by the growth of an historical mythology which often accompanies a successful revolution. The central theme of the myth was the belief that those early workers were inspired by radical European political ideologies and, particularly, were led by the PLM in an effort not only to overthrow the Díaz regime but the repressive capitalist system as well.[11] In order to verify the extent to which this belief is correct, we need to reexamine the events of the years between 1906 and the fall of the regime in 1911.

First, a closer examination of economic changes prior to 1906 reveals several important facts about the origins of labor unrest in the years that followed. The recession of 1900 had driven many marginal producers out of business and encouraged the survivors to cut wages, introduce more efficient and costly machinery, and instigate more regimented and restrictive work routines. The results were worsened working conditions at the same time that the economy began to pick up—after 1902. Workers found that, while working conditions were deteriorating, jobs were more plentiful. Therefore, they could organize and strike without the same fear of unemployment that made such advances difficult during hard times. The economy did not decline again in central Mexico until mid-1907.[12] By that time the industrial peace enforced by the Díaz regime had been shattered by the great strikes of 1906–1907.

In reviewing the events of those years, the most obvious evidence of PLM influence is in the important copper-miners strike in Cananea, Sonora, in June, 1906.[13] Clearly, the leaders of the striking workers were PLM members and supporters, who hoped to spread the PLM's influence among Mexican miners. Just as clearly, however, the strike itself began spontaneously, without encouragement or instigation from local PLM leaders. More importantly, PLM strength at Cananea benefitted considerably from proximity to the American Southwest, where it enjoyed widespread support among the Mexican-American community. The great bulk of Mexican industry, however, was located on the central plateau far from the PLM strongholds on the border. In other words, the myth is reasonably correct for the Cananea strike, but not for understanding the Mexican labor movement as a whole.

The second major incident during 1906 was a strike in July involving the mechanics on the Mexican Central Railroad. Led by the *Unión de Mecánicos Mexicanos,* based in Chihuahua, the strikers closed down repair shops throughout north-central Mexico and were soon joined by nearly three thousand other employees of the line. It lasted until mid-August and finally ended with the intervention of President Díaz himself. Although James Cockcroft's work on the PLM claims that these workers belonged to the PLM, there is no apparent evidence that this is so, and Cockcroft himself presents little evidence in support of his claim. His assertion that European syndicalism was influential among the workers also is without support in many documents.[14]

The third crucial strike of that year took place in the textile mills of Puebla and Orizaba. In the latter industrial city, PLM supporters were among the founders and early leaders of the textile workers union, the *Gran Círculo de Obreros Libres* (GCOL), organized in April, 1906.[15] These leaders were forced out in early June, during a government crackdown, and were replaced by political moderates led by José Morales of the Río Blanco Mill. The GCOL, however, continued to pressure the mills, expanding its membership throughout the textile factories of central Mexico. A GCOL branch in Puebla struck the mills of that area in December, a strike that eventually led to an industry-wide lockout by the owners. Violence swept the Orizaba mills in early January, 1907, as the government tried to impose a settlement on recalcitrant industrialists and reluctant workers. Troops were called in and a number of workers were killed—shot down in the streets or executed by firing squads. Because these events began with the burning of the company store at the Río Blanco Mill outside of Orizaba, the episode is known in Mexican history as *la huelga de Río Blanco* (the Río Blanco strike).[16]

Historians have long viewed the Río Blanco strike as a precursor of the Mexican Revolution of 1910, one initiated and led by PLM workers.[17] However, instead of viewing the violence at Río Blanco in terms of radical politics, it is more reasonable to look at it as the result of a combination of interrelated factors: years of bitterness toward the mill owners and company stores (which were all burned to the ground during the strike); rivalry between workers from the Santa Rosa and Río Blanco factions for control of the union; frustration from economic hardship imposed by the lockout; and the anger felt by those who believed that the Díaz arbitration award failed to meet their needs. Admittedly, some of the violence may be attributed to PLM supporters, or to anarchists who blamed the entire capitalist-bourgeois system of production and ownership, just as some of the violence may have been the random acts of psychopaths who liked to burn and throw rocks. But it seems to me that neither of these last two explanations ranks high in any reasonable priority arrangement of causes and influences.[18]

There were, as we know, PLM supporters among the thousands of workers in the textile mills around Orizaba, but most were not radical—certainly not anarchists—or at least do not appear so in any of the information that is available. Many of the martyrs killed during the violence in early January, 1907, were from the large anti-Morales faction at the Santa Rosa Mill, but that did not make them radicals. Three years later, in fact, workers at the Santa Rosa factory supported liberal presidential candidate, Francisco I. Madero, in his quixotic campaign against Porfirio Díaz.[19]

There are two aspects to this situation. First, from 1904 through 1907, the PLM hid its increasingly anarchist leanings behind the facade of a progressive liberal political philosophy. Publicly, the PLM supported a return to democratic government and moderate social reforms. What most workers knew about the PLM came mainly from its widely circulated July Declaration of 1906, containing relatively mild labor proposals. The declaration called for an eight-hour day, minimum wages (lower in some cases than what the workers themselves were demanding), and the abolition of Sunday work— a demand which already had been accomplished in most industrial occupations. The declaration did not call for the right to organize, or strike, or to bargain collectively, all of which were contemporary labor demands.[20]

As a result of this subterfuge, most PLM supporters and party members in Mexico were unaware of their exiled leaders' conversion to anarchism. Even as late as the election of 1910, a PLM supporter chastised the PLM newspaper, *ALBA,* for attacking Madero's Anti-Reelection Party, noting that the latter was "as liberal as ourselves."[21]

The second aspect to this question is that even after 1907, when the PLM's anarchist leanings found their way into print more often than before, their propaganda only rarely reached its destination. North American post office and customs officials cooperated with Mexican authorities to prevent much of the PLM's literature from entering into Mexico. Therefore the true picture of the PLM's emerging radicalism was never fully revealed to its Mexican sympathizers.[22]

Another piece of evidence indicating that Mexican workers were little influenced by PLM anarchism was the vigorous campaign that organized labor waged, demanding government intervention to settle industrial disputes. When textile workers of Puebla struck in December, 1906, they immediately requested presidential arbitration; when Silvino Rodríguez's mechanics struck the Mexican Central in July, 1906, they requested government intervention, as did their comrades during the boilermakers' strike in June, 1907, and the important railroad strike in April, 1908.[23] Anarchist and syndicalist philosophy generally was opposed to cooperation with the state, and the PLM concurred. PLM activist and former textile worker Juan Olivares wrote a friend in Orizaba, criticizing the current union leadership for "continuing to resort to the authorities in order to better the situation of our comrades."[24]

Historian James Cockcroft admits that active relations between working-class groups and the PLM declined after 1907. He blames this, however, on governmental repression and surveillance, contending that "a significant number of workers remained in a state of revolutionary anticipation after the 1906–1908 strikes."[25] Surveillance and suppression there certainly were, but this is not prima facie evidence that the workers were repressed. During the political campaigns of 1909–1910, in fact, workers did join the opposition, but it was Madero's Anti-Reelection Party, and not the PLM. Indeed, at least thirty-one Anti-Reelectionist clubs were founded among such militant workers as those at the Río Blanco and Metepec (Puebla) mills and the Cananea copper mines. When the revolution broke out in November, 1910, there were pro-Madero uprisings among various groups of workers throughout Mexico. The Madero forces were able to defeat the Díaz regime by May, 1911, precisely because they had broad support from Mexicans of all classes.[26]

The PLM, on the other hand, apparently was not able to get its message across to most of its potential supporters, particularly in central Mexico. Therefore, its support lay mainly in the north, because of its proximity to PLM strongholds in the United States. Furthermore, PLM supporters were concentrated among middle and lower middle class people, and among many artisans, perhaps because their way of life came increasingly under challenge from the industrial production fostered by the Díaz government. There is not yet any systematic study of the PLM's social makeup, but some interesting evidence does exist. The Mexican government compiled a list of PLM supporters in Monterrey, the leading industrial city of the north. Of the fifty-one names on that list, only seventeen were listed as specifically working class. Of those, thirteen were artisans; there were four industrial workers.[27]

The key to why Mexican industrial workers were not attracted to radical politics lies in their having only a vague sense of class but a strong sense of identity with their nation and its past, especially the Reform Era. In terms of loyalty, most politically conscious workers were *juaristas*, not *magonistas*.

Many workers had a strong, stubborn faith in the Constitution of 1857 and the liberal reform movement which gave it birth, symbolized by Benito Juárez. In nearly everything they wrote, these juaristas invoked the names of the liberal heroes of the past and demanded that the government restore what they believed to be the rights granted them during the reform. Striking mill hand, Flavio Arroyo, referred to the "constitution of Benito Juárez" as the hard core of his goals.[28] A railroad worker requested justice in the names of those liberals who had fallen in battle during the reform, giving "their blood and their life on the altar of liberty."[29] And there are many more examples.[30]

Why did workers identify with the reform? After all, the reform was based on nineteenth-century liberalism, an ideology clearly hostile to working-class interests. On speculation, they were probably identifying with the nationalist struggles of that era—against Spain, the United States, and France. Certainly, many of their own conflicts were with the foreigners who owned the mills and mines of Mexico. Their nationalism, therefore, strengthened their own position and placed their fight squarely in the mainstream of Mexico's historical experience.

Even more importantly, however, they viewed the reform not simply as a movement for political democracy but as a quest for social justice as well, a quest which they believed, if revived, would lead to a resolution of their problems.[31] One worker alluded to this when he wrote to President Díaz: "If the justice of our nation sleeps in the far off, dusty past, we will awaken it with our message and force it to finish its sacred mission."[32] In other words, Mexican workers felt no need for foreign doctrines or radical solutions to their problems because they believed, rightly or wrongly, that their own political system, if it were made to function correctly, would do the job. What they needed, they believed, was a restoration of past principles.[33]

Whatever the truth of the matter, a myth has a life of its own and a constituency which, for its own reasons, has an interest in keeping the myth alive. The constituency changes over time, of course, and, therefore, the promotion and growth of any myth differs from one period to another, and from one group to another. The first to label the labor movement as "anarchist" and "revolutionary" was the Díaz government, which saw those dreaded specters behind every strike and worker organization. In part, their fear of an alliance between disgruntled workers and the PLM has helped to convince historians that such an alliance existed. The conspiracy theory of history attracts strange bedfellows.

PLM supporters, on the other hand, had good reason to deny such links during their exile in the United States prior to 1911, especially when there was violence involved. To acknowledge involvement in the Cananea or Río Blanco strikes would have given the United States and Mexican authorities more ammunition with which to attack the PLM. Not only did the PLM publicly deny any connection with labor violence but, interestingly, its private letters as well revealed the same position.[34] Although a private detective maintained that he had obtained a confession from one PLM leader that the group had been involved in the labor unrest, the fact that he was a paid informant of the Mexican Government during the trial of PLM leader, Manuel Sarabía, tends to reduce his credibility.[35]

After the Díaz regime fell in 1911, the myth lay dormant, nurtured by occasional polemics which denounced the old regime and exaggerated the political consciousness of prerevolutionary working-class movements.[36]

In 1923, labor-leader-turned-historian Rosendo Salazar published his *Las pugnas de la gleba,* an account of the previous two decades of labor activities. In his book, Salazar told the story of the PLM's attempt to revolutionize and radicalize Mexico's working class, prior to 1910. Because Salazar went on to become the nation's leading labor historian, his work took on the aura of a classic despite its lack of documentation, and therefore effectively canonized the myth of class-consciousness among Porfirian workers, and its corollary, their adherence to the *magonista* cause.[37]

Soon the myth became doctrine, spread in the 1920s and 1930s by the publication of a number of popular histories of the labor movement. Those works, perhaps by design, served as ideological adjuncts to the rise of a politically oriented labor movement. This was particularly true during the presidency of Lazaro Cárdenas (1934–40), when the government officially published many of those histories.[38]

Meanwhile, North American scholars came to rely on Marjorie Clark's 1934 study of organized labor in Mexico as their source on prerevolutionary labor, even though her major emphasis was clearly the postrevolutionary era. As Clark accepted the Salazar thesis, an entire generation of graduate students dutifully accepted the myth as true.[39] Actually, until the 1950s, few works in either Spanish or English dealt seriously with working-class history prior to 1910, and none even partially utilized the wide range of potential primary sources.

In the mid-fifties, an able young Mexican historian, Moisés González Navarro, published an outstanding social history of Porfirian labor. Although he did not deal directly with the myth, he nonetheless reaffirmed the Salazar thesis. Antonio López Aparicio's widely used history of Mexican labor, published at about the same time, did much to give the myth further credence.[40] In 1968, James Cockcroft's influential study of the PLM became the most ambitious effort yet, to attempt to demonstrate the class-consciousness of Porfirian workers and their essentially radical ideological perspective. For the most part, historians have accepted Cockcroft's version of working-class ideology.[41]

The leading expert on Mexican anarchism, Professor John M. Hart, in his award-winning article in *The Americas,* published in 1974, came out in support of the Cockcroft thesis, claiming that during the labor unrest from 1906 to 1910 "Mexican labor returned to the militant—revolutionary—and anarchist stance that was inherited from the precursors of the nineteenth century."[42] Hart's work, so essential in clarifying the origins of Mexican anarchism in the 1860s and 1870s, added no new primary research on the era after 1900 and before the fall of Díaz.

In the end, if the myth is false, it is, far more importantly, presumptuous. By implication, the myth takes away from the workers of Porfirian Mexico the only right they really enjoyed—the right to act on their own. There is no reason to believe that Mexican workers needed middle-class intellectuals writing from St. Louis or Los Angeles to tell them that their lives were unnecessarily miserable or that their work was unnecessarily hard and unrewarded.

The key error in perspective that has permitted the myth to grow is that the historian has accepted the PLM's belief about its role in raising working-class consciousness to a stage of revolutionary readiness, rather than posing the question from the point of view of Mexican workers themselves. Indeed, there is every reason to believe that the actions of Mexican workers affected the PLM far more than the reverse. For one thing, it was the strike at Cananea, the troubles on the railroads, and the bloodshed at Río Blanco that gave the PLM ammunition to use against the regime. Moreover, those events revealed to the PLM the potential of working-class support for their movement. Prior to 1906, the PLM rarely talked about the possibility of an alliance with workers. After the events of 1906 and early 1907, PLM supporters mentioned such a possibility more and more frequently.

It makes at least as much sense, therefore, to suggest that Mexican workers influenced the consciousness of the PLM leadership as it does to say that the PLM had an impact on working-class motives and goals. There is a clear possibility that the radicalization of the PLM occurred in response to the militancy of a determined working-class movement, in an effort to change the misfortunes of their lives. All true and lasting changes in the paradigms by which we live come from below.

NOTES

[1] The works which most strongly argue this to be the case are: James D. Cockcroft, *Intellectual Precursors of the Mexican Revolution, 1900–1913* (Austin, Texas: University of Texas Press, 1968), and John M. Hart, "Nineteenth Century Urban Labor Precursors of the Mexican Revolution: Development of an Ideology," *The Americas*, 31 (1974):298–318.

[2] Cockcroft, *Intellectual Precursors*, pp. 92–120.

[3] *Ibid.*, p. 162.

[4] Quoted in *Reforma, Libertad y Justicia*, June 15, 1908, contained in Ambassador Thompson to secretary of state, United States Department of State, Record Group 59, n.f. 8183, enclosure 100–104, United States National Archives. For a detailed coverage of the PLM's activities between 1905 and 1910, see Cockcroft, *Intellectual Precursors*, pp. 120–169.

[5]Charles C. Cumberland, *Mexico: The Struggle for Modernity* (New York, 1968), p. 227; Fernando Rosenzweig, "La industria," in Daniel Cosio Villegas, ed., *Historia moderna de México*, 10 vols. (México, 1956–1971), vol. 7, *El Porfiriato. La vida economica*, by Nicolau d'Olwer et al., pp. 314–15.

[6]El Colegio de Mexico, *Estadisticas economicas del Porfiriato. Fuerza de trabajo y actividad economicas por sectores* (México, n.d., circa 1965), p. 29. John Coatsworth, "Railroads, Landholding, and Agrarian Protest in the Early Porfiriato," *Hispanic American Historical Review*, 54 (February 1974):48–71.

[7]Information on health condition in the factories and mines are numerous. On mines, see article in *La Palanca* (Mexico City), January 15, 1905, and G. Nava Oyeo, "La mineria" in d'Olwer, *El Porfiriato*, p. 256. On tobacco shops, see Moisés Gonzalez Navarro, *El Porfiriato. La vida social*, vol. 4 of Cosio Villegas *La historia moderna de México*, p. 295. On conditions in the cities, see Alberto Pani, *Hygiene in Mexico: A Study of Sanitation and Educational Problems*, trans. Ernest L. de Gogorza, (New York, 1917), pp. 34–37, 43–44, 71–73, 192–99; *El México Obrero* (Mexico City), September 1, 1909.

[8]*Diario de los debates de la Camara de Diputados*, Congreso 18 vol. 3:211.

[9]For the early phase of the labor movement, see John M. Hart, *Los anarquistas mexicanos, 1860–1900* (México: SepSetentas, 1974), and Hart, "Urban Labor Precursors," pp. 298–318. See also Gaston García Cantu, *El socialismo en Mexico* (Mexico: Ediciones era, 1969). The best overviews of labor in the Porfiriato are Moisés González Navarro, *El Porfiriato: La vida social*, vol. 4 of *Historia moderna de México*, edited by Daniel Cosio Villegas (México: Editorial Hermes, 1957): Jorge Basurto, *El proletariado industrial en México (1850–1930)* (México: Universidad Nacional Autonoma de México, 1975): Alfonso Lopez Aparicio, *El movimiento obrero: Antecedentes, desarollo y tendencias* (México: Fondo de Cultura Economica, 1945).

[10]For a detailed study of those years, see Rodney Anderson, *Outcasts in Their Own Land. Mexican Industrial Workers, 1906–1911* (DeKalb, Ill. Northern Illinois University Press, 1976).

[11]The most important proponents of this interpretation are: Cockcroft, *Intellectual Precursors;* John Hart, *Los anarquistas*, and "Nineteenth Century Urban Labor Precursors;" Marjorie Ruth Clark, *Organized Labor in Mexico* (Chapel Hill, N.C.: University of North Carolina Press, 1934); Lopez Aparicio, *El movimiento obrero;* Victor Alba, *Las ideas sociales contemporaneas en México* (México: Fonto de Cultura Economica, 1960); Basurto, *El proletariado industrial;* Barry Carr, *El movimiento obrero y la politica en México, 1910–1929*, 2 vols., (México: SepSetentas, 1976); Rosendo Salazar and José G. Escobedo, *Las pugnas de la gleba 1902–1922* (México: Editorial Avante, 1923).

[12]Anderson, *Outcasts*, p. 95.

[13]For Cananea, see Lyle C. Brown, "The Mexican Liberals and Their Struggle Against Díaz Dictatorship: 1900–1906," *Anthology Mexico City College, 1956* (Mexico: Mexico City College Press, 1956), pp. 328–43, and the personal account of one of the leaders of the copper miners, Esteban Baca Calderon, *Juicio sobre la guerra del yaqui y genesis de la huelga de Cananea* (México: Ed. del Sindicato Mexicano de Electricistas, 1956).

[14]For the railroad mechanics' strike, see Anderson, *Outcasts*, pp. 117–119.

[15]*Ibid.*, pp. 103–107.

[16]*Ibid.*, pp. 107–110; 130–171.

[17]The earliest proponent of that view is Salazar and Escobedo, *Pugnas*, p. 13.

[18]The most balanced view of the Río Blanco strike is Moisés Gonzalez Navarro, "La huelga de Río Blanco," *Historia Mexicana*, 6 (1957):510–533.

[19]For a coverage of workers involvement in the Anti-Reelectionist movement, see Anderson, *Outcasts*, pp. 254–267.

[20]*Ibid.*, p. 121. See also, however, Cockcroft, *Intellectual Precursors*, pp. 131–33, 239–45. For evidence of the PLM July Program circulating among workers, see flyer "Contra El Despotismo Mexicana," GPDC, 34:8880, and material in GPDC, 35:1766 and 1299; 81:1644 and 1550.

[21]Ignacio J. Nendiola to M. L. Escamilla, May 10, 1910, Brownsville, in General Villar to Díaz, May 31, 1910, Matamoros, General Porfirio Díaz Collection (The University of the Americas, Cholula, Puebla), 35:7911.

[22]Anderson, *Outcasts*, pp. 202–3, 268–69.

[23]For details of these strikes and others, see Anderson, *Outcasts*, pp. 140–44, 190–201, 212, 215, 224–29.

[24]Juan A. Olivares to Rafael Rosete, September 2, 1906, El Paso, Texas, Archivo General de la Nación, Ramo de Gobernación (AGN–Gob), "Asuntos diversos magonistas y revolucionarios, 1907–1908," leg. 12.

[25]Cockcroft, *Intellectual Precursors*, p. 143.

[26]Anderson, *Outcasts*, pp. 254–67, 275–97.

[27]Subsecretary of Gobernacion (Miguel S. Macedo) to General Bernardo Reyes, February 27, April 5, 1907, Archivo General Bernardo Reyes (AGBR), Mexico City, Correspondencia ministeria, 1903–1909. The list was compiled of those who subscribed to *Regeneración* or who had contributed money to the PLM cause. Of the two-thirds who were not listed as having a working-class occupation, a few were described as "gente del pueblo"—clearly not middle class but with no specific occupation—but most were obviously middle class, by virtue of their occupations or the property they owned.

[28]Cited in *La Lucha Obrera*, (Puebla), December 16, 1906.

[29]J. Trinidad Nav (indistinct) to Díaz, March 10, 1910, GPDC, 35:4058.

[30]See, for example, Santa Rosa workers to Ramon Corral in letter dated October 29, 1906, AGN–Gob, leg. 817; "Los obreros en huelga," *El Paladín*, January 7, 1909; flyer "A los Proletarios del Segundo Círculo de Obreros Libres," Puebla, November 11, 1906, AGN–Gob, leg. 817; *El Constitucional*, February 6, 1910, pp. 20–21; "La unión es fuerza," Cruz Villafranca, in *Mexico Nuevo*, April 19, 1910; "Cantos de un obrero," in *El Diablito Rojo*, February, 1908.

[31]Evidence of the workers' nationalism abounds. See several excellent examples in Jose Neira, "In the Arena," in *Revolución Social* (Río Blanco), cited in Hubierto Pena Samaniego, "Apuntes historicos de Río Blanco," in *El Clarín* (Orizaba), August 19, 1958, and letter to the editor of *México Nuevo* (Mexico City) from Metepec textile workers, May 16, 1909.

[32]Workers of La Hormiga to Díaz, March 2, 1909, GPDC, 34:4661.

[33]For statements from workers calling for restoration of lost rights, see Antonio Cárdenas, in Archivo Espinosa de los Monteros, Mexico City, CCLIX:540; "Los obreros en huelga," in *El Paladín* (Mexico City), January 7, 1909; Aquiles Serdan, "Convocatoria a la clase obrera," from the Serdan museum, Puebla; Juan Ramírez, letter in *México Nuevo*, August 6, 1909; "Antiguos tejedores de Río Blanco" in *El Paladín*, March 13, 1910; "Los obreros de la Republica," flyer from cotton textile union, Río Blanco, November 6, 1906, AGN–Gob, leg. 817. For a more detailed and diverse discussion of this theme, see Rodney Anderson, "Mexican Workers and the Politics of Revolution, 1906–1911," *Hispanic American Historical Review*, 54 (February, 1974):94–113.

[34]See R. F. Magon to Gabriel Rubica, May 27, 1906, Department of Justice, RG 60, exp. 30, Appel. Case 21153, United States National Archives, for a letter from Ricardo to a follower in Cananea. For the Río Blanco strike, see R. M. Caule (pseudonym for Ricardo Flores Magón) to an unknown recipient, enero 17, 1907, Archivo Central de la Secretaria de Relaciones Exteriores, Ramo de Ricardo Flores Magon, L–E–924, 7:23–24, for a letter in which Flores Magon denies responsibility for, or prior knowledge of, the strike.

[35]Thomas Furlong to assistant secretary of state (Robert E. Bacon), July 5, 1907, Justice, RG 60, no. 90755, United States National Archives. Sarabia had been kidnapped by Mexican agents from Douglas, Arizona, and taken across the border to stand trial in Mexico. United States officials forced the Mexican government to return him to the United States.

[36]See particularly Carlo de Fornaro, *Díaz, Czar of Mexico* (New York: International Publishing Co., 1909); Lazaro Gutierrez de Lara and Edgcumb Pinchon, *The Mexican People: Their Struggle for Freedom* (Garden City: Doubleday, Page and Co., 1914); John Kenneth Turner, *Barbarous Mexico* (Chicago: C. H. Kerr and Co., 1911).

[37]Salazar had been an active labor leader in the post-1911 era but not during the Díaz period.

[38]See especially German and Armando List Arzubide, *La huelga de Río Blanco* (México: Depto. de Biblioteca de la Sec. de Educación Pública, 1935) and León Díaz Cárdenas, *Cananea, primer brote del sindicalismo en México* (México: Depto. de Biblioteca de la Sec. de Educación Pública, 1935).

[39]Clark, *Organized Labor*, pp. 6–12.

[40]See Gonzalez Navarro, *El Porfiriato* (1957), and López Aparicio, *El movimiento obrero* (1952).

[41]Besides those already cited in note 11, see Dawn Keremitsis, *La industria textil mexicana en el siglo xix* (México: SepSetentas, 1973); Jean Meyer, "Los obreros en la Revolución Mexicana: Los 'Batallones Rojos,'" in *Historia Mexicana*, 20 (July–September 1971):1–32; R. Th. J. Buve, "Protesta de obreros y campesinos durante el Porfirato: unas consideraciones sobre su desarollo e interelaciones en el este de Mexico Central," translated by Anneke Roos, *Boletín de Estudios Latinoamericanos* 13 (1972):1–25. Only Buve has added substantive support to Cockcroft's position.

[42]Hart, "Urban Labor Precursors," p. 318.

Mexican Migrant Workers
in the United States

David R. Maciel

MEXICAN IMMIGRATION TO THE UNITED STATES, continuous from the days of the California Gold Rush, has followed certain cyclical trends. From these trends, a relative but particular periodization emerges: 1880–1910, 1910–1929, 1930–1942, 1942–1965, and 1965 to the 1980s. All of these periods relate to the labor needs of the United States, the socioeconomic situation in Mexico, and changing American immigration laws.

In reviewing the principal characteristics of the cycles of Mexican immigration, factors must be considered in both Mexico and the United States which have determined and influenced the flow. It is assumed that the continuing migration of workers from Mexico to the United States is an institutionalized phenomenon, which is a result of the dependency of Mexico and the structural nature of its economic and social growth. At the same time, Mexican workers have consistently proved a cheap, abundant, and readily available labor supply to be brought in when convenient or sent back to Mexico when not employed.

1889–1910: THE ORIGINS OF MEXICAN IMMIGRATION

The period 1810–1910 reflected large-scale penetration of the Mexican economy by foreign-owned industries. This development significantly altered the economic organization and relations of production. As a consequence of this penetration, Mexico was more closely linked to the international economy and the effects of international cycles, whose periodic recessions affected the national economy. There followed increasing inflation and massive unemployment.[1] During the reign of Porfirio Díaz (1876–1910), the population and cost of living in Mexico rose significantly, while wages of the average worker remained relatively static. It was estimated that real wages were only a fourth of what they had been a hundred years earlier.

Close to 90 percent of the Mexican working class earned twenty to twenty-five cents a day. At the same time, between 1891 and 1908, the price of many basic food items more than doubled.[2] This general economic situation in Mexico led to an increase of agrarian revolts, organized political opposition to the Porfirio Díaz regime, labor stoppages, and strikes.[3] Most of these manifestations were put down harshly by the police and army, suggesting the difficulty of bringing about social and economic change within the existing political structure.

The economic hardship facing the working class in Mexico coincided with the rise of the American Southwest as an important region. The mineral, industrial, and agricultural development of the area accounted for the process of immigration from Mexico and the increasing dependence of United States firms on recruitment of Mexican labor. Two additional factors were to contribute significantly to the increase of Mexican immigration to the United States: United States federal legislation, and the building of an extensive railway system, connecting Mexico and the United States.

In 1902, Congress passed the Newlands Reclamation Act, which provided federal funds for the construction of large-scale irrigation and reclamation projects throughout the Southwest. Arid desert areas became useful for the production of citrus fruits and vegetables.[4] Another pertinent article of legislation was the Gentlemen's Agreement of 1907. Its purpose was to restrict Japanese nationals' entry into the United States. The law complemented the Chinese Exclusion Act of 1882. Asian labor supply to the United States was now severely restricted and the way opened for recruitment of Mexican workers.[5]

United States immigration legislation has consistently reflected the overall need of the economy for Mexican labor. The principle function of immigration laws has been to regulate and control the process of immigration—that is, the supply of labor. The United States Departments of Labor, Agriculture, and State have worked closely with organized interest groups, invoking policy and practices that have affected migration patterns and Mexican workers on both sides of the border.

Prior to 1882, there existed no federal restrictions or quota laws regulating immigration. Two basic liberal concepts determined this open-door policy: the United States was to be an asylum and a place of opportunity for all; and the migrants of any nationality would be absorbed into the giant melting pot. During those years of economic growth, there existed the need for mass labor without restriction, and the practice worked well until the turn of the century.

In 1882, the first general immigration law was enacted. It established a head tax and provisions for the exclusion of certain categories of people who, because of one or another liability, could not work and were considered a burden to the state.[6] Xenophobia and nativism began to assert themselves in the dominant society. In 1882, furthermore, Congress passed the Chinese Exclusion Act which underscored the existing and increasing racism of segments of the society, the exclusivist character of some American unions, and the lack of class consciousness on the part of labor.[7] As can be noted, characterizing aspects of United States labor regulation and racism were visible in legal and political practice by the 1880s.

Three years later, Congress repealed the first alien contract labor law. The goal was to prevent employees from importing "cheap foreign labor" to replace Anglo workers. This law was enforced with regulatory descretion. In the Southwest, a similar maneuver was Arizona's "80 percent law" of the years 1914–1916.[8] Industry was forced to guarantee that 80 percent of its employees were American citizens, suggesting the interrelatedness of politics, economics, and attitude toward alien workers. A referendum approving the measure, proposed by the Arizona State Federation of Labor, was overwhelmingly passed by the voters, as a result of a coalition of so-called "progressive" Democrats, labor unions, and the Socialist Party. This was obviously an uneasy coalition which held two things in common: concern with the above-normal, 12 percent unemployment and a strong focus on the Mexicans, at whom the law was aimed, although it applied formally to all non-United States citizens. The United States Supreme Court eventually nullified the law, at a time when the cycle had shifted to a need for Mexican labor.[9]

1910–1929: THE GREAT EXODUS

Immigration from Mexico reached its height during the period 1910–1929. Three paramount reasons for this were the overall effects of the Mexican Revolution of 1910; the economic growth of the Southwest; and increased labor demands in the United States because of World War I.

"In 1910, a social and political upheaval erupted in Mexico."[10] As a political movement against the dictatorship of Porfirio Díaz, the upheaval had a significant role in the shaping of the modern Mexican state and society, but it more immediately affected the process of immigration. Intense internal warfare brought chaos to an already fragile economy. Agriculture production fell drastically as did other sectors of the Mexican economy, while unemployment and poverty increased. Many haciendas and agricultural fields were disrupted.[11] Laborers were pulled away from the factories and countryside and pressed into the armies. Armed conflict intensified the already harsh economic conditions for the majority of the Mexican people and increased the numbers of "a mobile labor force." With the mobility of the armies, provided largely by the railroad system, warfare and economic disruption added to the mobility of the working class.[12] Workers had geographical mobility, but little security.

As the fighting intensified, the movement northward did also. People in large numbers began leaving Mexico in search of security and subsistence.[13] Those on losing sides of the battles left for fear of reprisals. Immigration officials in the United States reported that an "inconsiderable" number of Mexicans sought refuge. It has been estimated that about 1/3 million Mexicans immigrated between 1910 and 1920. The breakdown is shown in Table 1.

Along the border in the southwestern United States, thanks to technology, the economy was flourishing.[14] World War I induced labor shortages which could be filled by Mexican workers in non-agricultural areas within industry and services. Some Mexicans were employed in such relatively skilled occupations as core makers, machinists, mechanics, finishers, job press workers, painters, and upholsterers.[15]

With the expanding economy, markets, and need for workers, the recruitment of Mexican labor became a business. Employment agencies were created with this as a sole assignment. The largest of these agencies worked for the railroads. The agencies would seek out potential workers and furnish them with food, clothing, and transportation to the United States. Once the workers arrived on the job, the railroads would deduct the expenses of their journey from their salaries and pay the agencies. The agencies sought out the workers in various interior states of Mexico.[16]

In 1917, Congress enacted a literacy test, providing for the exclusion of all aliens over sixteen who did not read English or some other major language. While industry needed literate workers, agriculture did not. In 1918, the requirements of the immigration laws were waived for Mexican laborers by the commissioner general of immigration.[17] This was to establish two significant precedents: the relaxing of immigration laws when it was advantageous to import Mexican workers; the restricting of provisions when it appeared necessary to exclude Mexicans from immigrating on a permanent basis.

Shortly thereafter, European and Asiatic immigration decreased substantially, as a result of the restrictions established by the Emergency Quota Act of 1921, and the Immigration Act of 1924.[18] This legislation established a quota system which numerically restricted immigration on the basis of a national origin formula. The concern was for a racial and ethnic balance within the United States. Despite arguments that this racial conceptualization was undemo-

TABLE 1

Legal Mexican Entrants Into the United States, 1910–20

Year Ending June 30	Immigrants	Non-Immigrants	Total
1910	17,760	3,327	20,997
1911	18,784	3,581	22,365
1912	22,001	3,701	25,702
1913	10,954	4,541	15,495
1914	13,089	3,990	17,079
1915	10,993	7,649	18,642
1916	17,198	7,963	25,161
1917	16,438	9,442	25,880
1918	17,602	14,147	31,749
1919	28,884	15,932	44,776
1920	51,042	117,350	68,392

Adapted from Commissioner General of Immigration's Annual Reports from 1910 to 1920; idem. Annual Report, 1920, pp. 707–21; James Davis, secretary of labor, to Representative Cole, April 25, 1924, in Congressional Record (January 6, 1925), pp. 1366–67.

Cited in Lawrence A. Cardoso, *Mexican Emigration to the United States 1897–1931* (Tucson, 1980).

cratic, the 1924 act set a standard for United States immigration policy. The 1917 act represented the theory of qualitative regulation; the 1924 act embodied the quantitative restriction.

Needing a large pool of low cost labor to expand the rising economic empire of the Southwest, industrialists continued to encourage the movement of Mexicans into the area. The owners and growers sought and eventually secured an abundant supply of labor and a constant industrial reserve, as markets and needs expanded. The desire for Mexican labor was not restricted to the Southwest; capitalists in the Northwest and Midwest also began seeking it out.[19]

During the 1920s, the number of Mexican immigrants reached a peak. Approximately 427,000 Mexicans were admitted legally into the United States in the period from 1920 to 1929.[20] The socioeconomic condition of Mexico and the wage differential between Mexico and the United States continued to spur immigration. In 1925, a cost-of-living study revealed that agricultural workers in most parts of Mexico did not earn salaries "sufficient to afford a livelihood." The study further showed that a Mexican worker's purchasing power was only one-fourteenth that of an Anglo worker.[21]

With the expanding numbers came one of the first in a series of anti-Mexican xenophobic campaigns. Some social scientists argued that Mexicans were a threat to the cultural and genetic fabric of the society. Organized labor opposed any further immigration from

Mexico, believing that Mexican workers displaced Anglos in the labor market by working for lower wages. These views were in turn supported by "objective scientific" studies, which sought to demonstrate inferior qualities of the Mexicans and an alleged negative effect on United States society.[22]

Urged on by labor leaders and certain politicians, the first "repatriation" campaign against Mexican migrants was put into effect. It has been estimated that between 1921 and 1929, close to 100,000 Mexicans were repatriated to Mexico.[23] Again the situation changed in the late twenties, mainly due to the economic growth of southwestern agriculture. Two other factors also spurred this immigration cycle: The Cristero rebellion in Mexico, a result of bitter church-state conflict; and additional lines of communication between the United States and Mexico, such as the newly completed railroad linking Guadalajara, Jalisco, with Nogales, Arizona.

1930–1940: THE GREAT DEPRESSION AND REPATRIATION

Workers during the 1930s experienced increased unemployment and politicization, in both Mexico and the States, as a result of worldwide depression. Mexican immigration subsided as a result of unemployment and depression in the United States. Wages were reduced to subsistence levels across the country. In contrast, subsistence was somewhat easier in Mexico, since jobs could still be secured in agriculture and service occupations. In the United States, seasonal and migrant workers became more and more marginal as Mexicans were displaced by Anglo workers. Many believed that the Mexican workers became public scapegoats of the policy to repatriate thousands of workers.[25] This was to be one of the most intensive deportation movements. Although some Mexicans returned on their own incentive, much of this reverse migration seemed to be a systematic campaign by United States authorities and private agencies. Many methods were used in repatriation—persuasion, intimidation, and force. Studies estimate that more than 415,000 Mexicans were repatriated by force and as many as 85,000 more left through intimidation.[26]

THE BRACERO PROGRAM

In the 1940s, renewed interest in securing Mexican labor gave rise to the Emergency Farm Labor Program. The Bracero Program was established through the 1942 Bilateral Agreement between the United States and Mexico.[27] In June, 1942, the United States De-

TABLE 2

Braceros Admitted from Mexico 1942–1964

Year	Braceros	Year	Braceros
1942	4,203	1953	201,380
1943	52,098	1955	398,650
1944	62,170	1956	445,197
1945	120,000	1957	436,049
1946	82,000	1958	432,857
1947	55,000	1959	437,643
1948	35,345	1960	315,846
1949	107,000	1961	291,420
1950	67,500	1962	194,978
1951	192,000	1963	186,865
1952	197,100	1964	177,736

Sources: Wayne A. Cornelius, *Mexican Migration to the United States: Causes, Consequences, and U.S. Responses.*

partment of State and the Mexican government signed an agreement which provided for the importation of 50,000 Mexican workers to the Southwest.

The provisions of the agreement included several stipulations. Mexican workers were not to be used to displace domestic workers, but only to fill proven shortages. Recruits were to be exempted from military service. The round-trip transportation expenses of the worker were to be guaranteed, as well as living expenses enroute. Hiring was to be done on the basis of a written contract between worker and employer, and the work was to be exclusively in agriculture. *Braceros* were to be free to buy merchandise in places of their own choice. Housing and sanitary conditions were to be adequate. Work was to be guaranteed for three-fourths of the duration of the contract.[28]

World War II stimulated all phases of industry; a large labor force was critically needed, and Mexican immigration resumed on a broad scale. United States businesses and the federal government wanted more regulation over Mexican labor, and the Bracero Program seemed to provide the necessary controls. Through a formalized bilateral agreement, an employment infrastructure was created for agricultural labor, and large-scale importation of Mexican workers was resumed for temporary jobs.[29]

Concurrent with the formalized programs, undocumented immigration also increased for three reasons: Mexican workers could save the time and expense of going through official channels; owners could avoid the red tape of the Bracero Program; those who could not qualify simply came over despite the program. In addition, immigration through permanent visas also increased: 16,500 came in during the first half of the forties and 38,000 during the second half.[30] Although Mexican labor was welcomed, the attitudes toward people of Mexican origin did not change. Racial conflict erupted in parts of the Southwest and especially in Los Angeles.

In the early 1950s, as undocumented migration increased in the midst of recession, anti-Mexican sentiment again developed and would eventually evolve into a massive campaign to curtail such migration through "operation wetback." This so-called operation was begun in 1954, having as its priority not just to curtail further immigration, but also to apprehend and deport a maximum number of undocumented immigrants.

The Border Patrol (assisted by federal, state, and county officials, the FBI, and the Army and the Navy supported by aircraft and special units) launched an extensive campaign against a highly vulnerable Mexican labor force.[31] Yet, throughout the decades of the fifties and sixties, the open and shut gate mechanism of labor recruitment and deportation continued to operate. As soon as the recession passed and industry began to flourish, Mexican workers —whether legal or illegal—were again welcomed.

The years 1955–1965 were a high point in the United States economy, and a constant demand for Mexican labor occurred despite the setback of the Korean War and several minor economic recessions. As the economy of Mexico became more dependent on the United States, there was a greater interaction between Mexican workers and the labor force in general. Furthermore, as the economy changed, Anglo workers left marginal and semiskilled occupations, and Mexicans occupied these jobs. This was concurrent with the continuing rise in undocumented immigration. Internal migration from the interior of Mexico to the north also rose dramatically.[32]

The *bracero* agreement was amended several times. On July 13, 1951, Public Law 78 was signed, authorizing further employment of Mexican workers. Further legislation in 1955 extended the agreement until December 31, 1964. By the beginning of the 1960s, however, opposition to the Bracero Program began to mount. The United States Department of Labor, responding to heavy pressure from various sectors such as organized labor, religious groups, and the Immigration Service, began issuing much more restrictive conditions for the hiring of Mexican migrant workers. Finally, as the pressure intensified against the program, Congress voted to end the *bracero* agreement altogether.[33] Additionally, a new immigration law was passed in 1965, which restricted legal immigration from the western hemisphere.

1965 TO THE PRESENT: INSTITUTIONALIZED CRISIS

In the early seventies, in the wake of a growing recession, high inflation, unemployment, and a real threat of economic depression, the issue of illegal or undocumented migration from Mexico was fomented by politicians, the INS, and certain organized interest groups. Because of opportune use of the media, the issue caught the attention of the general public. In 1972, Congressman Peter Rodino introduced H. R. 14831 as an amendment to existing immigration legislation. This bill, known as the Rodino Bill, sought to make the employment of undocumented workers a crime, and provided penalties for employers who knowingly hired illegal workers. But although the bill passed the house of representatives on two occasions, it failed to receive ratification by the senate.

On July 29, 1974, Senator Edward Kennedy introduced Senate Bill 3827. If enacted, the bill would have:

1. provided authority to regulate the status of illegals who had been physically present for at least three years
2. placed sanctions on the employers of illegal aliens
3. provided for adjustment of status of nonimmigrant aliens from western hemisphere countries on the same basis as nonimmigrant aliens from eastern hemisphere countries
4. amended the Civil Rights Act of 1964 to bar job discrimination.

Many of these provisions would be included in the 1976 "Carter Plan," but Kennedy's proposal itself never became law. In October of 1976, Congress passed Public Law 94–571, known popularly as the Eilberg Bill or the 1976 amendments to the Immigration and Nationality acts. Effective January 1, 1977, the law had five major provisions. First, numerical limits of 20,000 permanent resident visas were placed on all countries in the Western Hemisphere, effectively cutting Mexican legal permanent immigration by 60 percent. Second, the exception from labor certification (skills and job requirements), enjoyed by parents of United States citizens and immigrant residents, were eliminated. This lessened the chances for family reunification. Third, the preference system (priority categories) was made the same for both Western and Eastern Hemispheres, but 60,000 fewer visas were allotted to the Western Hemisphere (i.e. 120,000 versus 180,000). Fourth, labor certification was established for professionals. Fifth, adjustment of status (from nonpermanent to permanent visa) was limited to persons who had engaged in authorized employment while in the United States. This meant that those who had worked illegally could not legalize their residence in the United States. In sum, the Eilberg Bill, though applicable to all immigrants, particularly affected the Mexican immigrant, by reducing the number of legal immigrants and the possibility of family reunification.

In the late seventies, with inflation rising and the economic recession worsening in the United States, the Mexican undocumented worker was once again singled out as a scapegoat and one of the causes of economic ills. The propaganda that arose against the undocumented worker alleged that Mexican undocumented workers displaced natives, were a burden on public and social services, contributed to increasing crime, and helped to maintain low wages. One statement claimed that Mexican workers and their families were a threat to the "American way of life" and the homogeneity of United States culture and society.[34]

Such propaganda and public pressure by officials led to still another legislative solution. President Carter presented a "message" on undocumented "alien" workers in the United States to the members of Congress. The plan centered on four recommendations: to regain better control of the United States borders by adding at least 2,000 more immigration officers; to limit the employment opportunities of those undocumented workers who supposedly competed with natives; to register and regulate the undocumented workers already in the United States; and to intensify international cooperation for economic development and the creation of more employment opportunities. Registration would "promise some sort of tangible benefits and would be implemented via a national ID card. Those who had been in the United States before 1970 would be eligible for permanent resident status, and those who entered after the beginning of 1977 would be subject to repatriation. Those who entered between January 1, 1970, and December 31, 1976, would be forced to register and remain in a state of immigrant limbo for a period of five years, but there was no assurance that they could remain in the United States.

The Carter Plan was nothing new, but it did provide for more repression and for control and regulation of labor, and it appealed to big business and public opinion. For the industrialists, the plan offered cheap labor without any benefits or rights for workers. The plan totally excluded the workers from the rights of social services like pensions, health benefits, unemployment insurance, and injury compensation.[35]

Later, labor-regulatory bills introduced in the Senate offered similar measures and were sponsored by senators Schmitt, Hayakawa, and Goldwater under the general title of the United States Good Neighbor Act for 1979. The measures encompassed the following:

1. the granting of temporary work visas which would permit aliens to perform temporary services of labor in the United States for a period not to exceed 180 days during any calendar year
2. the issuing of penalties for violation of the above in the form of a five-year restriction on eligibility for mere violation and a ten-year restriction for illegal immigration
3. the legal use of immigrant labor to employers who demonstrated to the attorney general that such labor would not supplant domestic workers
4. the setting of numerical quotas by the attorney general.

The tone of the proposed legislation was one of immigration restriction rather than worker protection. Thus, from a Mexican point of view, it is fortunate that the bills had not made their way through the United States Congress by 1981.

When Mexico discovered vast new deposits of oil during the early eighties, the emphasis of Mexican-American relations shifted rather dramatically from immigration restriction to oil importation. The Carter administration began talking of a North American common market and did everything in its power to appease the suddenly powerful petroleum exporter to the south. It even listened to the criticisms of American Chicano organizations which condemned a policy of repairing fences along the American-Mexican border; the long-heralded repair project was quietly shelved. In the meantime, study groups on both sides of the border began looking into the problem of immigration.[36]

In the United States, the Carter government formed the Selection Commission on Immigration and Refugee Policy. The commission, after two years of study, recommended that the number of aliens legally admitted to the United States be increased by 40 percent. It also recommended that all persons eligible to work in the United States be required to have a special work identity card, also that employers who knowingly hired undocumented workers be fined heavily, and that the existing ceiling on annual admissions of 270,000 immigrants be raised to 450,000. Lastly, the commission proposed that the existing 4–2 guest worker program be expanded from about 30,000 to 50,000 workers each year.

On the Mexican side, President López-Portillo consistently emphasized that his administration was working toward creating more jobs to integrate additional workers into the labor force.[37] He also acknowledged that near to total employment probably will not occur until the end of the century. Meanwhile, to provide a basis for future policy, the Mexican president authorized a most sophisticated and far-reaching analysis of Mexican-United States immigration practices to be completed by the end of 1981. Until its findings become public, it appears that the immigration conflict has reached a stalemate.

THE ROLE OF ORGANIZED LABOR

One factor has not been seriously considered—the role of organized labor on both sides of the border. The historical experience of organized labor had demonstrated that racism and national chauvinism have most often been the tools of management, tools used to break the labor movement. Unionists in both Mexico and the United States can counter this by recognizing the importance of undocumented workers to the future of the union movement. The move should be to organize all the unorganized, as was the resolution to engage unorganized workers in the concerns of the labor movement in the first International Immigration and Public Policy meetings held in 1977 in San Antonio.[38]

The undocumented, or unorganized workers, also, have developed, at least embryonically, a labor organization—El Comite Obrero en Defensa de Indocumentados/das en Lucha (CODIL). Numerous social, educational, and legal defense groups (e.g., those in Houston, Texas) have been actively struggling in the early 1980s for the immigration of undocumented workers.[39] Sectors of the labor movement, such as the Farm Labor Organizing Committee (Ohio), the United Farm Workers of America, the International Longshoremen and Warehousemen, the International Ladies Garment Workers, and the United Auto Workers, have developed their own programs to organize undocumented workers. Labor, or at least a portion of labor, has acknowledged that the universal call to organize the unorganized refers to Mexican workers, whether they are legally or illegally in the United States. Independent farm-worker unions, such as the Texas Farm Workers Union and the Arizona Farm Workers Union have already tried to implement this goal.

As of 1981, much of organized labor, however, clings to the belief that only restriction will solve the immigration problem. To the south, undocumented immigration has been often viewed as a safety valve rather than a challenge to organized labor and the state alike. The key question and issues have come to be regarded by others as the role of the Mexican economy and the undocumented Mexican immigrant in a world dominated by American capital. They believe that if the problem is ever to be solved it will be bilaterally, with emphasis on the international character of labor as it moves back and forth across the border. They further believe that the issues will be resolved not through legislation, but through organization and efforts made by the immigrants themselves.

NOTES

[1]Charles C. Cumberland, *Mexico: The Struggle for Modernity* (New York, 1968), pp. 223–226. Other important studies on the harsh socio-economic conditions of the Porfiriato regime, for the majority of the working class, are the masterful synthesis of Luis Gonzáles, "El liberalismo triunfante" in the *Historia general de México* III (Mexico, 1976), pp. 163–245; and Moisés Ochoa Campos, *La Revolución Mexicana,* 2 vols., (Mexico, 1966).

[2]Ochoa Campos, *La Revolución,* pp. 259–266.

[3]Moisés Gonzáles Navarro has published two key studies on the Díaz period: *Historia Moderna de México. El Porfiriato. La Vida Social.* (México, 1957), and *Las huelgas textiles en el Porfiriato* (Puebla, 1970). They deal in depth with unrest and resistance of the agriculture and labor sector.

[4]For a detailed analysis of the socio-economic transformation of the Southwest at the turn of the century, see the authoritative sensitive work of Carey McWilliams, *North From Mexico* (New York, 1968), and W. Eugene Hollon, *The Southwest: Old and New* (Lincoln, 1968). Each devotes various chapters to the phenomenal growth of agriculture, mining, and industry in the Southwest in the late 1800s and early 1900s.

[5]Lawrence A. Cardoso, *Mexican Emigration to the United States, 1897–1931* (Tucson, 1980), pp. 20–22. For a masterful discussion of the rise of nativism in the United States during this time, John Higham, *Strangers in the Land* (New Brunswick, 1955), remains invaluable.

[6]Leo Grebler, *Mexican Immigration to the United States: The Record and its Implications* (Los Angeles, 1966), p. 19.

[7]David R. Maciel, ed., *La otra cara de México: El pueblo chicano* (México, 1977), pp. 246–249.

[8]Mark Reisler, *By the Sweat of their Brow* (Wesport, 1976), pp. 33–36.

[9]*Ibid.,* p. 39.

[10]Most of the studies of this period that deal with immigration usually concentrate on one factor over another. To date, no single work exists which integrates all the three "push-pull" factors in a comparative perspective.

[11]The great majority of scholars of the Mexican Revolution have pointed out the profound disruption and chaos of the economy brought about by the military conflict. Yet, like John Womack asserts in his suggestive article, "The Mexican Economy During the Revolution, 1910–1920: Historiography and Analysis," *Marxist Perspectives* I:4 (Winter, 1978), there was much more economic activity and movement of Mexican society than has been previously perceived.

[12]Many firsthand accounts narrate the change in geographical movements brought about by the wide use of the railroads during the revolutionary years. One such tale is John Reed's *Insurgent Mexico* (New York, 1969).

[13]Again, memoirs and narrative accounts describe the exodus of Mexicans to the United States for political reasons. Two of the most illustrative are: José Vasconcelos, *Ulises Criollo* (Mexico, 1934); and José Antonio Villareal, *Pocho* (New York, 1959).

[14]Grebler, *Mexican Immigration,* pp. 20–21.

[15]Reisler, pp. 3–14.

[16]*Ibid.,* pp. 15–17.

[17]Reisler, *By the Sweat of Their Brow,* pp. 8–10.

[18]Ricardo Romo, "Responses to Mexican Immigration, 1910–1930," *Aztlan* VI:2 (Summer, 1975), pp. 180–181.

[19]*Ibid.*, p. 183.

[20]David R. Maciel, ed., *La otra cara de México: el pueblo chicano* (Mexico, 1977), pp. 121–125.

[21]Romo, "Responses to Mexican Immigration," pp. 185–187.

[22]The most comprehensive demographic history of twentieth-century Mexico, which cites this report of socio-economic conditions during the 1920s and other decades, is the two volume, *Población y Sociedad en México, 1900–1970* (México, 1974) by Moises Gonzáles Navarro.

[23]Romo, "Responses to Mexican Immigration," p. 189.

[24]Cardoso, *Mexican Emigration*, pp. 129–143.

[25]Jean Meyer, noted specialist in the Cristero Rebellion, in a conversation mentioned that he had interviewed many excristeros who had crossed to the United States to escape the reprisals of government troops.

[26]Two recent studies investigate in detail the repatriation process and the period. Abraham Hoffman, *Unwanted Mexican Americans in the Great Depression* (Tucson, 1974) concentrates on the campaign and politics of repatriation of Mexicans within the United States, particularly in California and Texas. Mercedes Carreras de Velasco, *Los Mexicanos que devolvió la crisis 1929–1932* (México, 1974) focuses on repatriation and Mexican migrants, from a Mexican perspective. The two complement each other nicely.

[27]Reisler, *By the Sweat of Their Brow*, pp. 49–56.

[28]*Ibid*, pp.57–59.

[29]Gilbert Cardenas, "United States Immigration Policy Toward Mexico: An Historical Perspective," *Chicano Law Review* 2 (Summer, 1975), provides an in-depth analysis of this point.

[30]Reisler, *By the Sweat of Their Brow*, pp. 198–204.

[31]Jorge Bustamante has published extensively on the effects on Mexican migrant workers of the creation of the border patrol. For the most comprehensive treatment, see his *Espaldas mojadas: materia prima para la expansión de capital Norteamericano* (México, 1975).

[32]Maciel, *La otra cara de México*, pp. 255–257.

[33]Craig, *The Bracero* p. 142.

[34]For a most perceptive analysis of this question, see Estevan T. Flores, "The Immigration Crisis and the Repression Interface: A Salient Issue for the Chicano Community in the 1980s," paper presented at the Symposium on Mexican Undocumented Immigration to the United States, Mexico City, September 6–8, 1980.

[35]For a critique of the Carter Plan and other labor regulation laws, see the important anthology edited by Antonio Rios Bustamante, *Immigration and Public Policy: Human Rights for Undocumented Workers and Their Families* (Los Angeles, 1977).

[36]For more detail on this aspect, see the outstanding study by Peter Baird and Ed McCaughan, *Beyond The Border: Mexico and the United States Today* (NACLA, 1979).

[37]In spite of increased revenue from oil, Mexico suffers from structural problems that have maintained inflation at over 20 percent, population growth is still high, and agriculture and the rural sector is in a critical state.

[38]Estevan T. Flores has developed this theme in "Multinational Mexican Workers, The Multidimensional Attack on Them and Possible Responses," *Zerowork* Political Materials 3, (Fall, 1979).

[39]David R. Maciel, in *Al Norte del Río Bravo. Pasado Inmediato.* (México, 1980), traces various labor struggles of Mexican workers in the United States in detail.

V

Labor and Politics

Politics and the
Western Labor Movement

LABOR HAS ALWAYS BEEN IN POLITICS. The first political club in the nation, the Society of Tammany, was founded in 1789, as a society of anti-Federalist, New York mechanics. By the 1830s, labor had its own party in the form of various workingmen's parties which supported Jackson and others. Indeed, so committed was labor to the political realm that Samuel Gompers' declaration of voluntarism in the 1880s seemed a dramatic reversal of history to most unionists. Even Gompers' sacred principles of voluntarism, principles which declared that unions would dedicate themselves to the economic rather than the political world, would be reversed by the American Federation of Labor in the first decade of the twentieth century. The situation was much the same in the American West.

West of the Rockies, unions began with the miners on the Comstock, and those miners' unions were quite political. The mine unions were among the first California pressure groups to agitate for a Chinese Exclusion Act, to prevent the free entry of low-cost Chinese labor into the Golden State, and labor would continue to be active throughout the 1860s, 1870s, and 1880s, in a variety of causes. Unions took the lead in the western push for an eight-hour day; Nevada affiliates of the Western Federation of Miners carried on a long and hard fight for eight hours in the 1890s, as did their WFM allies in Colorado and Montana. However, it was not the miners alone who turned to politics in the West. The organized trades demanded and received workmen's compensation laws in California and, later, Arizona; mechanic's lien laws; and occupational safety legislation. Railroad unions agitated successfully for a number of national legislative reforms. Even the radical unions had some political success in the era of strong progressive sentiment.

However, political success was not to be a long-term labor development in the American West. With the onset of World War I, the union movement in the West received political and economic assaults which rendered it powerless in many states for years to come. Arizona witnessed the Jerome and Bisbee deportations of union miners during 1917, a move which was strongly supported by many segments of the state. In Montana, the lynching of Frank Little went unpunished the same year. Years before, Labor's political protest over the deportation of hundreds of Colorado strikers was squelched by the famed lame-duck legislature of 1904. Even liberal California was convulsed by the complexities of the Tom Mooney case, a case that continued to draw antiunion lightning until Governor Culbert Olson pardoned Mooney in the late thirties. Labor unions themselves were becoming a political issue, particularly when those unions were of a radical nature.

Obviously, the Industrial Workers of the World were feared by much of the western middle class. Wobbly exploits were usually covered by as much sensationalism as Hearst had reserved for the Spanish-American War. When wobblies were involved in an affair, even the most ordinary function was branded as bolshevik—by newspapers and management alike. Thus, an ordinary strike of miners at Bisbee became an antiwar plot by sinister German (or perhaps red) agents, and deportation was viewed by much of Arizona as a perfect counter to such a plot. A strike dedicated to catching up with wartime inflation became a frightening "bolsheviki" action, when Seattle's mayor perceived that IWW influence was rampant in the 1919 general strike. The simple demands of Wheatland became revolutionary, when they were presented by IWW leaders.

In the face of revolutionary threats, whether real or perceived, western states responded with a series of antisyndicalism laws. Mere advocacy of the tenets of the IWW constitution became a felony in states as diverse as California, Idaho, and Minnesota. California prosecuted more than 100 IWW members under its anti-IWW law, and sent the whole lot to prison. One of these, Nicolaas Steelink, remembers being thrown in a cell with the famed McNamara brothers, for an IWW career which centered around Los Angeles fruit and vegetable markets. Somehow, the subversion of cantaloupe appeared to be a major felony to California's dedicated anti-IWW prosecutors. While Steelink was a sincere and brilliant wobbly, his threat to the safety of the sovereign state of California did not justify a twenty-year sentence (interview with Nicolaas Steelink, Tucson, Arizona, March 6, 1977). Yet the antiwobbly campaign was just one symptom of the pervasive antiunion feeling in the political West.

The first paper in this section deals with the congressional career of Carl Hayden, Arizona's long-term resident of both the house and senate. The interesting thing about the early years of Hayden's career was his profound prolabor bias. Before the First World War, Hayden was a dedicated WFM supporter and ardent wooer of labor votes. Yet, even in his prolabor days, Hayden resorted to an antired campaign when he was threatened by an even more prolabor candidate. It was almost as if Carl Hayden had been carrying around a red-tag labor speech from the beginning and was only itching for the opportunity to use it.

Labor's political fortunes did not improve much in the twenties. The American Plan was abroad in the nation, a program carefully pushed by the National Association of Manufacturers, to substitute company employee representation plans for independent unions and the open shop for the closed. A simultaneous attack on labor's legal protection, incorporated into the Clayton Anti-Trust Act, proved particularly successful in the western case of *Truax v. Corrigan,* in which the Supreme Court ruled that Arizona's statute forbidding an antilabor injunction was unconstitutional. Perhaps the neatest play of the twenties was the beginning of a concerted antiunion push, under the cloak of patriotism. The open shop was patriotic; it was part of the "American" plan. Such careful use of the language would continue into the forties, with the invention of the term "right to work."

The thirties will long be remembered as the decade of the New Deal and the era of the reborn labor movement. Nationally, unions received a tremendous boost with the enactment of the National Labor Relations Act and the Fair Labor Standards Act. In the West, dormant unions such as Mine-Mill were revived, and many of these were less than careful about the political beliefs of their new members. The thirties would also be remembered as the decade of the CIO, the new labor federation whose western affiliates would become as important as those of the East. (What history of California would be complete without some mention of Harry Bridges and the International Longshoremen's and Warehousemen's Union?) The CIO's significance was also very political; in fact, the new federation had decided as early as 1936 that its future was in politics.

CIO politics however, did not have much direct impact on the Southwest in the early days. After all, CIO membership was quite weak in the mountain states. Yet, the CIO's dedication to political spending, at first in the 1936 presidential race and later in the 1944 Roosevelt campaign, made it a logical target for southwestern antilaborites. Texan Martin Dies served as chairman of the controversial House Un-American Activities Committee, a committee which had shown more dedication in hunting down wayward liberals than in finding Nazi spies. With the creation of the CIO's Political Action Committee in 1943, Dies set his sights on Sidney Hillman of CIO–PAC, the man who many claimed had cleared the vice-presidential nomination of Harry Truman. The CIO, on the other hand, considered Dies a prime candidate for replacement. The 1944 defeat of Congressman Dies turned the CIO and its Political Action Committee into the nemesis of Texas politics almost overnight. It is the antilabor politics of the post-Dies era in Texas which George Green examines in the second essay in this section.

The antilabor push in politics did not end with Texas or the CIO–PAC. As important as the American Plan was in the twenties, the right-to-work drive proved equally important in the forties. Florida started the campaign with the enactment of the first such law in 1944, and Arizona followed suit two years later. Eventually, some twenty states enacted antiunion security measures, which were given national sanction by the 1947 Taft-Hartley Act. An important antilabor ally in the right-to-work drive was the long-standing issue of labor's leftist bias. The issue which had arisen to plague the IWW was now hung on the leadership of the CIO.

What did the antired decade have to do with western labor? Dies began calling the CIO a Communist organization in 1944, and, although his charges did not stick, the issue became a favorite of both Republicans and conservative Democrats in the period from 1946 to 1954. It was during that period that the Southwest produced such leading anti-Communist crusaders as California's Richard M. Nixon, Arizona's Barry Goldwater, and Nevada's Pat McCarran, none of whom was known as a defender of unions. Nixon won his first campaign by attempting to tag his opponent as a supporter of the CIO–PAC; Goldwater, a right-to-work advocate, had called his mildly prolabor opposite a "Socialist" (a charge dreamed up by Carl Hayden's old campaign manager); and McCarran had shocked even Harry Truman with his proposal of anti-Communist legislation, which was ultimately overturned by the Supreme Court. Obviously, it was not a good time for organized labor.

Confronted with the anti-Communist decade, CIO leaders decided that the best way to win back the confidence of the American people was to purge the leftist unions from its fold. The decision was not made lightly by CIO President Phillip Murray. A call for such a purge had first gone out in the early 1940s, when certain communist locals in the United Auto Workers had defied the CIO's patriotic, no-strike pledge. Among the CIO leaders who asked for such a purge were James Carey, long-time CIO secretary-treasurer, and Walter Reuther, the UAW's president in the postwar years. A similar purge demand was made by a group of Catholic labor leaders and clergymen in the late forties, who had united themselves under the title of the Association of Catholic Trade Unionists. With pressure building by the moment and the 1947 enactment of labor legislation, which denied Communist-led unions the protection of the NLRB, Phillip Murray approved of the move to purge in late 1948. Within a year, three major and eight minor unions were brought up on charges of anti-CIO activity. The expulsion of the offenders followed in 1950. Two of the three major unions expelled by Murray were western— the Mine-Mill and Harry Bridges's ILWU. Both would survive the expulsion.

The final essay is, itself, an interesting historical document. Father Charles Owen Rice was at the center of the expulsion controversy in 1948. As Phillip Murray's confessor and a sympathizer of the ACTU, he was tagged by many as the power behind the throne in 1948, particularly when Murray expelled the third of the powerful leftist unions—the United Electrical Workers. Father Rice's eloquent statement on the purge of the CIO's United Electrical Workers may ultimately be viewed as the final work in the CIO's long-running controversy. Even though he does not deal with either the IUMMSW or the ILWU, it must be remembered that Father Rice's statements on the UE situation could just as well be said for the western duo that was purged.

What can be said about western labor in politics? Twenty years after the red scare, western labor has still not regained its former political strength. Carl Hayden, the prolabor politican of the teens, retired from the United States Senate in the 1960s, with a reputation far removed from that of a labor radical. Few of his colleagues from the Southwest differed markedly from him in their views of labor. In fact, nothing seems to have changed in the last twenty years except that the importance of communism in politics has steadily diminished. Dies and McCarran are gone, Nixon has retired, and Barry Goldwater acts more like a diplomat every day. The unions can always hope for the future.

Labor Politics, Hayden Style

Paul Mandel

IT WAS A TIME OF REFORM, that period which began in the wake of populism and came to an end on the bloody battlefields of the First World War. America had turned progressive and reformers could be found everywhere—in corporate boardrooms, across the farms of the Midwest, and in the picket lines. It has never been easy to define this controversial period, but most progressives agree that organized labor played a prominent role. "If the banner of the Kingdom of God is to enter through the gates of the future," said Walter Rauschenbusch, the progressive social reformer and theologian, "it will have to be carried by the tramping hosts of labor." In the real world of the political arena, Carl Hayden, the progressive congressman from Arizona, wrote, "so long as I am a member of Congress, every just bill in which organized labor is interested will receive my active support and that I will vote and work against all measures which are detrimental to the workingmen ...."[1]

Carl Trumbull Hayden's career in the United States House of Representatives spanned the years from 1912 to 1926, the first fourteen years of Arizona statehood. During those years, organized labor in Arizona was at the peak of its influence on the state political scene. At the same time, Carl Hayden was clearly the most successful politician in the state, leading the Democratic ticket in most elections. A review of union organization in Arizona during those years and a study of one aspect of Hayden's early career—his "courting" of the labor vote—would illuminate the role the labor movement in early Arizona politics. It would also reveal the attention that successful Arizona politicians gave to an important part of Arizona's progressive constituency—the union labor vote.

Labor unions had not always been a political power in Arizona. Territorial politics were dominated by a host of powerful interest groups and, indeed, it was not until the 1880s that the first unions even appeared on the scene. As the frontier territory grew from the land of the farmer-prospector into the copper capital of the West,

[206]

mine unions sprang up from Tombstone to Globe. The turn of the century saw Arizona copper companies among the world's leaders in the mining industry; it also saw the emergence of the Western Federation of Miners in the deserts of the Southwest. The federation, about to enter its most militant phase, held the allegiance of almost 30,000 miners from British Columbia to California. By 1911, over 2,000 union miners carried cards with Arizona locals, the largest of which boasted a membership of 600 in and around Globe.[2] Carl Hayden and other successful Arizona politicians quickly discovered that union miners could be a potent political force.

The miners, however, were not the only powerful labor group in Arizona. The labor movement also contained growing organizations among railroad workers and building tradesmen. The trainmen in Arizona organized around 1900 and, within a few years, the railroad brotherhoods made their presence felt on the political scene with support for legislation dealing with the length of the trainmen's workday. In the meantime, the building trades in the capital city of Phoenix had been well organized, with the bricklayers claiming 100 percent organization of their trade and a large and aggressive carpenters' union characterized as "cheerfully militant." In January, 1912, delegates claiming to represent approximately 7,000 union men gathered in Phoenix and organized the Arizona State Federation of Labor.[3] As these Arizona unions gained strength in the economic sphere, they began to make their mark in local politics.

Labor first emerged as an important political factor in Arizona in 1909. The increasing use of the antilabor injunction led workers to seek remedies through political activity. Beginning with the Pullman Palace Car Company strike of 1894, injunctions based upon the "conspiracy in restraint of trade" wording of the 1890 Sherman Anti-Trust Act were used more and more frequently by the courts. Unions found that even simple boycotts had become effectively illegal. In 1902, the United Hatters Union declared a boycott of the D. E. Loewe & Company, Danbury, Connecticut, and were found guilty of conspiring to restrain trade under the Sherman Act. The company successfully claimed triple damages from individual members of the striking union. These cases and others made the injunction issue a national concern for labor. "The American labor movement did not organize its political power," noted Samuel Gompers, "until we encountered political obstacles interjected into our economic activity."[4] The injunction was just such a political obstacle.

In July, 1910, union representatives and labor supporters met in Phoenix and formed a third political party—the Labor Party. What the Laborites wanted was a state constitution that provided for the popular democratic reforms of initiative, referendum, and recall (especially the latter, which would give labor a chance to recall injunction-prone judges); women's suffrage and popular election of United States senators; and important labor-related issues such as antiblacklist laws, employers' liability, and an anti-injunction statute. The Democrats, through the efforts of prolabor leaders such as George W. P. Hunt, agreed to adopt many of the Labor Party planks into their own platform and brought the unions into the Democratic fold. As a result of the Democrat-Labor fusion, the Labor Party withdrew from the field and, with a few exceptions, threw its support behind the Democratic candidates in the upcoming election for delegates to the state constitutional convention.[5]

The joining of the Democrat and Labor political parties helped to make the Democrats the majority party in Arizona, but it was a party with two distinct factions. The conservative wing of the party tended to represent the corporate mining and railroad interests, while the liberal wing became the voice of labor, the small businessman, and farmer. These two factions came into conflict early in the constitutional convention, over the contest for president of the convention. E. E. Ellinwood, an attorney whose clientele included large mining and railroad companies, opposed Hunt, the prolabor Democrat from Globe; the latter emerged the victor.[6]

The new state constitution devised by Hunt and the liberals contained the key features of popular democracy: the initiative, referendum, and recall (including the recall of judges). It also included important labor provisions such as an eight-hour day for public employees; child-labor regulation; an abrogation of the common-law, fellow-servant doctrine; employers' liability; and a prohibition of the antilabor blacklist. Other more radical labor proposals failed to gain acceptance. For example, a proposed constitutional provision which banned the use of injunctions against strikers, and a clause which placed the right of workers to strike and boycott against their employers as a part of the constitution's bill of rights were disapproved by the convention.[7]

Under this new constitution, Arizona held its first general election for state and national officials in December, 1911.[8] In this first election, the Democratic candidate for Congress, Carl Hayden, began to court the labor vote in earnest. Hayden was comfortable with the labor position, advocating the popular democratic issues of the initiative and referendum. He had supported these reforms as a young man graduating from Tempe Normal School in 1896. By 1911, he also favored the recall, especially of judges—an issue dear to labor. At a campaign rally in Tucson, Hayden carried his support for judicial recall one step farther. "If it is right to recall a state judge," Hayden said, then "it is also proper to recall a federal judge, and I will vote for the recall of the federal judiciary."[9]

In addition to campaign rallies, appeals to the labor vote were made through extensive newspaper advertising and electioneering which went directly into the union hall. Full-page newspaper advertisements lauding Hayden's position on labor issues declared,

> He has pledged himself in the public prints and from the platform, if elected, to vote for an employers' liability act, a compulsory compensation law, the abrogation of the fellow-servant doctrine, and for the extension to the limits of the federal jurisdiction of all provisions contained in the Arizona Constitution for the benefit of labor.[10]

Campaign circulars, written by Secretary J. W. Stinson of the Jerome Miners' Union, praising Hayden and the other Democratic candidates, went to every Arizona local of the large and active Western Federation of Miners.[11] Efforts like Stinson's helped to achieve a Democratic victory, and Carl Hayden went to Washington as Arizona's first congressman.

Over the next fourteen years and in subsequent campaigns, Carl Hayden's courting of the labor vote revolved around a number of key features, which he developed into a fine political art. Beginning with his favorable stance on issues of importance to the labor movement, Hayden built political support based on his actual voting record—his performance when bills considered crucial to labor's interest reached the halls of Congress. He swiftly moved to include all of the officers of every union local in Arizona in his statewide political "network," an immense group of Hayden loyalists made up of local officeholders, precinct committee people, postmaster appointees, friendly newspaper editors, and countless friends from all walks of life. These supporters played a key role in courting the labor vote, through their active campaigning in union halls and among workingmen throughout Arizona. Finally, there was Hayden's personal friendship with important union leaders, on both state and national levels.

Evidence of Hayden's association with Arizona union leaders and their willingness to aid in his campaign efforts appeared during the summer of 1912. J. Tom Lewis, three-term president of the Globe Miners' Union and executive board member of the Western Federation of Miners, wrote to Hayden, "Send me your nomination papers here and I will only be too glad to help you all I can." After Lewis's aid in the 1912 election, Hayden placed the names and addresses of the secretaries of every union local in Arizona affiliated with the American Federation of Labor on his regular mailing list.[12]

This mailing list brought union officers within the scope of Hayden's political network and enabled him to circulate his voting record to all union men. By 1914, he could send out campaign letters, which proclaimed his strong support of legislation "for the benefit of American labor." His campaign speeches also brought home the message of his prolabor voting record. "It is not necessary for me to enumerate all of the bills that have been passed in behalf of American labor," declared Hayden. "It is sufficient to say that in 1904 [sic], the American Federation of Labor submitted a bill of grievances to Congress, and that, with the passage of the Seaman's bill through the House last September, every one of these grievances...has been satisfactorily answered by the Democratic party."[13]

Carl Hayden's art of courting union labor would be put to the test in the divisive campaign of 1916. The Democratic primary of that year was the scene of a bitter struggle between the conservative and liberal factions of the majority party. The primary contest for governor, between George A. Olney and the incumbent, Governor George W. P. Hunt, reflected the alignment of the "corporation v. producer" in the Democratic Party. The battle was "all over the high-toned democrats going against Hunt," wrote M. C. Schalm, president of the Globe Central Labor Council, and "It is drifting to a party fight of capital against labor...." Carl Hayden was drawn into this factional controversy by the alleged activities of his postmaster appointees, who were campaigning against the liberal candidate, Governor Hunt. Hayden found it necessary to explain, defend, or repudiate the actions of his postmaster appointees, who were also hard at work campaigning for him and making it appear that Hayden backed the conservative, Olney, in the governor's contest.[14] For Carl Hayden, however, the postmaster controversy soon lost its importance, when Albinus A. Worsley, a representative of the liberal-labor wing of the Democratic Party, declared his candidacy for Congress and presented Hayden with what would prove to be the only serious primary challenge in the first fourteen years of his congressional career.

Albinus A. Worsley's credentials as a representative of the liberal faction of the Democratic Party were impeccable. Born in Wisconsin in 1869, Worsley first tested the political waters at the age of twenty-four, by running for governor of Wisconsin on the Labor-Populist ticket. After moving to Arizona, he played a role in the formation of the Labor Party, and ran as that party's candidate for election as a delegate to the state constitutional convention of 1910. In the first election under the new state constitution, he was elected to the state senate, where he served as chairman of the Labor Committee. Although labeled by his opponents as a radical, socialist, "red flagger," and anarchist, Worsley could not be dismissed so easily by Hayden. Congressman Hayden had a serious competitor for the crucial labor vote.[15]

Albinus Worsley declared his candidacy in the summer of 1916 and campaigned statewide as a labor candidate—openly appealing to the union labor vote. If Worsley were able to "form an alliance with the miners and other labor unions," wrote William Beck, a long-time Hayden supporter, "there is no denying the fact, that he will prove to be a formidble (sic) candidate."[16] Arthur W. Davis, Hayden's cousin and an active campaigner, warned:

> Now this man Worsley is one talker he is also well known and you are going to see the union bunch flock to him.... Worsley is a regular Bryan when it comes to talk and you know he stumped the state for a lot of railroad measures + they all carried so he has a union following that may be hard to beat.[17]

In some mining communities, Worsley's campaign notices appeared on the stationery of the local Miners' Union and were signed by the union secretary. Leon Jacobs, a Phoenix attorney and former state legislator estimated that at least 75 percent of the approximately 15,000 labor votes in Arizona would go to Worsley, labor's "champion."[18]

To offset the campaign appeal of a champion of labor, Carl Hayden first cemented his own standing as a friend of labor in the halls of Congress. He began with an extensive campaign through the mails, that put copies of his outstanding prolabor voting record into the hands of all Arizona union officials and as many workingmen as possible. Fifty thousand circular letters, containing copies of Hayden's voting record as compiled by the National Legislative and Information Bureau of the Railway Brotherhoods, were sent to voters throughout Arizona. Hayden felt sure that he would "get good support from the ranks of organiz[e]d labor if it is made known that I have always been on the square with the working man." He also advertised his voting record, via the offices of friendly newspaper editors and through his connections with the Washington office of the American Federation of Labor. Letters from the AFL's Washington office proclaimed, "You will find upon examination of this record that Mr. Hayden has been true to Labor and voted regularly for all the measures which have been under consideration.[19]

Hayden capitalized on the issues of the impending nationwide railroad strike (eight-hour day and compulsory arbitration) in early September, 1916, to demonstrate to the trainmen that they had a champion in Congress. He reported to Chairman T. T. Cull of

Yuma's Order of Railroad Telegraphers that Congress supported the principle of the eight-hour day, and that compulsory arbitration was "but another name for involuntary servitude, a condition which was abolished with slavery by the Thirteenth Amendment to the Constitution and which I shall never favor no matter how it is labeled." Cull informed Hayden that even though the railroad organizations in Arizona held Worsley in high regard, "I feel sure that you will receive the majority of the railroad votes at the coming primaries."[20]

As the primary campaign advanced, Hayden's record as a friend of labor began to bring forth results. "I have always appreciated the favorable action you have taken on the labor measures coming before the United States Congress," declared C. E. Tracy, secretary-treasurer, Phoenix Typographical Union No. 352. M. C. Hankins assured Hayden, "Most of the railroad boys are going to support you." W. P. Mahoney, vice president of the WFM's Snowball Miners' Union, wrote to Hayden, "I showed your record to many of the miners here and they were satisfied you were OK on labor."[21]

While Carl Hayden remained in Washington, more of his supporters reported on their successful campaigning for the labor vote. Thomas A. Feeney, a Hayden postmaster appointee and active campaigner in Miami, Arizona, exemplified the spirit of the Hayden campaign. Feeney attended a campaign rally where Worsley "stated that the railroad boys asked him to run." After listening to Worsley's speech, Feeney reported, "I made him come over to the office with his few socialists friend [sic] and I pulled that letter of yours from [sic] the legislative representatives of the railroad boys and it made that bunch sit up and take notice."[22] Feeney's campaign work probably went far in helping to destroy Worsley's credibility among the union voters of Miami.

As reports such as Feeney's poured into Hayden's Washington office, the odds against Worsley taking the labor vote away from Hayden increased. When the September 12 primary election drew near, Hayden felt confident that he would hold the sizable block of union voters, even though "Mr. Worsley will get practically all of the votes of the Socialists who have registered as Democrats." Hayden wrote to M. C. Hankins, "I am satisfied that Mr. Worsley will get all of the red flag vote...." Albinus Worsley, it turned out, polled over 7,000 votes in the Democratic primary.[23] This was not enough to defeat the popular Hayden; but the election did demonstrate the powerful lure the labor vote held in 1916.

Carl Hayden's successful courting of the labor vote in 1916 was a tribute to his political dexterity. Not only did he campaign as a friend of labor, but he also worked for support from the Arizona Chapter of the American Mining Congress. This group of mine operators, under the leadership of Phelps Dodge was organized in 1915, to take the offensive against the growing power of Arizona unions and drive the Western Federation of Miners out of Arizona's copper industry. In 1917, using the war as a patriotic expedient and capitalizing on the alleged threat from the radical Industrial Workers of the World, the Arizona corporate interests waged an effective campaign against organized labor, and virtually eliminated the once-powerful miners' union (now the International Union of Mine, Mill, and Smelter Workers) from the Arizona scene.[24]

In the summer of 1917, the most dramatic moment in the history of the Arizona labor movement occurred in the mining towns of Jerome and Bisbee, as union men and sympathizers were kidnapped and deported from the towns in cattle cars. Arizona's two United States senators, Henry Ashurst and Marcus A. Smith, both expressed their approval of the deportation as a means of dealing with the radical and disruptive Industrial Workers of the World. Although opposing the radical union, Congressman Hayden disapproved of vigilante action to settle industrial disputes. He took an unusually independent stand on the floor of Congress, when he offended Arizona mining interests by introducing legislation "to prohibit and punish the interstate deportation of laborers and other persons." Hayden's action did little to endear him to the jingoist National Security League, which campaigned strongly against him in 1918. His declining majority that year showed that some of the Hayden political following was as offended as the league.[25]

The period following the First World War proved to be labor's "lean years." For the working men and women of America, normalcy meant the American Plan, open shop, yellow-dog contracts, and a time of prosperity, when workers' wages failed to keep pace with rising productivity, profits, and dividends. In Arizona, the once influential IUMMSW, racked by internal schism and battles with employers, was but a shell of its former self. The nationwide drive for the open shop carried into Phoenix and Tucson. "I think we have got to come to the open shop," said Clinton Campbell, president of the Organized Builders Exchange of Phoenix. "Look at Los Angeles, famous as an open-shop town for a number of years." With Los Angeles as their example, Phoenix businessmen began the battle for the open shop in the spring of 1920, to crack the strength of the powerful building trades organizations. Labor was also on the defensive in the courts. As far as organized labor was concerned, William Howard Taft, chief justice of the Supreme Court, commented, "That faction we have to hit every little while...." The chief justice made good on his word, as the court used the Fourteenth Amendment to invalidate the anti-injunction provisions of the Clayton Anti-Trust Bill of 1914. The Supreme Court, also declared Arizona's anti-injunction law, passed by the first state legislature, to be unconstitutional (*Truax v. Corrigan*, 257 U.S. 312 [1921]).[26]

Faced with such overwhelming legal and economic onslaughts, Arizona's trade unions suffered declining membership and relative insignificance on the political scene. By the advent of the twenties, organized labor had lost its political clout. More and more, successful politicians such as Carl Hayden turned their backs on labor, to court the more conservative elements which now controlled the state's power structure. Indeed, so complete was Hayden's shift, that Barry Goldwater chose Hayden's campaign manager, Steven Shadegg, for his conservative stance, when Goldwater first ran for the Senate in 1952. The state which had once been known for its militant miners had become the national symbol of right-to-work. Labor had became a liability in the world of politics, Hayden-style.

NOTES

[1]Walter Rauschenbusch, *Christianizing The Social Order* (New York: The Macmillan Company, 1919), p. 449; and campaign letter, August 10, 1916, 644/12, Carl Trumbull Hayden Papers, Arizona Collection, Hayden Library, Arizona State University, Tempe, Arizona (hereafter cited as CTHP).

[2]Western Federation of Miners *Official Proceedings of the Nineteenth Annual Convention of the Western Federation of Miners, Butte, Montana, July 7 to August 4, 1911*, pp. 197–201.

[3]Michael S. Wade, *The Bitter Issue, the Right to Work Law in Arizona* (Tucson: The Arizona Historical Society, 1976), p. 12; Carlton H. Parker, "A Report to the United States Commission on Industrial Relations on a Labor Trouble in Phoenix, Arizona," 1914, p. 5, Wisconsin Historical Society Library, Madison, Wisconsin; and (Phoenix) *Arizona Republican*, January 21, 1912, sec. 1, p. 12.

[4]H. A. Hubbard, "The Arizona Enabling Act and President Taft's Veto," *Pacific Historical Review 3* (1934):138; and Samuel Gompers, *Seventy Years of Life and Labor*, 1957 edition, ed. by Philip Taft and John A. Sessions (New York: E. P. Dutton & Company, 1925, 1957), p. 253.

[5](Phoenix) *Arizona Republican*, July 13, 1910, p. 5; Hubbard, "Arizona Enabling Act," pp. 320, 322; Wade, *Bitter Issue*, p. 14; Jay J. Wagoner, *Arizona Territory, 1863–1912, A Political History* (Tucson: University of Arizona Press, 1970), p. 464; and Alan V. Johnson, "Governor, G. W. P. Hunt and Organized Labor" (M.A. thesis, University of Arizona, 1964), p. 25. For a study of a 1910 election campaign in which the Labor Party failed to support the Democrats, see Mary Dale Palsson, "The Arizona Constitutional Convention of 1910, the Election of Delegates in Pima County," *Arizona and the West* 16 (Summer, 1974):111–24.

[6]Steven A. Fazio, "Marcus Aurelius Smith: Arizona Delegate and Senator," *Arizona and the West* 12 (Spring, 1970):54–55.

[7]"Proposed Constitution of Arizona, 1910," pp. 33–34, 502/3, CTHP; Rufus K. Wyllys, *Arizona, the History of a Frontier State* (Phoenix: Hobson & Herr, 1950), p. 307; and "Propositions to Constitutional Convention, 1910," No. 71, introduced by Thomas Feeney of Cochise County, box #16/folder #1, George W. P. Hunt Papers, Arizona Collection, Hayden Library, Arizona State University, Tempe, Arizona.

[8]The story of President Taft's veto of the Arizona statehood resolution due to his opposition to the recall of judges is well known. Arizona voters vented their displeasure with Taft in the 1912 election, when they placed him fourth behind Woodrow Wilson, Theodore Roosevelt, and Eugene Debs—the candidate of the Socialist Party.

[9]*Phoenix Daily Herald*, June 11, 1896, p. 2; and (Tucson) *Arizona Daily Star*, November 26, 1911, p. 1.

[10](Tucson) *Arizona Daily Star*, December 2, 1911, p. 5.

[11]J. W. Stinson to Carl Hayden, November 15, 1911, 644/1, CTHP; and campaign circular signed by J. W. Stinson, 644/1, CTHP.

[12]J. Tom Lewis to Carl Hayden, July 25, 1912, 630/2, CTHP; and names and addresses of union secretaries in Arizona from locals affiliated with AFL, 644/10, CTHP.

[13]Campaign letter, 1914, 644/10, CTHP; and Hayden speech, 1914, 502/7, CTHP.

[14]Henry M. Woods to Carl Hayden, August 16, 1916, 644/13, CTHP; M. C. Schalm to Carl Hayden, August 14, 1916, 644/13, CTHP; W. P. Doheney to Carl Hayden, August 19, 1916, 643/10, CTHP; Wilson T. Wright to Carl Hayden, August 17, 1916, 644/12, CTHP; and Carl Hayden to M. C. Schalm, August 21, 1916, 643/10, CTHP.

[15]Jo Connors, *Who's Who in Arizona* (Tucson: Press of the Arizona Daily Star, 1913), p. 369; and Palsson, "1910 Election, Pima County," p. 114. For comments on Worsley as a radical, socialist, red flagger, and anarchist, see W. C. Hedgpeth to Carl Hayden, August 25, 1916, 643/11, CTHP; E. E. Ellinwood to Carl Hayden, August 26, 1916, 643/11, CTHP; and W. A. O'Connor to Carl Hayden, August 25, 1916, 643/11, CTHP.

[16]William Beck to Carl Hayden, August 4, 1916, 644/12, CTHP.

[17]Arthur W. Davis to Carl Hayden, August 11, 1916, 644/12, CTHP.

[18]Dan Augius to Carl Hayden, August 18, 1916, 655/12, CTHP; and Leon Jacobs to Carl Hayden, August 17, 1916, 644/12, CTHP.

[19]Campaign letter with copy of labor voting record, August 10, 1916, 644/12, CTHP; Carl Hayden to Arthur W. Davis, August 28, 1916, 643/10, CTHP; Carl Hayden to L. S. Williams, August 14, 1916, 643/12, CTHP; M. C. Hankins to Carl Hayden, August 18, 1916, 644/12, CTHP; W. P. Doheney to Carl Hayden, August 19, 1916, 643/10, CTHP; and A. E. Holden to Carl Evans, August 24, 1916, 644/12, CTHP.

[20](Phoenix) *Arizona Republican*, September 1, 1916, p, 1; Carl Hayden to T. T. Cull, September 6, 1916, 643/10, CTHP; and T. T. Cull to Carl Hayden, August 31, 1916, 643/10, CTHP.

[21]C. E. Tracy to Carl Hayden, August 19, 1916, 643/13, CTHP; M. C. Hankins to Carl Hayden, August 23, 1916, 643/11, CTHP; and W. P. Mahoney to Carl Hayden, August 23, 1916, 643/13, CTHP.

[22]Thomas A. Feeney to Carl Hayden, August 9, 1916, 644/13, CTHP.

[23]Carl Hayden to Arthur W. Davis, August 28, 1916, 643/10, CTHP; Carl Hayden to M. C. Hankins, August 28, 1916, 643/10, CTHP; and election results, 703/10, CTHP.

[24]J. H. Robinson to Carl Hayden, August 10, 1916, 644/13, CTHP: J. H. Robinson to Carl Hayden, August 26, 1916, 643/11, CTHP; and James W. Byrkit, "Walter Douglas and Labor Struggles in Early 20th Century Arizona," *Southwest Economy and Society 1* (Spring 1976):18–20. For wartime labor conflicts in Arizona mining communities, see John H. Lindquist, "The Jerome Deportation of 1917,'" *Arizona and the West* 11 (Autumn, 1969):233–46; Daphne Overstreet, "On Strike! The 1917 Walkout at Globe, Arizona," *Journal of Arizona History* 18 (Summer, 1977):197–218; and James W. Byrkit, "The IWW in Wartime Arizona," *Journal of Arizona History* 18 (Summer, 1977): 149–70.

[25]Alice McKinney, "Arizona's Congressional Delegation, 1912–1921" (M. A. thesis, Stanford University, 1955), p. 67; U.S., Congress, House, 65th Cong. 2d sess., December 3, 1917, *Congressional Record* 56:8; U.S., Congress, House, Extension of Remarks of Representative Carl Hayden, "Voting Record on War Measures," 65th Cong., 2d sess., September 24, 1918, Appendix to the *Congressional Record* 56:628. Total vote for Hayden in 1916 was 34, 377, and in 1918 was 26,805 (election results, 703/10, CTHP).

[26]Vernon H. Jensen, *Heritage of Conflict: Labor Relations in the Nonferrous Metals Industry up to 1930* (Ithaca, New York: Cornell University Press, 1950), pp. 452–53; International Union of Mine, Mill and Smelter Workers, *Official Proceedings of the Twenty-fourth Consecutive and Fourth Biennial Convention of the International Union of Mine, Mill and Smelter Workers, Denver, Colorado, August 2 to August 12, 1920*, p. 295; (Phoenix) *Arizona Republican*, March 4, 1920, p. 1; and Henry F. Pringle, *The Life and Times of William Howard Taft*, 2 vols., (New York: Farrar & Rinehart, Inc., 1939), 2:967.

Anti-Labor Politics in Texas
1941–1957

George N. Green

CORPORATE INTERESTS HAVE BEEN POWERFUL IN TEXAS since the Civil War. Though many cotton fortunes were destroyed in the war, they were replaced by ranching, railroad, and lumber fortunes. Then along came the oil, gas, and sulphur interests, as well as the banks, insurance companies, and utilities. All these groups were adept at protecting their activities from state interference, but they were curbed by occasional outbreaks that placed populistic or progressive politicians in the state house. The last of these was the "New Deal" governor, Jimmie Allred, 1935–1939, who taxed the chain stores and blocked the passage of a state sales tax. In the Democratic gubernatorial primary of 1938, conservative, corporate interests took over Texas, perhaps for years to come. They were often termed "the establishment," a loosely-knit plutocracy of Anglo businessmen, oilmen, bankers, and lawyers. The leaders—especially during the 1940s and 1950s—were dedicated to a regressive tax structure; low corporate taxes; antilabor laws; political, social, and economic oppression of black and Mexican-Americans; alleged states' rights; and extreme reluctance to expand state services. Essays have been written about the Texas Establishment,[1] but no study has revealed the political strategies it utilized to sustain itself in office during its heyday.

In 1938, the usual clutch of politicians entered the Texas gubernatorial lists, but they were overwhelmed by a radio crooner and flour salesman, W. Lee O'Daniel. The upstart candidate never denied that one of his aims in the campaign was to sell more flour. Running on a platform of the Ten Commandments, along with an aggressive promise of $30-a-month pensions for everybody over sixty-five, O'Daniel's country-boy image was mostly a pose. He was, in fact, a business college graduate, worth half a million dollars. The public did

not know that some of the richest corporate leaders in the state persuaded him to enter the race. After winning and serving two years as
governor, during which time he surrounded himself with corporate
lobbyists and almost got a sales tax into the state constitution, O'Daniel
perceived that his posturing against "professional politicians" had
about run its course. Feeling the need for another target in the spring
of 1941, he discovered union racketeering.[2]

Unions had risen to power in the nation suddenly, during the
1930s, and some union leaders had committed abuses. Yet, in Texas,
still a predominantly agrarian state, unions were weak. As of mid-
April, 1941, not a single man-hour of labor had been lost on any
defense job, due to strikes or labor disturbances. Then, unexpectedly,
O'Daniel asked for an immediate joint session of the legislature on
March 13, 1941. The governor delivered an emotionally charged
speech about "labor leader racketeers," who were threatening to take
over Texas and were crippling Britain's struggle against the Nazis. He
called upon the legislators to pass his antiviolence bill before they left
the room. The bill did almost pass at that moment, even though no
one had read it. The final version of the law forbade the use or threat
of force or violence for the purpose of preventing someone from
working. Assemblies near locales where labor disputes were taking
place were also illegal, and violators could serve from one to two years
in the state penitentiary. Thus, if a picketer used violence to prevent
a strikebreaker from entering a plant, he had committed a felony
and was subject to imprisonment. But, if a strikebreaker slugged a
picketer, it was still a misdemeanor.[3]

If O'Daniel was truly sensitive about America's defense efforts, it
was not reflected in his earlier allusion to the war as a European howl-
ing that would have no effect on the United States, or in his later
opposition to the draft bill. It appears that the governor simply in-
vented a labor crisis as justification for an antiunion law which
boosted him politically. He had coordinated his antilabor drive with
that of Dallas Congressman Hatton Summers, and obviously yearned
for an opportunity to appear on the national slate himself and play
the antiunion issue for all it was worth.[4]

Upon the sudden death of Senator Morris Sheppard in April,
1941, O'Daniel got his chance. During the special election, pitted
against New Deal Congressman Lyndon Johnson among others,
O'Daniel really began riding the labor issue. He claimed that, after the
passage of his antistrike law, the "labor agitators...scurried out of
Texas overnight"; yet, he simultaneously bemoaned that the "radical,
wild-eyed labor leaders" were supporting other candidates. The bulk
of the labor vote, such as it was, undoubtedly went to Johnson, though

he had taken his first antilabor potshots and thereby convinced several unions not to endorse him. Another candidate was Congressman Martin Dies, who hurled spectacular charges of communist subversion at the CIO and other agencies and institutions. He siphoned off so much of O'Daniels' rural east Texas support, that the governor had to depend upon the arrival of thousands of suspicious, tardy ballots before he squeaked past Johnson.[5]

O'Daniel introduced a series of anti-labor bills in Congress, none of which got more than four votes, and then faced a serious threat to his reelection in 1942. During his second campaign for the senate, "Pappy" O'Daniel became more aware of the Communist menace in Texas. At first, he revealed that his opponents, former governors Dan Moody and Jimmie Allred, were financed by "communistic labor-leader racketeers," a phrase he used as often as sixteen times in one speech. The senator finally alleged that he faced a multimillion dollar conspiracy, comprising Moody, Allred, the professional politicians, the politically controlled newspapers (including the Dallas *News*), and, of course, the "communistic labor-leader racketeers." Backed by most of the corporate establishment and tremendous support from the countryside, O'Daniel came close to a majority but was forced into a runoff with Allred.[6]

Given the antilabor miasma of the day and a certain amount of anti-New-Deal sentiment, Allred could not afford the public embrace of either group, especially labor. In a hotel conference with Austin New Deal mayor, Tim Miller, and Texas State Federation of Labor secretary, Harry Acreman, Allred informed them that his financiers wanted him to take a couple of shots at labor. He thought he might criticize the CIO, since that union was going to vote for him anyway. Miller agreed that he had to, but Acreman warned that CIO leaders and members would "go fishing" on election day. Probably a few did, angered by Allred's proposals to prohibit compulsory unionism in defense industries and to limit dues to $1 a month. It is doubtful that labor defections made any difference in the outcome, however, and Allred lost by only 433,203 to 451,559.[7]

Another labor setback occurred the next year, even though wartime governor Coko Stevenson was more sympathetic to labor—or at least to the AFL—than his predecessor. The governor strengthened the unemployment compensation system, and, during the height of the growing antilabor feeling, negotiated a no-strike agreement with organized labor. Even so, in 1943, when the Manford Bill sailed through the house and was rammed through the senate in unseemly fashion by Lieutenant Governor John Lee Smith, Stevenson allowed it to become law (without his signature). The law required unions to

file comprehensive annual reports with the state, and forbade contributions to political campaigns. The reports, which were to include all financial and organizational records, were virtually open to
the public.[8]

In 1944, many leading oil men and corporate lobbyists, irate at
Roosevelt's economic policies and at the Smith v. Allwright Supreme
Court decision that allowed Blacks to vote in the Democratic primary,
fomented a successful coup and nominated Democratic presidential
electors who were uninstructed. Since their sympathies were anti-New
Deal, the electors would be expected to vote for Republican nominee,
Tom Dewey, or for ultraconservative Virginia Democrat, Harry Byrd.
Most Texans would then be completely disenfranchised in the general
election. If they crossed out the names of the Democratic electors, the
Republican electors would vote Republican. If they crossed out the
names of the Republican electors, the Democratic electors would vote
Republican or for Byrd. Jimmie Allred and others led a New Dealer's
counterrebellion and purged the disloyal electors at the fall state convention. The anti-New Dealers then organized a third political party,
the Texas Regulars, whose first two planks (out of eight) were aimed
at labor: restoration of the Democratic party to the integrity "taken
away by Hillman, Browder, and others," and "protection of honest
labor unions from foreign-born racketeers who have gained control
by blackmail." They were aided by various corporate front-groups, all
of which were exposed by congressional investigating committees, but
the administration evidently thought it sufficient to embarrass them
in public hearings rather than prosecute them under the Corrupt
Practices Act. Roosevelt's popularity as wartime commander was still
enormous in Texas, and the Regulars were brushed aside with only 12
percent of the vote.[9]

Besides aiding in the reelection of F.D.R., Texas labor enjoyed
another success that year; Martin Dies, head of the labor-baiting
House Un-American Activities Committee, was forced into retirement. In Dies' southeast Texas district, apathy and the poll tax usually
combined to limit the voting to about 5 or 10 percent of the population. But the CIO undertook a massive poll-tax drive and asked a
distinguished judge to run for Congress. Dies soon announced his
retirement, due to ill health and fear of becoming a professional
politician.[10]

In 1946, thousands of Texas workers, like those elsewhere, bolted
off their jobs in an attempt to keep up with the rising cost of living.
Moreover, by June of that year, the CIO seemed well on its way to
unionizing the state's biggest industrial plants. Hundreds of workers
successfully struck the Waco factory of General Tire and Rubber and

the Fort Worth plant of Consolidated Vultee Aircraft. The only pro-labor candidate in the governor's race that year was Homer Rainey, recently deposed as president of the University of Texas. In addition to defending organized labor's rights, Rainey embraced academic freedom and better treatment of black citizens. These three positions became the main campaign issues, as the other candidates zeroed in on the New Deal-Fair Deal champion. In the cities, Rainey was backed by an emerging coalition of labor and minority groups. The Dallas precincts that Rainey carried, or even ran well in, were heavily infused with lower-income Blacks, Chicanos and, to a lesser extent, organized labor. In Houston, Rainey ran especially well in the black precincts and also carried other areas that were an admixture of union and nonunion labor and minority groups. Rainey was trounced in the runoff, however, by Railroad Commissioner Beauford Jester, who was heavily supported by oil and other corporate interests. Labor-backed candidates lost all over the state, many of them in bitter campaigns against the "left-wing political terrorists of the CIO–PAC.[11]

Antiunion sentiment crested in 1947, when the Texas Manufacturers' Association, regional Chambers of Commerce, and right-wing extremist groups successfully lobbied for a spate of regulatory laws. The solons obliged, with a right-to-work law, an anticheckoff act, an antisecondary boycott law, a law subjecting unions to antitrust statutes, and an anti-mass-picketing act (defining mass picketing as more than two pickets either within fifty feet of the plant entrance or fifty feet of any other picket). The legislative move reached absurdity when a prolabor member of the house offered an amendment which would have abolished unions, confiscated union members' property, sent their families to concentration camps, and lined up all union members against a wall and had them shot. The house voted it down sixty-three to eight.[12]

In the presidential election year of 1948, labor matters were unimportant in the Dixiecratic rebellion against the Truman candidacy, but they were crucial in Texas' disputed senatorial election that year. Congressman Lyndon Johnson's vote for the Taft-Hartley Bill was instrumental in nailing down corporate financial support in Texas, support increased during the campaign because his conservative opponent, Coke Stevenson, had reservations about the constitutionality of the law. More importantly, Stevenson had privately promised a railroad union leader that he would not embrace the Taft-Hartley Bill, which secured for him the surprising public endorsement of the State Federation of Labor. Johnson slammed the endorsement, alleging a secret deal, while benefitting from the more effective help of the CIO. At least one Johnson brochure even berated Stevenson as the CIO

candidate. Lyndon Johnson was essentially an establishment conservative by 1948, and, of course, Stevenson had always been one. Although Johnson won the race, and although most urban workingmen
probably preferred the enigmatic congressman to "Calculatin' Coke,"
labor was a clear loser in the public eye.[13]

For the next few years, labor-baiting took a back seat to the tide-
lands question in Texas politics, but it dramatically resurfaced in three
straight elections during the mid-1950s. By 1954, Governor Allan
Shivers' administration had been embarrassed by insurance company
scandals and the governor's dubious real estate transactions in the Rio
Grande Valley, but the governor nevertheless declared for an unprecedented third term. The liberal challenger, Ralph Yarborough, solidly
backed by labor, waged a spirited campaign but soon found himself connected with a communistic labor menace, conjured up by
Shivers. A CIO retail workers strike in Port Arthur had evidently
been helped by a couple of Communists or ex-Communists whom
the CIO had quickly replaced. But the tainted connection enabled
Shivers to escalate an ordinary strike situation (ordinary outside
Texas and the South) into a Communist conspiracy that threatened to
take hold of the state. The governor could then assert that, "While I
know my opponent is not a Communist, I feel that he is a captive of
certain people who do not approve of being tough on Communists."
The governor also exploited segregationist attitudes, stirred by the
Brown decision of the Supreme Court which was handed down in the
midst of the Texas primary. Yarborough forced Shivers into a runoff,
which no previous incumbent governor had won.[14]

With less than two weeks to go in the runoff, the governor's
closest advisor informed him that he still needed a burning issue for
the finish. As for segregation, he said, "I don't believe that old dog will
hunt again," and the "outside labor bosses" hadn't caught on either.
The aide suggested "using the Port Arthur story as a threat to businessmen everywhere," and using "the farm-labor unionization threat,
especially in West Texas." The former meant switching from opposition to the union because it was "red-controlled," to opposition to "the
union, period." The farm-labor gambit was risky because of the governor's personal involvement with ranches that used cheap wetback
labor, but "it's the only thing we have that can be made to appeal
to the west Texas (especially South Plains) farmers, who are pretty
solidly against you...."[15] This strategy was followed in the runoff.
Teams of Port Arthur businessmen appeared on radio and television
around the state, describing their city as a ghost town because of the
Communist picketing. Mass meetings of merchants were told that
their towns would be next, unless Shivers was reelected. A televised

"Port Arthur Story" showed deserted streets in the coastal town. Yarborough claimed, and a Shivers staff man later admitted, that the film was taken at 5:00 A.M. Assisted also by enormous donations from corporate interest groups and by the editorial support of ninety-five of the state's one hundred daily papers, Shivers beat Yarborough 775,088 to 683,132.[16]

Racial issues, perhaps, had slipped past labor as an establishment whipping post by the 1956 governor's race. Conservative Democrat Price Daniel often seemed confused over the identity of his opponent. Although challenged by Ralph Yarborough, Daniel usually spoke as though he were running against the NAACP and Walter Reuther. The Daniel forces paraded a photograph of Reuther giving a $75,000 check to the NAACP. They did not parade the information that the transaction took place in Detroit and had nothing to do with the Texas elections. The NAACP, in fact, had not endorsed Yarborough, since he had come out against "forced" integration. Daniel appealed to the farm vote with the old, absurd charge that the CIO was about to take over the state's farms and ranches. Daniel was backed by big oil and the customary monolithic support of the Texas press. Yet, Yarborough almost beat the establishment, polling 694,830 to Daniel's 698,001. The next year, he did win Daniel's vacated seat in the United States Senate, primarily because the establishment could not pressure either of two conservatives (one a Republican) out of the one-shot election and failed in the effort—in the middle of the campaign—to change the election law to require a runoff.[17]

Looking back on the politics of that period, one historian of the labor movement in Texas attributes the antilabor laws to urbanizing influences, and notes that the cities were run by businessmen. Most prolabor votes during the crucial 1947 session, he notes further, came from the rural legislators.[18] But this analysis does not really hold up. In 1941, three of the four senate votes against the O'Daniel Act were cast by rural solons, but, in the house, thirteen urbanites voted against it while only four of their more numerous rural colleagues did so. In 1943, rural senators cast six of the nine votes against the Manford Act, but, in the house, twenty-four urbanites opposed it as against only twenty-one rural legislators. And a composite vote on labor bills in the 1947 session shows that only one rural senator out of twenty-two cast a slight majority of votes in labor's favor, while one urban senator out of nine had a perfect seven-to-zero labor record. In the house, twenty-five rural representatives out of one hundred four (24 percent) voted in accordance with union interests on a majority of the labor bills, and seventeen out of forty-six (37 percent) urbanites did the same.[19] Moreover, dozens of politically active oil operators from east and west

Texas were anything but urban-oriented. Both O'Daniel and Stevenson considered themselves rural spokesmen, and neither could depend on a durable urban base of support in contested elections. On the other hand, Jester and (especially) Shivers depended heavily on urban corporate support. The point is, the corporations simply rendered rural-urban differences irrelevant. Rural and urban legislators and governors could be handled in precisely the same fashion.

The leading economist of the Texas labor movement in the 1950s asserted that Texas' antiunion laws, albeit more numerous than in any other state, had little effect on the economy. The legislative battles were traceable to corporate desire to prove that they could pass the statutes.[20] Doubtless, the establishment's antilabor stance was more symbolic than real, in the sense that the economist stated it, but the establishment position was real enough in most elections of that day. Labor-baiting was the conservatives' most dependable winning tactic in Texas in virtually every contested election for governor and senator from 1941 through 1957, as well as in a number of other elections.

The establishment hasn't been quite the same since the election of Yarborough and the simultaneous collapse of the white-hot phase of resistance to integration. After a generation of practicing demagogic politics, the conservatives "cleaned up their act." Every governor since that time has made overtures to organized labor (and the minorities) until finally, with the election of Dolph Briscoe in 1973, the Texas AFL–CIO more or less became part of the establishment, or at least the arm of it that dominated the Democratic party. By the 1970s, the establishment had become, of course, a more moderate and mature power complex than the one that had prevailed during the more primitive years of the 1940s and 1950s.[21]

NOTES

[1]See Hart Stilwell, *Texas* (Austin: Texas Social and Legislative Conference, 1949), booklet in Brotherhood of Locomotive Firemen and Enginemen Files (Texas Labor Archives, University of Texas at Arlington); Neal Peirce's chapter on Texas in *The Great Plains States of America* (New York: Norton, 1972); Theodore H. White, "Texas: Land of Wealth and Fear," *Reporter*, X (June 8, 1954), pp. 30–37; Margaret Carter, column in the *Texas Observer*, January 24, 1964. See also, G. N. Green, *The Establishment in Texas Politics* (Westport, Connecticut: Greenwood, 1979).

[2]Dick West, column in the Dallas *Morning News*, May 25, 1969; T. A. Price, column in the Dallas *Morning News*, August 14, 1938; Sam Kinch and Stuart Long, *Allan Shivers* (Austin: Shoal Creek Press, 1973), pp. 33; John Ferling, "The First Administration of Governor W. Lee O'Daniel" (unpublished M. A. thesis, Baylor, 1962); Frank Goodwyn, *Lone Star Land* (New York: Alfred A. Knopf, 1955), p. 269.

Regarding O'Daniel and the corporate lobbyist interviews with Robert Calvert, Austin, December 23, 1976; Bill Lawson, Austin, September 14, 1976; and letter from Stuart Long, November 11, 1976; see *Texas Spectator*, October 18, 1946.

³*House Journal,* 47th Legislature, Reg. Sess., 1941, I, 1440; *Senate Journal,* 47th Legislature, Reg. Sess., 1941, p. 690; Austin *American,* April 18, 1941; John Wortham, "Regulation of Organized Labor in Texas, 1940–1945" (unpublished M. A. thesis, University of Texas at Austin, 1947), pp. 29–32; Grady Mullennix, "A History of the Texas State Federation of Labor" (unpublished Ph.D. dissertation, University of Texas at Austin, 1955), pp. 390–391.

⁴Fort Worth *Star-Telegram,* June 30, 1942; John Gunther, *Inside U.S.A.* (New York: Harper and Brothers, 1947), p. 851; letter from W. Lee O'Daniel to Hatton Sumners, April 4, 1941; and "Resolution Adopted by State Democratic Executive Committee in Session at Houston," March 29, 1941, in letter from E. B. Germany to Hatton Sumners, March 31, 1941, in the Hatton Sumners Papers, Drawer 14 (Dallas Historical Society).

⁵O'Daniel quotes from *W. Lee O'Daniel News,* June 23, 1941, and O'Daniel speech, June 4, 1941, in the James V. Allred Collection, Box 158 (Special Collections, University of Houston); "Analysis of the 1941 Texas Senatorial Election by Texas Surveys of Public Opinion,"confidential poll by Joe Belden, 1941, in the Lyndon Johnson Papers, House Years, Box 9 (Lyndon B. Johnson Library, Austin).

On labor, see *Texas State Federation of Labor-Proceedings, 1941* (Austin; n. p., 1941), pp. 41, 85, 174–175; letters from W. H. Winchester to Texas Legislative board members, May 16, 1941; and from Joe Steadham to John Connally, June 5, 1941, in the Brotherhood of Locomotive Firemen and Enginemen Files; and letters from J. M. Arnold to Lyndon Johnson, September 14, 1941, from Simeon Hyde and P. F. Kennedy to Johnson, June 24, 1941, from Harry Bernhard to Johnson, April 15, 1941, and from J. L. M. to Edward Keating, May 3, 1941, in the Johnson Papers, House Years, Boxes 7, 8, 10, and 11 respectively.

⁶*W. Lee O'Daniel News,* August 14, 1942; S. S. McKay, *W. Lee O'Daniel and Texas Politics* (Lubbock: Texas Tech Press, 1944), pp. 565, 566, 569, 581, 590, and 611; on corporate support for O'Daniel, see letters to Jimmie Allred from John McCarty, August 16, 1942, and Bert King, September 1, 1942, in Box 136, from Emil Corenbleth, July 27, 1942, in Box 141, from Frank Harrison, August 7, 1942, and Henry Flagg, August 24, 1942, in Box 174, and letters to Claude Wild from Clarence Lohman, August 11, 1942, Box 144, and from J. P. Cox, July 16, 1942, in Box 157, and letter from Bill Kittrell Jr. to Ed Flynn, August 7, 1942, in Box 141. All boxes are in the Allred Collection.

⁷Interview with Harry Acreman, Dallas, August 38, 1969; interview with John Crossland, Houston, November 17, 1976; "Hasten the Day of Victory," Allred brochure, 1942, in Box 156, and Claude Wild telegram to Jimmie Allred, May 15, 1942, in Box 174, and letter from W. A. Combs in Sam Low, August 12, 1942, in Box 136—all boxes in the Allred Collection; *Texas Almanac, 1943–1944* (Dallas: A. H. Belo, 1945), pp. 253–255.

⁸Mullennix, p. 394; Austin *American,* March 26, 1943; unidentified paper, February 17, 1943, in the John Lee Smith Papers (Southwest Collection, Texas Tech University, Lubbock); Wilbourn Benton, *Texas* (Englewood Cliffs, New Jersey; Prentice-Hall, 1961), pp. 522–523; "An Agreement," the no-strike compact of March 2, 1943, in the Texas AFL–CIO Papers, 110–15–1–6.

⁹S. S. McKay, *Texas Politics, 1906–1944* (Lubbock: Texas Tech Press, 1952), pp. 430–438; *Proceedings of the State Democratic Convention* (anti-New Deal convention), May 23, 1944; Austin American October 6, 1944; "Prominent Lawyers Who Were Leaders at the Convention Held in the Senate Chamber, May 23, 1944," list in the Lyndon Johnson Papers, House Years, Box 38; *Texas Almanac, 1946–1947,* pp. 531–533; Alexander Heard, *A Two-Party South?* (Chapel Hill: University of North Carolina Press, 1952), p. 258; Stanley Schneider, "The Texas Regular Party of 1944" (unpublished M.A. thesis, University of Chicago, 1948), pp. 57–59, 97–101, 195. For the exposure of front groups, see United States Senate, Committee Investigating Campaign Expenditures, *Investigation of Presidential, Vice-Presidential, and Senatorial Campaign Expenditures,* Report No. 101, 79th Cong., 1st Sess., 1944, and United States House of Representatives, Special Committee to Investigate Campaign Expenditures, *Hearings: Investigation of Campaign Expenditures,* Parts 7, 8, and 10, 78th Cong., 2d Sess., 1944.

[10]Green, pp. 74–75; James Foster, *The Union Politic* (Columbia, Missouri: University of Missouri, 1975), p. 28.

[11]Waco *Times-Herald,* June 2, 1946; Fort Worth Star-Telegram, May 11, 1946; *CIO News,* February 10, 1947; David Botter, column in the Dallas Morning News, August 27 and 28, 1946; Gunther, p. 841; quote in Dallas *Times-Herald,* August 23, 1946; precinct returns in Green, pp. 214–217. See also, S. S. McKay, *Texas and the Fair Deal* (San Antonio: Naylor, 1954), pp. 119–130.

[12]Benton, pp. 523–526, 529; *International Oil Worker,* May 19, 1947; *Texas Industry,* June, 1947; Hart Stilwell, "Will He Boss Texas?" *Nation,* 173 (November 10, 1951), p. 399; Frederick Meyers, *"Right-to-Work" in Practice* (New York: the Fund for the Republic, 1959), p. 3.

[13]Lyndon Johnson election brochure, 1948, in the Johnson Papers, House Years, Box 94; McKay, *Fair Deal,* pp. 200–201, 223; letter from Jimmie Allred to Claude Wild, June 26, 1948, in the Allred Collection, Box 172; V. O. Kay, *Southern Politics* (New York: Alfred A. Koopf, 1949), p. 258; Roland Evans and Robert Novak, *Lyndon B. Johnson: The Exercise of Power* (New York: the New American Library, 1966), pp. 23–24; Green, p. 113.

[14]Transcript of "Facts Forum State of the Nation," December 1, 1953, in the Allan Shivers Papers, 4–9/55 (Texas State Archives, Austin); Dallas *Morning News,* January 24, 1954; Goodwyn, pp. 316–317; *State Observer,* January 11, 1954; Austin *American,* November 28, 1953; quote is from Shivers speech, July 15, 1954, in Shivers Papers, 4–10/23; Shivers' first segregationist speech was the dramatic Lufkin address, June 21, 1954, in the Shivers Papers, 4–9/145, and others are in 4–9/153, 4–10/23, and 4–10/24.

[15]Memo from Weldon Hart to Allan Shivers, August 15, 1954, in the Shivers Papers, 4–10/33.

[16]Stuart Long, "'Scared Money' Wins an Election in Texas," *Reporter,* XI (October 21, 1954), pp. 23, 26; Dallas *Morning News,* August 12, 14, 21, 22, 1954; Kinch and Long, p. 148; *Texas Observer,* May 2 and 16, 1955; "The Port Arthur Story," movie housed in Texas State Archives as part of Shivers Papers; D. B. Hardeman, "Shivers of Texas, A Tragedy in Three Acts," *Harper's* 213 (November, 1956), p. 54; for a glimpse into financing, see H. E. Chiles report to Shivers, August 13, 1954, in the Shivers Papers, 4–10/33; "Texas," *New Republic,* 131 (September 13, 1954), p. 5; Texas Almanac, 1956–1957, pp. 117, 141–154, 532–533.

For actual donations from the state's coporate establishment, see the Shivers Papers, 4–15/333 and 4–15/334. Included are the donations from Houston corporate attorney Jack Binion ($1500), Houston oil men K. S. "Bud" Adams ($1000) and John Mecom ($1000), Orange banker Edgar Brown ($1000), Fort Worth financier J. Lee Johnson ($1000), Charles Beard, the president of Braniff ($500), etc., plus unknown amounts from such well-known oil millionaires as H. L. Hunt, Hugh Roy Cullen, and Palmer Bradley. One corporation slipped and actually sent in a contribution under its own name, a violation of both state and federal law—see letter from Floyd Ard, Jr., of the Ard Drilling Company, to M. W. Acers, August 14,1954, and attached memo. It was listed as a contribution from another individual.

[17]*Texas Observer,* July 4, 18, 25, 1956; Jimmy Banks, *Money, Marbles, and Chalk* (Austin: Texas Publishing Company, 1971), p. 141; George Fuermann, *Reluctant Empire* Garden City, New York: Doubleday, 1957), pp. 59–61; Austin *American,* July 22, 1956; J. C. Martin, "The First Administration of Governor Price Daniel," (unpublished M. A. thesis, University of Texas at Austin, 1967), pp. 31, 51; *Texas Almanac, 1958–1959,* pp. 461–463.

On 1957 shenanigans, see "Confidential Interview, 1964," and "Closed Manuscript," in possession of Dr. Ben Procter, Texas Christian University; *Texas Observer,* February 5, 12, 19, 27, and March 6, 1957; Dallas *Morning News,* January 16, February 1, 3, 16, 19, 1957; interview with Ralph Yarborough, Austin, November 24, 1975; *Austin Report,* February 3 and 9, 1957; letter from Ben Bock to Jim Lindsey, March 25, 1957, in the Texas AFL–CIO Papers, State Democratic Executive Committee folder (Texas Labor Archives, University of Texas at Arlington).

[18]Tom Brewer, "State Anti-Labor Legislation: Texas—A Case Study, Labor History, 11 (Winter, 1970), pp. 58, 66, 73, 76.

[19]*Twentieth Biennial Report of the Joint Railway Labor Board of Texas and the Texas State Federation of Labor,* 1941–1942, pp. 13–24; *Twenty-First Biennial Report of the Texas Joint Railway Labor Legislative Board, 1943,* pp. 10–18; and *Twenty-Third Biennial Report of the Texas Joint Railway Labor Legislative Board,* 1947, pp. 12–20; B.L.F.E. Files, 38–4–1; *Texas Almanac, 1943–1944,* pp. 70–85; and *Texas Almanac, 1949–1950,* pp. 372–375.

The definition of "urban," of course, is both arbitrary and crucial. The author considers a senator or representative to be an urbanite if his district comprised one or more counties in which one urban complex equaled about half the population or more. Urbanites included representatives from Brownsville, Wichita Falls, and Texarkana, but not, say, from Waxahatchie.

[20]Meyers, p. 4.

[21]These points are based on innumerable conversations with politicians and labor leaders, as well as the author's own participation in Texas political affairs.

The Tragic Purge of 1948—
A Personal Recollection

Monsignor Charles O. Rice

WHEN I WAS BRAVELY BATTLING COMMUNISM in the labor movement a long generation ago, little did I think that, when my days were "in the yellow leaf," I would look back on the episode with considerably less than pride.

My involvement was not simple, actually it was...involved. My platform was the position of Chaplain of the Pittsburgh Chapter, Association of Catholic Trade Unionists. One vehicle was the Catholic Press—chiefly, *The Pittsburgh Catholic,* and secondarily, *Our Sunday Visitor*—which had national circulation. More than that, I traveled throughout a wide area. I met with trade unionists, organized the rank-and-file in opposition to Communist leadership (or what I deemed to be such), and dealt with trade union leaders—principally Phillip Murray, president of the United Steel Workers and the CIO.

For a period of over a year, I transmitted funds from Phil Murray to John Duffy. Duffy was a militant trade unionist, who happened to be, also, a militant anti-Communist. When his local union, Allis Chalmers in Pittsburgh, voted to leave the UE, he gave up his job to concentrate on the struggle. John wanted to preserve the UE but change the leadership. Incidentally, although he was opposed to the Communists ideologically, he admired many of them as trade unionists.

It is unlikely that I would have remained as deeply involved but for John. At one juncture, Al Fitzgerald, UE president, had me almost persuaded, but John turned me around again.

This anti-Communism was hard work. For the most part, the rank-and-file was nonideological and was interested in bread and butter, which the leftist leadership provided as well as any and better than most.

There are only so many natural leaders in any group, and they tend to be loyal to whomever first moves them to action and directs them reasonably. Not too many of these natural leaders became Communists, but most of them insisted on judging their leaders on performance as union leaders.

You may not be able to muster up a great deal of sympathy but a sincere prolabor anti-Communist propagandist had it hard. There were anti-Communists and anti-Communists; we thought that we were the good kind. We made a point of not bothering folks unless they were Communists or followed the Communist party line faithfully, and we distinguished between followers and the real article. The others, the bad anti-Communists, called all kinds of people Communists, including us. There is some truth in the Communist joke about the fellow, caught in a red-baiting campaign, who protested "but I'm an anti-Communist" and got told, "We don't keer what kinda Communist you are, just git outa here!"

The Communists eased our task by one of their characteristics. There was a Communist line. In domestic affairs, you might mistake it, but in foreign affairs, it was clear-cut. It followed the interests of the Soviet Union. Communists had an orthodoxy with hard edges and were serious about it. That was about all we had to go on, really, and we were not able to upset the rank-and-file with our discreet use of it. Something else turned them off, and I shall get to that before I finish.

We made hay out of the Molotov-Ribbentrop Pact, in which Stalin made a deal with Hitler, and the change in the rhetoric was quickly observable in the Communist labor press; we trumpeted loud and long the counterchange which came when Hitler brutally involved Russia, June 21, 1940.

Communist controlled, or influenced, unions veered then from intransigence to labor-management cooperation. Domestically, their national politics changed, as did their union politics. John L. Lewis was their darling one moment and their villain the next, while Phillip Murray rode the other end of the see-saw.

We used to blame one strike on the noncooperation policy, that at North American Aviation.

I began my anti-Communist activities before World War II. Some of the old-timers at Westinghouse Local No. 601 drew me into the squabble, when the leadership was getting ready to dump Jim Carey from the UE presidency in 1941, and I kept my hand in until the early fifties.

During the war, few would listen to me. The Communist-related unions and factions grew strong, along with the rest of labor, but it was a false strength. Since the Soviet Union had a certain wartime popularity, especially with workers of Slav extraction, the domestic

Communists gained also, and many workers who were ideologically unaffected felt strongly that, Communist or not, a man deserved a fair hearing and fair treatment.

At one time, I reckoned the Communist strength as quite formidable: one-fourth to one-third of the CIO, with strength here and there in the AFL. The UE we felt, was under solid control, and, at one time, the Auto Workers were close to being controlled. Farm Equipment was like the UE. There was some strength in steel. We felt that they were very strong in the entertainment unions, and they were strong in the Newspaper Guild. They had a base in the government workers and some white-collar operations. They had some good cannery locals and hospital locals. They had Mike Quill's Transport Workers and Joe Curran's Maritime Union. We, of course, exaggerated their strength, sincerely. We accepted some of the mystique of our enemy, just as we adopted tactics that we talked of as being their sort of thing.

Anti-Communism of the better sort—ours, that is—was a minor industry and I was a resource. I compiled information and had correspondence with people from many parts of the country and even the Canal Zone. I interfered in the affairs of many a union, always for the best, I then thought.

Two or three articles written by me for *Our Sunday Visitor* brought much correspondence and information on Communists or their followers far and wide. That Catholic paper had a truly national range. It was horribly conservative and played with the bad sort of anti-Communism more happily, and far more often, than it did with me and mine. God forgive me, I did not mind using it to reach people I would not otherwise have reached.

The Association of Catholic Trade Unionists had significant chapters in two other cities—New York and Detroit. The Detroit one was almost an appendage of Walter Reuther's caucus. Mine in Pittsburgh was open to the charge of being that for Phil Murray and his Steel Workers. I hope the charge was not totally true. I assure you, that I was pushing Murray to move against the Communist power, rather than the reverse.

The chapter in New York, which was the founding chapter, was a real outfit, with a variety of members and resources. It was in the Communist fight but it, also, performed nobly against trade union crooks and mob control. It fought with Cardinal Spellman over the cemetery strike, where he smashed a local that was affiliated with a Communist-connected international. I inferred publicly that he was a scab and I suffered a little. I'm not simpering; I had it coming for other reasons.

Socialists were big in anti-Communism. Actually, I think they pumped me up. They had long factional memories and they had their own network. Many Socialists were the most bitter against Communists and the followers of the party line—incredibly bitter. Some local men and women in Pittsburgh could be included in that category and, also, national figures such as Victor Riesel, with whom I was very good friends.

The question naturally arises: if the Communists ran rather good unions, and if their rank-and-file was content, why bother them? They were aggressive for one thing, and they projected themselves as part of an international movement that was on the march. They were effective and they grew and they had policies which they pushed. They were very visible. Among other things, they rewarded the good and punished the wicked—their good and their wicked. I honestly thought that they had a shot at gaining control of American labor. I was opposed to Soviet Russia and this was not entirely for religious reasons. The purges bothered me and I knew some of the stories of torture and abuse to be true. I allotted Communists more than their quota of cynicism.

Believe me, I was not a devotee of capitalism, but I was more of an unblinking American-style patriot than I should have been. I could see through American-Legion-style rhetoric but, for several decades, I was not only a Cold-War liberal but an unforgiveably naive one to boot.

Where I was concerned, a great love of the labor movement played a part. I was one of those who hoped for great things from labor and felt that it was good. Consequently, I was adamant against elements that might give labor a bad name. But, if one was not careful, one found oneself whapping reds so that non-reds would respect you, and your defense of the labor movement would be more effective.

I was not trusted by the capitalists or their assistants. The FBI and Hoover did not trust me. The word apparently went out to tell me nothing. I had no cooperation from even the lower echelons of the FBI from 1941 onward. And not only the idiot fringe but the respectables in U. S. Steel and Duquesne University cut me down. An interesting story that, and one that I shall tell in some detail later.

Looking back, I am convinced that the very success of the Communists during the war helped to undo them. They were all out for production. Jim Matles's book, *Them and Us,* virtually ignores that time and those conventions. It was not the Communist left's finest hour, and it came back to haunt them. We used it against them with some effect.

Frank Emspak, in his paper, dwells on the CIO purge of 1948, in which the Communist unions were forced out because they broke ranks and supported Henry A. Wallace. That was important, but we must realize that the Wallace campaign was, in a way, an excuse. By supporting Wallace's third party, the Communist camp gave Phil Murray and his controlling faction a handy weapon, but, regardless, Phil would have found one. It was more comfortable for him to move on the basis of political revolt than ideological belief. Of course, Murray had emotional attachments to the Democrats, but he would not have split his movement for politics alone.

In the last analysis, however, the great Communist left (I use the adjective "great" deliberately and sincerely) was destroyed by the upsurge of American righteousness and arrogance, of which McCarthyism was merely a cheap expression. The United States, the darling of capitalism who held capitalism to be darling, was heeding the call of manifest destiny.

I sincerely believed, at the time, that Communism was a real threat and that Russia was the aggressor. It was my fault for not heeding independent journals of the non-Communist left. I was naive and was swept away with the flood of lies and deceptions. I could not believe that my country was spying, lying, and provoking.

It took a long time for me to realize that when the communistic unions were supporting Soviet Union positions in the Cold War, they were closer to reason than treason.

A word about my use of the words Communist and communistic. It is deliberate, if not always accurate. The issue was whether or not men in the trade-union movement and its leadership were to be permitted to profess Communism or support it. Then I thought "no"; now I think "yes."

It is tragic that there is not a strong left in American trade unions today. Was that more the fault of the Communists than of the likes of me? The Communists in the zesty days of the New Deal and the CIO gobbled up the left and attracted the eager young, so many of whom became disillusioned and abandoned the left entirely when they abandoned Communism. Others were simply beaten into submission. In those days, the Communists were not models of toleration themselves, and chewed up their opposition when they could.

Nonetheless, the American trade-union movement would be healthier today if Phil Murray had not purged the CIO and if a strong, broad-based Communist minority had been able to survive in the trade unions. The split of the UE was a loss, and so was the transformation of the UAW into a monolith.

What bothers me personally, most of all, is that, in the very bad days of the Cold War, The Day of the Toad, and Scoundrel Time, I did not defend all the victims. Of course, I fought McCarthy when he went after people I agreed with, but I did not defend brave people whose careers and lives were destroyed by McCarthyism because of membership, alliance, or mere flirtation with Communism.

I was not wrong all the time, and, in some good fights, I did not hesitate to stand along side Communists in trade-union battles, but I think I wasted a lot of time on a crusade that did more harm than good. Far better had I concentrated exclusively on building strong, honest unions, exposing crooks, organizing the unorganized, and confronting the might of unchecked monopoly and aggrandizement.

Index